The Rebirth of
Urban Democracy

The Rebirth of Urban Democracy

JEFFREY M. BERRY
KENT E. PORTNEY
KEN THOMSON

THE BROOKINGS INSTITUTION
WASHINGTON, D.C.

About Brookings

The Brookings Institution is a private nonprofit organization devoted to research, education, and publication on important issues of domestic and foreign policy. Its principal purpose is to bring knowledge to bear on the current and emerging policy problems facing the American people.

A board of trustees is responsible for general supervision of the Institution and safeguarding of its independence. The president is the chief administrative officer and bears final responsibility for the decision to publish a manuscript as a Brookings book. Publication of a work signifies that it is deemed a competent treatment worthy of public consideration but does not imply endorsement of conclusions or recommendations. The Institution itself does not take positions on policy issues.

Copyright © 1993

THE BROOKINGS INSTITUTION

1775 Massachusetts Avenue, N.W., Washington, D.C. 20036

Library of Congress Cataloging-in-Publication data:

Berry, Jeffrey M., 1948–
    The rebirth of urban democracy / Jeffrey M. Berry, Kent E. Portney and Ken Thomson.
     p. cm.
    Includes bibliographical references and index.
    ISBN 0-8157-0928-5 (cloth : alk. paper)—
    ISBN 0-8157-0927-7 (pbk. : alk. paper)
    1. Citizens' associations—United States. 2. Neighborhood government—United States. 3. Municipal government—United States. 4. Democracy—United States. 5. Political participation—United States. I. Portney, Kent E. II. Thomson, Ken, 1946– III. Title.
JS303.5.B47 1992
320.8′5′0973—dc20   92-37826
                                      CIP

9 8 7 6 5 4 3 2 1

Preface

IN 1985 WE EMBARKED with great expectations on our research for this book. The optimist in each of us hoped that we would discover exemplars of citizen participation in practice—those that did well to achieve the most highly valued goals of democracy—that could be transferred to other places. The realist in each of us understood that in contemporary America there may not be examples of participation that achieve the theoretical goals of democracy and that the conditions necessary to develop, support, and sustain citywide systems of public participation may not be easily transferred. And the scholar in each of us recognized that the research project needed to investigate the consequences of well-developed citizen participation would be extremely challenging.

With the gracious and generous support of the Ford Foundation, we were able to marshal the forces of social science research to the task of trying to understand what happens when cities' neighborhoods become part of citywide systems of public participation. We asked hard research questions, and we report their answers here. The answers are not always straightforward, and they ultimately raise many more questions still needing to be addressed.

Although we may not have found models of participation that can easily be transferred, we did find programs whose features can inform the design and practice of citizen participation elsewhere. We believe this book provides some important corrections to current skepticism about citizen participation in the United States. It suggests that these concerns, raised mostly in empirical analyses about democratic participation, are overstated. And it suggests that the expectations for practical democracy that grow out of normative theory are too high. Nevertheless, face-to-face forms of political participation can achieve much of what theorists suggest is worthwhile and can do so without producing significant negative consequences.

We would like to thank many people without whose contributions this project would have been impossible. First and foremost, we would like to thank the Ford Foundation, especially David Arnold, the program officer with whom we interacted most closely, and Michael Lipsky, who replaced David when he took another assignment. We would also like to thank Stuart Langton, former executive director of the Lincoln Filene Center for Citizenship and Public Affairs at Tufts University, whose efforts to help secure funding for this research are greatly appreciated, and Robert M. Hollister, the current executive director, for his continued support.

In order to obtain advice, criticism, and feedback on the initial research design, we established a research advisory panel consisting of Richard L. Cole, Thomas R. Dye, Lester W. Milbrath, Richard R. Rich, Hans B. C. Spiegel, Linda Williams, and Joan Wills. We thank these scholars for providing thorough and penetrating advice on the research design and for ultimately helping to make this project much more successful than it might otherwise have been.

In order to provide advice and direction in developing the practical application of the research findings, we established a working group panel consisting of David Arnold, Alan Beals, Barry Checkoway, William Cirone, Donald Davies, Frank Duehay, Andrea Kydd, Roy Laos, Douglas Lawson, Gail Levin, Joseph McNeeley, Charles Stith, and Ruth Wilson. These people provided invaluable direction to this project by specifying how we could maximize the application of the project's resulting information to day-to-day problems of citizen participation.

A special debt of gratitude is owed to Elizabeth Hall, who provided invaluable assistance and support as our advance person in each of the five cities where interviews were conducted. She made initial visits to the five cities and arranged many of the interviews before we arrived in each city. Thanks also go to Madeline Costanza and Jill Lepore, who also provided logistical support for the in-person interviews, and to Christine La Fiandra and Merilee Mishall, who assisted in conducting the in-person interviews in Dayton.

The public opinion surveys involved literally hundreds of graduate and undergraduate students at Tufts, too numerous to name here. A special note of thanks goes to Eric Bove, Catherine Corliss, Kevin Diehl, Joe Freeman, Jill Lepore, Merilee Mishall, and Michael Woodbridge, who supervised the surveys. We would also like to express our appreciation to Survey Sampling, Inc., in Fairfield, Connecticut, for providing assistance in the sampling of respondents for the surveys in the ten matched cities and to the Center for Urban Affairs at the University of Alabama in Birmingham, Columbia Information Systems in Portland, and L. Tucker Gibson and Associates, Inc., in San Antonio for the extensive assistance provided in conducting the surveys in their respective cities. Richard R. Rich and Abraham Wandersman shared much of their respective work with us so that we could build on what they had already learned. We would also like to thank Alma Powers and Marilyn Santiesteban for their work in creating the Spanish translations of the public opinion instruments.

Making sense out of the resulting data was no small task, and many people deserve special thanks for their assistance. These include Athena Bradley, who helped compile the enormous amount of information from more than 500 hours of taped interviews and conducted follow-up interviews; Christine Sanni, who tackled the task of coding and key-entering much of the information from the public opinion surveys; Lisa Tittemore, who helped code the in-person interviews; and Max Herman and Dorothy Shurmaster, who helped create coding schemes for and coded many of the open-ended questions.

Assistance in summarizing interviews, analyzing media reports, and coding surveys was provided by Karen Blackwell, Steve Faberman, Aleisa Gittens, Yvonne Hsu, Elizabeth Jones, Linda Kiene, Olya Kinney, Heather Ley, Bob Markel, Karen Massey, Pamela Mercer, Quynh-Giang Tran, and Li Na Wang. Our work identifying and describing model participation programs was greatly assisted by Eric Bove, Cheryl McCarter-Hoffman, and Christine Sumner. We also would like to thank Maria Figueroa, Jay Greene, and Tracy Turner for their contributions to the project. The follow-up interviews were conducted by Joanne Bissetta, Melisa Cahnmann, Elaine DeSario, Holly Isbitsky, Mathew Kushner, Christine Sumner, and Tom Webb.

We would like to thank all the people in the five cities whose cooperation made this project possible. In St. Paul, these include Jerry Jenkins and George Latimer; in Portland, Sarah Newhall and Rachel Jacky; in Dayton, Cilla Bosnak; in Birmingham, Betty Bock, Faye Dixon, and Ben Greene; in San Antonio, Helen Ayala, Beatrice Cortez, Maribeth Larkin, and Cathy Powell; and in all five cities, the officers and participants with whom we conducted interviews from the dozens of neighborhood associations.

We would also like to thank James Glaser, John Schneider, and Linda Williams for reading portions of the manuscript or conference papers based on the material later incorporated into the manuscript. Their comments and suggestions contributed to improving specific chapters of this book. Durwood Marshall provided extensive assistance in conducting the analysis associated with the reciprocal causation models reported in the book. Carolyn McGovern edited the manuscript, David L. Duffy verified its factual content, and Jean Moody prepared the index.

Last, but not least, we would like to thank our editor at the Brookings Institution, Nancy D. Davidson, for her unyielding support, and Matthew A. Crenson, Paul E. Peterson, and Kay L. Schlozman, who provided exceptionally detailed and helpful reviews of the manuscript. Inevitably, more advice was given than could be taken. And ultimate responsibility for errors of commission, omission, or interpretation lies with us. The views expressed here are ours and should not be attributed to the Ford Foundation, Tufts University, or the Brookings Institution.

JEFFREY M. BERRY
KENT E. PORTNEY
KEN THOMSON

Contents

FIGURES

The Rebirth of
Urban Democracy

CHAPTER 1

Participation and Democracy

WE WENT TO THE HEART of America to search for cities that are democratic. The cities we examined—Birmingham, Dayton, Portland (Oregon), St. Paul, and San Antonio—were chosen because each is characterized by an impressive commitment to the idea of participatory democracy. These five cities represent examples of how cities can reach out to their neighborhoods and successfully incorporate the participation of average citizens into public policymaking. In an era when government seems ever more remote and difficult to approach, the neighborhood associations in these cities have brought government closer to the people.

Participatory democracy may seem a hopelessly romantic notion, evoking Tocqueville's small-town America and visions of quaint New England town meetings, but conjuring up little that is relevant to the practice of government today. Yet nothing seems more crucial to the future of American democracy than to figure out some way of spurring greater citizen participation. And if ways can be found to increase people's involvement in government, we may then have the foundation upon which to build a true participatory democracy.

The Decline of Democracy

There is widespread agreement that democracy in America needs renewal. Too few people participate in the governmental process. Too few people seem to feel that they share responsibility for making government work better. Too many people are content to rely on their elected officials to solve society's problems, even though they are dissatisfied with the results of those officials' actions.

For many years the decline in voting has been viewed as the primary sickness eating away at American democracy. Between 1960 and 1988 the proportion of adults voting steadily dropped, until just one in two

Americans were exercising their right to vote. In the 1992 presidential election the voting rate was up; this is certainly encouraging news. Yet the problem is far from being solved. At stake is something much more fundamental: the nature of citizenship in America. Too many Americans define the responsibilities of citizenship as beginning and ending with voting. And many do not even go that far, choosing instead not to vote.

In recent years, reform efforts to expand the public's role in the democratic process have focused almost exclusively on voting. This is unfortunate, for voting is too meager an act to rebuild citizenship.[1] If substantially more people voted but did little else to try to influence government, it would be a rather hollow revival of democracy. Voting is a solitary act that takes a few minutes to perform every few years. The ballot has fixed choices and can be completed with minimal reflection. By itself, voting does little to build a sense of community; it may be an act of anger rather than a positive statement of the direction government ought to take. Rebuilding citizenship in America means that reform must move beyond getting more people into private voting booths to getting more people to public forums where they can work with their neighbors to solve the problems of their community. Once America has real citizens, increased voting will be sure to follow. And once we have real citizens, campaigns will be held to higher standards and elections will be more concrete manifestations of the people's will.

Although survey researchers have identified the correlates of participation and nonparticipation, they have reached little consensus as to why Americans do not participate more in the political process. Among normative theorists, however, a school of thought has emerged that is highly certain of both cause and remedy. In the eyes of scholars like Benjamin Barber and Michael Sandel, it is liberalism that has undermined citizenship. For Barber, liberalism has sanctioned "thin democracy" that "can conceive of no form of citizenship other than the self-interested bargain."[2] Sandel and other communitarian critics of liberalism attack it for fostering communities without shared values. Sandel laments a shift "in our practices and institutions, from a public philosophy of common purposes to one of fair procedures, from a politics of good to

1. Benjamin R. Barber, *Strong Democracy: Participatory Politics for a New Age* (University of California Press, 1984), p. xiii.
2. Barber, *Strong Democracy*, p. 24.

a politics of right, from the national republic to the procedural republic."[3] As a result, America produces citizens who are "strangers" to each other.[4]

The antidote to this sickness is building communities where neighbors talk to each other about politics. In face-to-face meetings, men and women can learn from each other, reason with one another, and search for common interests. Face-to-face democracy moves politics away from its adversarial norm, where interest groups square off in conflict and lobbyists speak for their constituents. Instead, the bonds of friendship and community are forged as neighbors look for common solutions to their problems.[5] Political participation becomes an educative device rather than an occasionally exercised civic obligation.

The communitarian theorists have a far from airtight case. Not everyone is convinced that community cannot exist under liberalism or that liberalism bears a lion's share of the blame for the decline of community. Claims for the curative power of community also seem naive. All the values that communities may come to share will not necessarily be virtuous ones; strong community bonds can lead to efforts to exclude those who do not fit the community's image of itself. And all too often, the idea of community is championed without any conception of how it might be achieved.[6]

Yet those theorists who push for more participation within true communities tap a responsive chord in American society. In their study of community in America, reported in *Habits of the Heart*, Robert Bellah and his colleagues found a society where "individualism may have grown cancerous."[7] At the same time, however, they found a great desire for

3. Michael J. Sandel, "The Procedural Republic and the Unencumbered Self," *Political Theory*, vol. 12 (February 1984), p. 93.

4. Michael J. Sandel, *Liberalism and the Limits to Justice* (Cambridge University Press, 1982), p. 183. See also Alasdair MacIntyre, *After Virtue* (University of Notre Dame Press, 1981).

5. Jane J. Mansbridge, *Beyond Adversary Democracy* (Basic Books, 1980).

6. See Amy Gutmann, "Communitarian Critics of Liberalism," *Philosophy and Public Affairs*, vol. 14 (Summer 1985), pp. 308–22; H. N. Hirsch, "The Threnody of Liberalism: Constitutional Liberty and the Renewal of Community," *Political Theory*, vol. 14 (August 1986), pp. 423–49; Michael Walzer, "The Communitarian Critique of Liberalism," *Political Theory*, vol. 18 (February 1990), pp. 6–23; and Mark Warren, "Democratic Theory and Self-Transformation," *American Political Science Review*, vol. 86 (March 1992), pp. 8–23.

7. Robert N. Bellah and others, *Habits of the Heart: Individualism and Commitment in American Life* (University of California Press, 1985), p. viii.

individuals to be "involved" and a perception that a return to small-town government was a remedy for America's ills. During the 1960s, this country's last period of agitation for political reform, there was a persistent call for a return to a governmental process built on the participation of ordinary citizens. The Port Huron Statement, the left's clarion call to action, argued that in a participatory democracy "politics has the function of bringing people out of isolation and into community, thus being a necessary, though not sufficient, means of finding meaning in personal life."[8] In the 1980s it was the political leaders of the right, Ronald Reagan and George Bush, who articulated the spirit of Tocqueville's America. Their summons for increased voluntarism—what Bush ineptly labeled a "thousand points of light"—spoke to Americans' desire to return to the good and decent values of small-town society.[9]

The quest for community extends beyond the rhetoric of activists and elected officials. The actions of Americans speak even more loudly to the appeal of working together with one's neighbors. A 1989 Gallup Poll reported that 41 percent of all citizens were involved in charitable or social service volunteer work, up from just 27 percent in 1977. Of those who do volunteer, fully 23 percent donate at least fifteen hours of work a month; another 24 percent donate at least six hours.[10] This commitment reflects a culture characterized by generosity and caring rather than narcissism and apathy.

Americans' attitudes toward their roles as citizens are thus complex. There is serious disaffection from the political process, and many people define their civic duties in the political realm in a very limited fashion. But community remains strongly appealing to Americans, who evidence a remarkable willingness to donate time to nonprofit organizations in their communities. The key to making America more participatory may be making political participation more meaningful in the context of the communities that people live in.

8. James Miller, *Democracy Is in the Streets: From Port Huron to the Siege of Chicago* (Simon and Schuster, 1987), p. 333. The SDS manifesto is reprinted in its entirety in the Miller book.

9. On the enduring appeal of citizen participation, see James A. Morone, *The Democratic Wish: Popular Participation and the Limits of American Government* (Basic Books, 1990).

10. Diane Colasanto, "Americans Show Commitment to Helping Those in Need," *Gallup Report*, no. 290 (November 1989), pp. 17–24.

Unleashing Participation

If America becomes more participatory, what will happen? Will we enter a golden age of government or be beset by destabilizing mass politics?

There are powerful and enduring arguments for and against participatory democracy. The central issue is not whether participation is good or bad—democracy requires widespread participation in some form. It is instead a question about how to balance the desire to maximize participation and popular control with the need for stability and efficiency in government.[11] The issue of what level of participation is best is ultimately an argument about the fundamental nature of people engaged in politics. If we bring more people into the governmental process, what will these people want? If we give people more authority to decide questions of public policy, will they prove themselves worthy of that responsibility?

Redemption

Proponents of participatory democracy view it as redemptive, while critics base their arguments on pragmatic and utilitarian grounds. Participation is seen as redemptive in three crucial ways. First, participation nourishes the democratic spirit of individuals. Second, it builds community, which in turn nurtures shared values such as compassion, tolerance, and equality. Third, and most broadly, participation transforms institutions so that they become more effective instruments of democracy.

Participation nourishes democracy because it is an educative force: people learn to be good citizens through practice. The most passionate arguments for participation, however, see it as teaching more than the responsibilities of citizenship. John Stuart Mill emphasized "the moral part of the instruction afforded by the participation of the private citizen." When an individual participates, he is forced "to weigh interests not his own; to be guided, in case of conflicting claims, by another rule than his private partialities; to apply, at every turn, principles and maxims which have for their reason of existence the general good."[12] The *expe-*

---

11. See Morone, *The Democratic Wish*.

12. John Stuart Mill, *Considerations on Representative Government* (Harper and Brothers, 1862), p. 79.

rience of participating in decisions is crucial to the potential for change. After examining the relevant empirical literature, Herbert Simon concluded that "significant changes in human behavior can be brought about rapidly only if the persons who are expected to change participate in deciding what the change shall be and how it shall be made."[13]

The idea that participation builds community is a recurring theme in western political thought. Rousseau emphasized the link between public service and the vitality of the state.[14] Similarly, Mill warned, "Let a person have nothing to do for his country, and he will not care for it."[15] Contemporary theorists are expansive in their claims for citizen participation. Jane Mansbridge maintains that in unitary democracies—those that rely on consensus—participation builds on bonds of friendship, and this dynamic leads to true equality within the community.[16] For Barber, the "noisy assemblies" of democracy will free citizens to discover their "common humanity."[17] The communitarians claim that the sense of shared purpose in a community helps people to find meaning in their lives beyond their own individual identity and accomplishments. Community then is not simply an abstract sense of belonging, but it is the wellspring of democratic values.

The most important impact of participation on the institutions of government is to make them more responsive to the preferences of citizens. For Rousseau, representative government was not an acceptable substitute for the direct democracy of the city-state. The decisions of government should embody the general will and "will cannot be represented."[18] Modern theorists who advocate greater participation have not had the luxury of assuming a world made of city-states. They have, however, found that political science has made too easy a peace with representative democracy. In particular, pluralism has been singled out for rationalizing that our system of interest group representation is a realistic approximation of what democracy can be in a modern complex society. The attack against pluralism maintains not only that interest group politics is biased in favor of those with the most resources, but

13. Quoted in Jack H. Nagel, *Participation* (Prentice-Hall, 1987), p. 14.
14. Jean-Jacques Rousseau, *The Social Contract* (Penguin, 1968), book III-15.
15. Mill, *Considerations on Representative Government*, p. 58.
16. Mansbridge, *Beyond Adversary Democracy*, p. 9.
17. Barber, *Strong Democracy*, p. 311.
18. Rousseau, *Social Contract*, book III-15, p. 141. Rousseau also argued that when citizens fail to recognize the general will, the act of participating in government makes it easier for them to accept the collective decisions that have been reached. Carole Pateman, *Participation and Democratic Theory* (Cambridge University Press, 1970), p. 27.

also that interest groups are habitually unparticipatory organizations. The critique of pluralism was a powerful part of the intellectual argument that pushed for political reforms during the 1960s and 1970s. Reforms such as the community action program (CAP) and changes in the rules governing political parties were aimed at making institutions truer reflections of "will" by expanding participation beyond interest group politics.

The False Hope of Participation

The arguments against participatory democracy attack the romanticism of participation and replace it with a steely logic that justifies a system where elites hold disproportionate power and the masses participate at a moderate level. From Plato onward, many theorists have insisted that government is best served by "guardians" who are qualified to govern because of their superior knowledge and skills.[19] At the polar extreme of this line of thinking was Mosca, whose crude determinism contended that all societies are divided between "a class that rules and a class that is ruled."[20] Joseph Schumpeter also advocated what critics deride as "elitism." He ridiculed Rousseau's notion that there is a common good that becomes clear as members of the community debate the problem before them. Schumpeter claimed that the public interest will always be defined differently by the various groups within society.[21] He extended his argument for realism by assailing the abilities of the common man: "The typical citizen drops down to a lower level of mental performance as soon as he enters the political field. He argues and analyzes in a way which he would readily recognize as infantile within the sphere of his real interests. He becomes a primitive again."[22]

The dangers of mass politics were echoed again when various political movements of the 1960s and 1970s challenged the capacity of government to adapt to new and conflicting demands. The expansion of political activism could not be easily consolidated into the existing channels of participation. The civil rights movement, the antiwar movement, Dem-

19. See, generally, Robert A. Dahl, *Democracy and Its Critics* (Yale University Press, 1989), pp. 52–79.
20. Gaetano Mosca, *The Ruling Class* (McGraw-Hill, 1939), p. 50.
21. Joseph A. Schumpeter, *Capitalism, Socialism, and Democracy*, 3d ed. (Harper and Brothers, 1950), p. 251.
22. Schumpeter, *Capitalism, Socialism, and Democracy*, p. 262. See also Peter Bachrach, *The Theory of Democratic Elitism* (Little, Brown, 1967).

ocratic party reformers, and public interest lobbies were all viewed by conservative thinkers as destabilizing forces in society. The leading proponent of this school of thought was political scientist Samuel Huntington, who warned against an "excess of democracy" that was damaging America's political institutions.[23] He suggested that the "surge of participatory democracy" had weakened American government because it had been unable to satisfy the conflicting claims made upon it.[24] This, in turn, made people cynical and disrespectful of government. In Huntington's mind, participatory democracy eventually leads to a crisis of authority.

Less apocalyptic has been the criticism that public involvement programs ultimately dilute the power of expertise and enhance the authority of ideological activists. In a world of complex problems like toxic waste and nuclear power, do we want administrators to share their authority with those who use citizen participation programs to promote their own personal political views? Advocates of public involvement programs claim that citizens are capable of being part of administrative decisions in the most advanced, technical policy areas. Still, to many students of public administration it makes little sense to reduce the role of competent, nonpartisan experts so that a modest number of people can participate in public policymaking. Elections are seen as the appropriate arena for political activity; administrative policymaking between elections ought to be based on the technical requirements of the issues at hand.

Fears of the great unwashed are an enduring part of American politics. These fears gain legitimacy, though, when proposals for participatory democracy surface. Then the burden of proof seems to fall on the shoulders of the proponents of participation, who have never fully allayed fears that participatory democracy would turn out to be an unruly and unpredictable form of government. Those who advocate reform must convince skeptics that widespread participation will not lead to disorder and that the technical expertise of professional administrators will not be ignored.

A Question of Scale

The debate over how much participation is desirable and practical is complicated by a further question: at what levels of government should

23. Samuel P. Huntington, "The Democratic Distemper," *Public Interest*, no. 41 (Fall 1975), pp. 9–38.
24. Samuel P. Huntington, *American Politics: The Promise of Disharmony* (Harvard University Press, 1981), p. 219.

this participation take place? Is participatory democracy possible at the national level, or is it realistically limited to local government? Even at the local level, can citizens of enormous cities like New York and Los Angeles reasonably expect to control their governments through citizen participation programs?

As modern societies have emerged, theorists have become less precise about the optimum size of a participatory government. Those who contemplated the city-state had a firmer grasp of the details. Plato, for example, said that the population limit for a unit of government was 5,040. Over that size, it was difficult for everyone to know each other. Aristotle said that all the people of a state should be able to assemble at a single location and be able to hear whoever was speaking. Thus, the size of the polity was determined by "the range of the unamplified human voice."[25]

The traditional view of American democracy is that the best conditions for extensive participation in government are to be found in small towns. For Tocqueville, the small towns of New England were an ideal setting for democracy, as the mores of these villages nurtured a sense of collective responsibility. He found that in these settings citizens "take part in every occurrence" when government is required to act.[26] The New England town meeting still captures our imagination as an example of true democracy in action. More generally, the small town remains fixed in our minds as a place where the bond of community allows those with differing points of view to come together and solve the problems they face.[27]

Empirical studies offer some clues but no definitive answer to the question of optimal size. Neither the rates of political participation nor people's feelings of personal political efficacy are correlated with the size of a country. One study done in Sweden, however, found that participation and sense of personal effectiveness were highest in densely populated communities of under 8,000.[28] Even so, this cannot be said to be the ideal size for the units of government. Communities of this size would not have the appropriate resources to attack all the problems of society. Given the differential scope of the problems any large, modern country faces, there must be a mix of political units of different sizes.

25. Robert A. Dahl and Edward R. Tufte, *Size and Democracy* (Stanford University Press, 1973), p. 5.
26. Alexis de Tocqueville, *Democracy in America*, ed. Richard D. Heffner (Mentor Books, 1956), p. 61.
27. Bellah and others, *Habits of the Heart*, p. 204.
28. Dahl and Tufte, *Size and Democracy*, pp. 135, 63–64.

Neighborhoods and Community

Since there is not now widespread citizen participation at any level of government, it is premature to draw a boundary between what is appropriate for participatory democracy and what must be left in the realm of representative democracy. As a society, we have not yet tested the limits of participatory democracy. But on the road to becoming a nation where people take their obligations as citizens seriously, how far we might go seems less clear than where we should start. The common denominator of large cities and small towns is that people in both live in neighborhoods.

Face-to-Face Democracy

Given that the empirical research has not demonstrated that there is a best size for democratic governments, is there any reason to believe that neighborhoods are a key to revitalizing democracy? The experience with neighborhood government is far too limited to make any definitive conclusions. What neighborhood government does have to offer, however, is the possibility of face-to-face interaction, which lies at the heart of the theory of participatory democracy.

The literature on face-to-face interaction is of crucial importance to constructing a plausible case for participatory democracy because it attacks the notion that individual behavior is based on self-interest. It offers a rationale for why people might be more likely to gravitate toward solutions that are best for the broader community rather than single-mindedly pursuing what is best for themselves. Experimental research shows that group identity is a critical variable in leading people away from self-interested behavior. People place a high value on benefits accruing to groups they identify with, and thus having the group reach a good decision can take on greater importance than having one's own preference chosen. Behavioral research has also shown that "ingroup biasing is a remarkably robust and easily elicited psychological phenomenon."[29]

Another important finding from this research is that the frequency of interaction is strongly related to the propensity for cooperative behavior. In his study of the prisoner's dilemma, Robert Axelrod concludes: "Here

---

29. Linnda R. Caporael and others, "Selfishness Examined: Cooperation in the Absence of Egoistic Incentives," *Behavioral and Brain Sciences*, vol. 12, no. 4 (1989), p. 693.

is the argument in a nutshell. The evolution of cooperation requires that individuals have a sufficiently large chance to meet again so that they have a stake in their future interaction."[30] It is simple human nature for individuals to behave differently with other people when they know they will be in extensive contact in the months or years to come.

Cooperation is also facilitated by the opportunity for discussion. Experimental research that places strangers in group situations and forces them to choose between courses of action that benefit themselves and those that benefit the group finds dramatic differences in outcomes when discussion is allowed. In one set of experiments, people could defect from the group anonymously by choosing an option on a secret ballot that could give them an individual financial payoff larger than the one they would get by choosing the option that would benefit the whole group. Discussion was the critical variable that bonded the group and led to cooperative rather than egoistic choices.[31] Personal interaction and discussion lead to trust, and trust underlies cooperation. Trust is an emotional commitment as well as a rational calculation of likely outcomes.[32]

It is important not to overstate the case: face-to-face interaction does not inevitably lead to cooperative, public-spirited behavior. A majority faction may use its numerical strength to override the concerns of others. In addition, face-to-face forums allow for peer pressure and decisions that mask real disagreements. And cooperative behavior does not necessarily signify completely altruistic behavior. In much of the theoretical work, self-interest and altruistic behavior are placed at opposite poles, but political behavior can incorporate both motives.[33] Moreover, for people to bring their own self-interested concerns to the political process is not inherently wrong. But if self-interest is assumed to be the dominant incentive that drives political behavior, then institutions and policymaking processes will be designed to facilitate the politics of self-interest. If it is assumed instead that self-interest is an important but not a dominant motivating factor in politics, then government may be structured quite differently.

---

30. Robert M. Axelrod, *The Evolution of Cooperation* (Basic Books, 1984), p. 20.

31. Robyn M. Dawes, Alphons J. C. van de Kragt, and John M. Orbell, "Cooperation for the Benefit of Us—Not Me, or My Conscience," in Jane J. Mansbridge, ed., *Beyond Self-Interest* (University of Chicago Press, 1990), p. 106.

32. Robert H. Frank, "A Theory of Moral Sentiments," in Mansbridge, ed., *Beyond Self-Interest*, pp. 71–96.

33. Jane J. Mansbridge, "On the Relation of Altruism and Self-Interest," in Mansbridge, ed., *Beyond Self- Interest*, pp. 133–43.

A decentralized city government, with considerable authority placed in the hands of the neighborhoods, represents a sensible compromise between the realistic needs of efficiency and scale for some services and the requirements of participatory democracy. Neighborhood-based government draws easily on people's sense of identity with the area they live in. People know they are going to have frequent interactions with their neighbors, so even if they attend meetings infrequently they have a powerful incentive to think about long-term relationships in addition to the policy questions at hand. The primary decisionmaking tool in neighborhood associations is, quite simply, discussion among the community residents who attend the regular open meetings. Thus neighborhood associations are institutions that are well suited to the face-to-face interaction that can nurture cooperative behavior.

Neighborhoods and Participation

This book is a study of five cities that take face-to-face democracy seriously. In these cities neighborhood organizations are the primary agent of political dialogue and citizen influence. This type of neighborhood system is a significant step toward strong democracy. And the systems work.

Each city has built a system of support and policy connections around the following neighborhood groups.

—Birmingham has a three-tiered system in which neighborhood officers in over ninety-five neighborhoods are elected every two years at the polls. The neighborhood associations form the base of the system. Broader "communities" encompass several neighborhoods apiece, and a citywide Citizens Advisory Board (CAB) is composed of representatives from each of these communities. Each association communicates with all households in its neighborhood through a monthly newsletter, decides how its community development block grant (CDBG) allocations will be used, and works with community resource staff to find solutions to neighborhood concerns. This structure was the first to bring blacks and whites in Birmingham together in a common vision for the city.

—Dayton has a system of seven Priority Boards whose members are elected by precinct through the use of mail ballots. Each Priority Board area is divided into neighborhoods, which overlap the precinct boundaries. The system is seen explicitly as a two-way communication channel between government and citizens. Through leadership training; a monthly council meeting of each board and representatives of major city agencies; annual neighborhood needs statements; and a wide range of neighborhood-oriented planning, initiatives, and self-help programs, citizens learn how to make their voices heard. In return, the city communicates its plans and progress to all the neighborhoods through a Priority Board staff based in a neighborhood office and makes its case for needed change on a wide range of matters from bond issues to city employee residency requirements.

—Portland has grown into a citywide system of autonomous neighborhood associations, with seven District Coalition Boards pulling together more than ninety neighborhood representatives. Each board, hiring its own staff and working out of its own office, is under contract with the city to provide "citizen participation services" to its own community. The administrative budget alone was more than $1.2 million in 1986–87. The system consciously balances the coalition advocacy, annual neighborhood needs reports, crime prevention teams, and individual neighborhood issues with a wide range of citywide participation initiatives. These initiatives include Budget Advisory Committees for every major agency plus the "big BAC" for the city as a whole, comprehensive neighborhood-based planning, self-help development grants, technical assistance, and a citizen mediation program. City officials take pride in the multiplicity of participation routes.

—St. Paul is divided into seventeen District Councils, each elected by residents of the council area. Every council has a city-paid community organizer and neighborhood office, but virtually all other efforts come from volunteers or additional funds raised by the council itself. The District Councils have substantial powers, including jurisdiction over zoning, authority over the distribution of various goods and services, and substantial influence over capital expenditures. A citywide Capital Improvement Budget Committee (CIB), composed solely of neighborhood representatives, is responsible for the initiation and priority ranking of most capital development projects in the city. Community centers, crime prevention efforts, an early notification system for all major city agencies, and a district newspaper in virtually every council area help to make the system one of the most coherent and comprehensive of any city we have seen.

—In San Antonio, Communities Organized for Public Service (COPS) is structured along parish boundaries of the Catholic church in the Hispanic sections of the city. Parallel but much weaker organizations exist in the remainder of the city, competing with independent neighborhood organizations. Citywide conventions and "actions" (demonstrations, meetings, and confrontations with public officials) of several hundred to several thousand people characterize COPS activity. The city initiates fewer programs in support of the neighborhood groups than do the other four cities, but over the course of twenty years, COPS has provided the Hispanic community, which had virtually no clout at city hall, with an organization that arguably has more political power than any other single community group in the nation.

In contrast to the critics' predictions, these strong participation systems have not functioned at the expense of governability. They do not produce policy gridlock or increased political conflict. The systems do not seem to introduce racial or economic biases into the policymaking process. There is no evidence that the city-supported neighborhood associations at the core of the systems in four of the five cities are less effective in translating citizen demands into governmental action than are independent citizen groups.

Instead of chaos, there is a degree of empowerment. Participation in these systems tends to increase confidence in government and sense of community. Within a certain range of issues—particularly land use and planning issues—neighborhoods generate city policy. High levels of face-to-face participation are linked to increased responsiveness by city hall.

After many years of operation, however, many participants and non-participants alike have criticisms of these systems. Some feel that they do not go far enough: the city does not listen to them on the important issues, the participation structures have become rigid, and too few people are involved. Indeed, our comparison surveys show that the overall numbers of people active in their community are little different in these cities from those in comparable cities with less extensive participation efforts, although more of this activity in the five cities is directed toward community and political issues than purely social interaction. Low-income people and those with lower education levels are still much less involved than higher income, more highly educated people. Many remain unaware of an opportunity to participate and skeptical of their ability to influence any political decision. Even the five cities are still far from achieving the ideals of strong democracy.

To explore the potential and realities of systems promoting strong participation, we constructed a multifaceted research design combining both surveys and fieldwork in the five cities. Our approach can only be described in the briefest of terms here; readers who want to know more about details of the research design may consult the Methodological Appendix.

The first task in studying neighborhoods and participation was to identify communities where well-functioning institutions facilitated citizen involvement in local government. Citizens have always organized on their own to try to influence government, and many individual citizen groups have had substantial impact on their city government's policy-making on a particular issue. As Paul Peterson has pointed out, though, city politics is generally "groupless politics."[34] Therefore the search was for cities that deviated from the norm of having politically inactive neighborhoods. The initial step in this selection process was a mailing to some 7,500 leaders of citizen participation efforts around the country. (A list of these leaders had been compiled over many years by the Lincoln Filene Center for Citizenship and Public Affairs at Tufts University.) From this effort more than 900 impressive citizen participation programs were nominated for inclusion in this study. This list was supplemented by a data bank at the Filene Center that catalogues citizen participation programs. From these lists 415 programs were culled and a one-page screening questionnaire was sent to each. Two primary criteria were used to create a short list from the responses received. First, did the program offer widespread outreach to citizens? Second, was there reason to believe that the program had a strong potential to greatly influence public policy?

Extensive research was done on each of the programs that remained to find those that were most impressive on these two counts. Initially, the search for exemplary participation efforts did not focus exclusively on programs that covered a large part or all of a city. However, as the search progressed, it became fairly clear that the criterion that such efforts have a strong potential to affect public policy screened out many programs that lacked this broad institutional scope.

Scholarly studies and other literature describing the programs were reviewed and program administrators were interviewed over the phone when we needed further information. A smaller short list left fifteen candidates. The final selections were made from those that seemed most impressive and offered some geographic diversity. We decided early on to select participation efforts that might yield information about participatory democracy that could be applied to fairly typical American cities. For this reason, only cities with more than 100,000 people were included,

34. Paul E. Peterson, *City Limits* (University of Chicago Press, 1981), p. 116.

and excluded were cities that are highly homogeneous in their socioeconomic makeup.

Each of the five cities was studied in the same manner. Surveys of approximately 1,100 citizens were completed during 1986 and 1987. The samples were stratified to ensure proportionate representation of respondents from each officially defined neighborhood of the city. Approximately eighteen months later an effort was made to reinterview everyone who had participated in the first round of the surveys. On average, these second-wave interviews included 66 percent of the original sets of respondents. Complementing these ten surveys was an eleventh that questioned a control group of 1,500 people. To create this sample, each of the five cities was matched with two others similar in size and socioeconomic characteristics. An average of about 150 individuals were randomly selected from each of the ten comparison cities and asked most of the same questions from the earlier surveys. These surveys provide needed information to serve as a control because none of the ten cities has an extensive citywide citizen participation effort. Altogether, over 11,000 interviews were completed as part of this study's citizen surveys.

Another major part of the research was in-depth fieldwork in the five cities. The authors spent time in each, conducting interviews with city administrators, city councillors, officials from the citizen participation programs, and citizen group leaders. Focus groups were also conducted with groups of activists in some of the neighborhood associations. Separate standardized questionnaires were used for administrators, city councillors, and the heads of citizen groups, but the three instruments shared many of the same questions.

This book is organized around three principal questions. The first asks if participatory democracy is possible. In part I we ask if previous experiments in promoting rank-and-file participation in policymaking have proven that participatory democracy is impractical. Does the empirical evidence from the five cities show that more people participate? Do people participate in different ways?

Part II examines whether the neighborhood associations are able to promote policy responsiveness on the part of the local governments. Who gets their issues on the agenda? Do the poor and minorities fare better in a political system built around neighborhood government? To what degree do the actual decisions of government conform to the preferences of the neighborhoods? Finally, does the responsiveness of the local governments to the neighborhood associations promote parochialism at the expense of the larger interests of the community?

Empowerment is the subject of part III. Does participation in the neighborhood associations increase the capacity of people to take part in government, or are the neighborhood associations simply vehicles for those who are already experienced and knowledgeable in the ways of the political world? If responsibility is turned over to the neighborhoods, is the result increased conflict among amateur politicians who do not understand the realities of the political process? To test Rousseau's belief that active participation leads to acceptance of the general will by those who initially disagreed with the majority, we compare participants with nonparticipants and measure their willingness to tolerate the views of those they disagree with. How does citizen participation affect people's confidence in government? In the same vein, does participation lead to a greater sense of community?

Beyond all these empirical questions lies a prescriptive one. From the experience of these five cities, what practical steps can be taken to increase political participation in urban America?

Part One

Is Participation Possible?

CHAPTER 2

A Legacy of Failure

MAKING THE CASE for participatory democracy on theoretical grounds is much easier than demonstrating that it will work. Only the naive would assume that simply creating new opportunities for participation will lead to expanded political activity, more knowledgeable and capable citizens, enhanced public confidence in government, or any of the other benefits promised by advocates of participatory democracy. Changes in opportunities need to be coupled with new efforts at political socialization and significant changes in the political culture. Yet politicians seem to have little incentive to expend their political capital to pursue structural reforms that may pave the way for more participation. Even sympathetic political elites are likely to reason that efforts at expanding participation have been tried before and have failed.

Concluding that efforts to expand citizen participation beyond the act of voting are doomed to failure is surely reasonable: many previous efforts in the United States have not been successful. Nevertheless, such a judgment is also unfair because genuine participatory democracy has yet to be tried. The efforts to institutionalize citizen participation during the 1960s and 1970s were far too constrained; people looking at these citizen participation structures understandably judged them to be superficial and not worth their time. Elected officials and program administrators paid lip service to the virtues of citizen participation, but ultimately they did not want to diminish their own authority by sharing it with others. Citizen participation failed because political elites wanted it to fail.

Even though elites designed programs that were predisposed to fail, they did not bear responsibility for the disappointing results. The legacy of the 1960s and 1970s is that public involvement programs failed because the public did not care to participate. Those who did participate were seen as either rabble-rousers or elites unrepresentative of the larger community. Unfortunately, this legacy of failure deters efforts to revitalize American democracy. If people remain convinced that these previous endeavors were unavoidable failures, this conviction unconsciously strengthens the notion that representative democracy is the only form of democracy.

In the chapters to come, the question of whether meaningful citizen participation programs can work will be explored in detail. The purpose in this chapter, however, is to set the record straight about the past. We do this because the programs in our five cities should not be viewed as anomalies against a broader background of conflict, apathy, and failure. Despite the impressive scope of the collective efforts of the 1960s and 1970s, they are not analogous to the programs studied here. Despite their rhetoric, these earlier programs were not aimed at rank-and-file citizens. Many of them only nominally involved face-to-face interaction. Most important, these earlier efforts did not offer citizens real *control* over governmental programs that affected their lives.

Misunderstanding's Misunderstandings

Community control, however, was theoretically at the heart of this nation's most ambitious attempt to promote citizen participation in public policymaking. Before Lyndon Johnson's declaration of war on poverty, efforts to expand political participation were largely restricted to trying to increase the number of people who voted. With the Economic Opportunity Act of 1964 came the community action program (CAP), intended to attack poverty by tapping the energies and imagination of those on the local level. The underlying strategy of the antipoverty efforts of CAPs was that local solutions would be tailored to fit local problems. This grandiose plan was at the center of Lyndon Johnson's effort to define his presidency as something separate from that of his fabled predecessor. The war on poverty was Lyndon Johnson's alone—it was not, like the 1964 civil rights bill or the food stamp program, a Kennedy plan that he had to work for to honor the slain leader's legacy. The war on poverty was to add luster to his presidency; therefore, as Johnson himself recalled, "It had to be big and bold and hit the whole nation with real impact."[1] It was and it did.

At the heart of the definition of a community action program in the statute creating the war on poverty was a simple requirement for citizen participation. Each CAP had to be "developed, conducted, and admin-

1. Lyndon Baines Johnson, *The Vantage Point: Perspectives of the Presidency, 1963–1969* (Holt, Rinehart and Winston, 1971), p. 74.

istered with the maximum feasible participation of residents of the areas and members of the groups served."[2] Out of this requirement came controversy concerning the real purpose of the program, and the criticism of maximum feasible participation contributed to the program's ultimate demise. Of all the criticism of citizen participation in the CAP, none was louder or more influential than that of Daniel Patrick Moynihan. His 1969 book, *Maximum Feasible Misunderstanding*, skewered the program by portraying CAPs as local free-for-alls, abetted by a vague law and conniving liberal social engineers.[3]

Moynihan's book deserves scrutiny not simply because of its notoriety, but because it accurately captured the charges being made against the program at the time it was written—charges that stuck to the program like glue. Among the critics Moynihan, now a U.S. senator from New York, had unusual credibility. He was a member of the Johnson administration at the time the war on poverty was created, and he was on the original task force that planned the program presented to Congress. *Maximum Feasible Misunderstanding* derives a great deal of its power from the personal present-at-the-creation-and-watched-it-go-wrong tone. Moynihan portrays the founding fathers of the program as his colleagues, even friends, who somehow led the country astray with their zeal to do good. As one review put it, "Moynihan's book provides a unique view," as the author is "analyzing events in which he was deeply involved."[4]

Moynihan, however, was not deeply involved in the creation of the war on poverty. The mutual antagonism between him and poverty czar Sargent Shriver and his group led Moynihan to retreat from the task force back to the Department of Labor, where he was an assistant secretary.[5] Although he calls his book a "personal memoir," much of the narrative about the development of the program is based on a senior thesis done by a Harvard undergraduate, Richard Blumenthal.[6]

2. Economic Opportunity Act of 1964 (P.L. 88-452), title II.

3. Daniel P. Moynihan, *Maximum Feasible Misunderstanding: Community Action in the War on Poverty* (Free Press, 1969).

4. Norman C. Thomas, review of *Maximum Feasible Misunderstanding, Journal of Politics,* vol. 32 (May 1970), p. 455.

5. Nicholas Lemann, "The Unfinished War," pt. II, *Atlantic Monthly,* January 1989, pp. 58–59.

6. Moynihan, *Maximum Feasible Misunderstanding,* pp. xiv–xvii. A version of Richard Blumenthal's thesis is published as "The Bureaucracy: Antipoverty and the Community Action Program," in Allan P. Sindler, ed., *American Political Institutions and Public Policy* (Little, Brown, 1969), pp. 129–79.

Moynihan makes four charges against community action. Each of them is serious, and cumulatively they constitute a devastating indictment. In broad terms community action is depicted as an inherently bad idea that was confusingly formulated into law and then badly implemented. More specifically, the problems that Moynihan cites are that community action promoted conflict and violence in the inner city, government did not have a conceptual understanding of what it was trying to accomplish, bureaucrats perverted congressional intent when they implemented the law, and the poor may never be ready to assume power. Each of these charges bears closer inspection.

Community Action Promoted Conflict and Violence

Looking back at the turbulent 1960s from the end of the decade, Moynihan identifies citizen participation in the community action program as a central cause of the turmoil in America's big cities. His logic is that the promise of community control led to rising expectations by inner-city residents; when those expectations were not met, frustration eventually led to anger, conflict, and violence. An epigraph at the beginning of the book quotes political scientist Aaron Wildavsky.

> A recipe for violence: Promise a lot; deliver a little. Lead people to believe they will be much better off, but let there be no dramatic improvement.[7]

Moynihan takes to task not only the planners of the war on poverty, but the social scientists whose ideas laid the foundation for the whole endeavor. Social scientists overpromised what their remedies could accomplish, and political elites then compounded the problem by establishing programs that promised much more than they could ever achieve.

The causal logic that rising expectations can lead to social and political upheavals is certainly sound. What is truly astonishing about Moynihan's critique is that it completely ignores the role of the civil rights movement. Rising expectations by inner-city blacks are viewed as something that white political elites mistakenly permitted to happen. In reality what community action contributed to rising expectations was relatively trivial

7. Moynihan, *Maximum Feasible Misunderstanding.*

compared with the torrent of demands for full equality that began in the 1950s. Community action was not a strategic mistake by program planners; there could be no antipoverty effort that did not build in some form of policymaking participation for those who lived in the inner city. A program targeted at inner-city blacks and controlled by white bureaucrats was not intellectually credible in 1964. The outrage from black intelligentsia and political elites would have crippled any effort of the government to go into black communities with programs that treated residents only as clients. As Marris and Rein note, the Office of Economic Opportunity (OEO) "could not have escaped conflict: it could only choose which battle to fight—against city hall or ghetto leadership."[8]

Moynihan's belief that citizen participation was one of the matches that lit America's urban tinderboxes is misguided as well. The urban rioting of that era began in earnest with the Harlem riot on July 18, 1964, before Congress had actually put the final touches on the Economic Opportunity Act.[9] The spread of disorders that summer may have underlined the gravity of doing something to combat poverty, but at the time the program had not yet been implemented, much less had a chance to fail.

Government Did Not Understand

In his book Moynihan treats citizen participation as an intellectual orphan. In his mind the whole idea of community action was "little noticed or understood at the time."[10] His conclusion does not mince words, claiming that "this is the essential fact: *The government did not know what it was doing.*"[11] This is quite a claim—and it is quite wrong. Policy planners certainly did not anticipate all that would happen with community action, but it was not merely a notion reflecting the momentary ascendancy of some liberal social activists. Rather, community action was grounded in two broad and recurring ideas in American political thought.

8. Peter Marris and Martin Rein, *Dilemmas of Social Reform: Poverty and Community Action in the United States,* 2d ed. (Chicago: Aldine, 1973), p. 260.

9. Edward C. Banfield, *The Unheavenly City: The Nature and Future of Our Urban Crisis* (Little, Brown, 1970), p. 193.

10. Moynihan, *Maximum Feasible Misunderstanding,* p. xvi.

11. Moynihan, *Maximum Feasible Misunderstanding,* p. 170 (emphasis in the original).

First, the design of the war on poverty reflected the underlying strength of the idea of federalism and the frequent political efforts to find a way to revitalize American federalism. The community action program was a forerunner of the Nixon administration's New Federalism with its emphasis on revenue sharing and block grants: federal money was to be coupled with local preference. Lyndon Johnson saw this clearly: "This plan had the sound of something brand new and even faintly radical. Actually, it was based on one of the oldest ideas of our democracy, as old as the New England town meeting—self-determination at the local level."[12] Theodore Berry, who directed the community action program for the OEO, explained the program in similar terms. He told Congress that "Community Action is rooted deep in the American tradition of local initiative—local answers to local problems and opportunities."[13]

Second, community action represented a traditional American perspective on welfare that people should help themselves rather than accepting handouts from government. Johnson would not entertain the idea of a "welfare" program. "You tell Shriver no doles," Johnson instructed Bill Moyers during the time the design of the war on poverty was being debated within the administration.[14] Robert F. Kennedy, Johnson's main rival for leadership of the party, felt the same distaste for welfare as did Johnson and actively promoted the idea of community control as an alternate solution to the problems of the ghetto.[15] Simply defined, CAPs were to be self-help programs. As John Wofford, one of the OEO's initial policymakers, put it, community action was "an opportunity program to assist the poor to begin to pull themselves up by their own bootstraps."[16] This was not just rhetoric from Washington—the local CAPs made self-help through participation the cornerstones of their operating philosophy.[17]

12. Johnson, *Vantage Point*, p. 74.

13. Prepared Statement of Theodore M. Berry, *Examination of the War on Poverty Program*, Hearings before the Subcommittee on Employment, Manpower, and Poverty of the Committee on Labor and Public Welfare, 90 Cong. 1 sess. (Government Printing Office, 1965), pt. 9, p. 2765.

14. Lemann, "The Unfinished War," p. 58.

15. Arthur M. Schlesinger, Jr., *Robert F. Kennedy and His Times* (Ballantine, 1978), pp. 842–45.

16. John G. Wofford, "The Politics of Local Responsibility," in James L. Sundquist, ed., *On Fighting Poverty: Perspectives from Experience* (Basic Books, 1969), p. 74.

17. Ralph M. Kramer, *Participation of the Poor: Comparative Community Case Studies in the War on Poverty* (Prentice-Hall, 1969), pp. 218–19.

Government knew what it wanted to do and why it made sense to do it. It failed in its attempt to end poverty, but not because it chose a solution divorced from the intellectual foundations of American politics.

The Bureaucracy Perverted
Congressional Intent

Moynihan is certainly correct in faulting Congress for not being more precise in defining "maximum feasible participation." His professed shock at such sloppiness is a bit disingenuous for a Washington insider though—Congress frequently fails to define key concepts in its statutes. Where Moynihan really misconstrues events, however, is in his interpretation of what happened as a consequence of the term's vagueness. Moynihan claims that the phrase was used by Shriver's bureaucrats to "sanction a specific theory of social change" never envisioned by the Congress. He claims that all that was intended by "maximum feasible participation" was the protection of Southern blacks from being excluded from "the *benefits* of the community action programs."[18]

Did OEO bureaucrats use an ambiguous "feel good" phrase in the statute as a license to rewrite the poverty program? The first step in assessing congressional intent is to examine the statutory record, especially the House and Senate reports accompanying the legislation; they typically spell out intent in their section-by-section analyses. Unfortunately, the committee reports issued as part of the 1964 legislation do not specify what the Congress wanted in terms of participation.[19] A year later, though, Congress passed some minor amendments to the Economic Opportunity Act that gave it a chance to add specificity, and more important, to rectify anything it did not like in the way the OEO was administering the maximum feasible participation requirement. Rather than saying that the OEO had gone too far in implementing maximum feasible participation, the House report chided it for not going far enough and gave a sweeping endorsement to the principle of participation by the poor:

18. Moynihan, *Maximum Feasible Misunderstanding*, p. 87 (emphasis in the original).
19. *Economic Opportunity Act of 1964*, H. Rept. 1458, 88 Cong. 2 sess. (GPO, 1964), pp. 10–11, 74; and *Economic Opportunity Act of 1964*, S. Rept. 1218, 88 Cong. 2 sess. (GPO, 1964), pp. 18–19.

It is the [Labor and Public Welfare] committee's firm direction that it is the responsibility of OEO and of local and State officials concerned with the program . . . to take the necessary action to correct any program in which the principle of maximum feasible participation of the poor does not extend to all levels and stages of planning and administration.[20]

There is nothing very ambiguous about a "firm direction" to ensure the participation of the poor at all "stages of planning and administration." Contrary to the argument in *Maximum Feasible Misunderstanding*, Congress seems to have been initially concerned about too little rather than too much citizen participation.

Further evidence of what Congress wanted comes from its subsequent reviews of the program and the changes it made in the statute. Congress commonly rewrites sections of a law either to revise or to give additional validity to program regulations.[21] In the years following passage of the Economic Opportunity Act, two major changes were made in the provision for citizen participation. First, in 1966, Congress passed an amendment sponsored by Representative Albert Quie, Republican of Minnesota, that required at least one-third of the membership of local antipoverty boards to be composed of poor people. This amendment was intended to *increase* citizen participation in the wake of reports that the White House wanted to pull back because some mayors were complaining about the independence of the community action agencies.[22] The second significant change, the Green amendment, did represent a curtailment of citizen participation. In response to the continuing criticism from mayors, a 1967 amendment by Representative Edith Green, Democrat of Oregon, gave cities the right to bring their community action program under local government control. Congress used the Green amendment to say that "community action" did not represent complete community control. Despite the complaints that preceded the amendment's enact-

20. *Economic Opportunity Act Amendments of 1965*, S. Rept. 599, 89 Cong. 1 sess. (GPO, 1965), p. 6. The House report endorses OEO policy on citizen participation as outlined in the program guide that it issued for use by local governments. *Economic Opportunity Act Amendments of 1965*, H. Rept. 428, 89 Cong. 1 sess. (GPO, 1965), p. 9.

21. Jeffrey M. Berry, *Feeding Hungry People: Rulemaking in the Food Stamp Program* (Rutgers University Press, 1984), pp. 106–07.

22. William G. Selover, "The View from Capitol Hill: Harassment and Survival," in Sundquist, ed., *On Fighting Poverty*, p. 172.

ment, few cities availed themselves of this option. Apparently, most of the aggrieved concluded that it was not worth the political cost to undo the working relationships that had already been established.[23]

Finally, Congress's real intent in regard to citizen participation can also be divined from its decision when it confronted the issue during the development of the model cities program in 1966. Although it had an opportunity to change its mind, Congress instead pressed ahead by calling for "widespread citizen participation" in model cities planning.[24] In short, citizen participation was not something that departed from congressional intent. Congress wanted meaningful and recurrent participation of the poor; it did not have to be dragged along by bureaucrats wishing to ignite a social revolution.[25]

The Poor May Never Be Ready

Moynihan uses *Maximum Feasible Misunderstanding* to teach a lesson: that the poor were not ready to participate in the formulation and administration of local poverty programs. Moreover, "It may be that the poor are never 'ready' to assume power in an advanced society: the exercise of power in an effective manner is an ability acquired through apprenticeship and seasoning." He carries this thought to an ominous vision of America: "We may discover to our sorrow that 'participatory democracy' can mean the end of both participation and democracy."[26]

A consistent strain in Western political thought has always emphasized the need for a more qualified class to lead those who are unqualified. What is noteworthy about Moynihan's book is not that it repeats this argument, but that it builds support for it by unfairly stigmatizing poor blacks. In Moynihan's view maximum feasible participation unleashed unruly behavior by those who were suddenly given a role in the policymaking process. Citizen participants are stereotyped as those interested in harassing the establishment rather than working with it.

23. Alan Altshuler, *Community Control: The Black Demand for Participation in Large American Cities* (Pegasus, 1970), pp. 111–12.

24. Debate within the Department of Housing and Urban Development immediately ensued as to what constituted "widespread citizen participation." Lawrence D. Brown and Bernard J. Frieden, "Rulemaking by Improvisation: Guidelines and Goals in the Model Cities Program," *Policy Sciences*, vol. 7, no. 4 (1976), pp. 455–88.

25. James A. Morone, *The Democratic Wish: Popular Participation and the Limits of American Government* (Basic Books, 1990), p. 250.

26. Moynihan, *Maximum Feasible Misunderstanding*, pp. 136–37, 164.

There were, of course, instances of prolonged conflict between community activists and city hall. The Green amendment is testimony to the anger of many big-city mayors about both the independence of CAPs and the criticism they were receiving from leaders of the poor. More than a thousand CAPs were in operation during the 1960s, but Moynihan does not assess how frequently conflict, rather than cooperation, occurred. He never considers that conflict may be an intermediate phase between quiescence and cooperative working arrangements. Conflict is inevitable in a democratic polity, but it is not inevitably chronic.

If the poor are not ready to rule, how are they to be prepared? Waiting until they are middle class hardly seems a satisfactory answer, but it is the one implied by Moynihan's Manichaean view. If Moynihan is right, then citizen participation schemes that give significant authority to low-income communities will always be endangered by the disruptive forces of those not ready to assume power.

Despite the exaggerations and inaccuracies of Moynihan's charges, the prospects for further experiments in participatory democracy for the poor were seriously damaged by his book. The impact of *Maximum Feasible Misunderstanding* was limited, however, to its assessment of public involvement for the poor. As will be detailed below, citizen participation for the middle class positively prospered in the wake of the failure of community action. For the poor, however, the indictment and the conviction came quickly: the poor cannot be trusted to behave responsibly in the governmental process. Unfair as it was, this perception became the historical reality.

The Undermining of Citizen Participation

Moynihan was, of course, quite right: the community action program was in most respects a failure. He was also right that it was designed to fail, although it was not the incorporation of public involvement that was responsible for its failure. The role of community residents was not sufficient to be blamed for the ineffective programs that were created in their neighborhoods. One early study of CAPs in medium sized-cities concluded that "there were *no* poor people, *no* residents of poverty neighborhoods, *no* members of the groups to be served involved in the initiation of the local community action agencies or in the initial program development in the twenty cities in this sample."[27]

27. S. M. Rose, *Community Action Programs*, thesis, Brandeis University, 1970, cited in Marris and Rein, *Dilemmas of Social Reform*, p. 258 (emphasis in original).

For representatives of the poor, the most important battle was the fight to be taken seriously. They did not develop the CAPs; rather, they often found themselves knocking on the door of the CAP that was created for them in their city. In San Francisco in 1965, not a single member of the CAP board or executive committee came from the CAP's target neighborhoods. By 1966, members from the target areas had majorities on both.[28] This was a common pattern as pressure from community activists and from the federal government (soon manifested in the Quie amendment) led to significant representation from poor neighborhoods. By 1967 Sargent Shriver could proudly tell Representative Quie that 10,000 poor people served on CAP agency boards and another 30,000 on neighborhood advisory councils.[29]

Representation on boards became a bureaucratically convenient indicator of whether the poor were participating. Broader participation beyond the small numbers in each community who sat on boards was quickly deemphasized by the OEO. In cities that had elections for membership on CAP boards during the OEO's first year, the turnout in the target neighborhoods ranged from about 1 percent to 5 percent. A study of why the elections were ignored by the poor concluded that the races lacked compelling issues and candidates and that community residents doubted the community action agencies would succeed where earlier antipoverty efforts had failed.[30]

The fulfillment of maximum feasible participation through board representation came much easier than the efforts of those boards to gain influence for their CAPs within city politics. What community action represented to the local politicians in power was an effort by Washington to establish decentralized government within their cities. Cities were not being given a program that could be used to expand political support for current officeholders through strategic deployment of the newly acquired federal resources. These resources were going not to city hall but to a community action agency that was not under the control of local government.

For many big-city mayors, the money was also going to the "wrong" constituency. Community action gave a forum to a new set of aggressive—often deemed "militant"—black leaders who had cut their political

28. Kramer, *Participation of the Poor*, p. 177.

29. *Economic Opportunity Act Amendments of 1967*, Hearings before the House Committee on Education and Labor, 90 Cong. 1 sess. (GPO, 1967), p. 81.

30. Sar A. Levitan, *The Great Society's Poor Law: A New Approach to Poverty* (Johns Hopkins University Press, 1969), p. 114.

teeth during the civil rights movement and were not easily co-opted by city hall. Even if city hall was doing business with the same black leaders they had always dealt with, those leaders made new demands upon them. Such established black leaders could not repudiate the calls for "black power" by younger leaders or even ignore the idea of black separatism that emanated from the black intelligentsia. All of this worked to upset the delicate balance of city politics. As Greenstone and Peterson note,

> For their part, the mayors and their allies saw a threat to the very foundations of urban government. The intensity with which these new community groups made their demands threatened to undermine the elaborate system of bargaining among established groups, making it extremely difficult to negotiate political compromise.[31]

Some big-city mayors were openly hostile to the administrative independence offered by the structure of the community action program. The legendary Richard J. Daley of Chicago said, "We think very strongly that any program of this kind, in order to succeed, must be administered by the duly elected officials of the areas with the cooperation of the private agencies." Mayor Robert Wagner of New York was also openly critical, asking that local government "have the power of approval over the makeup of the planning group, the structure of the planning group, and over the plan."[32] Other mayors were less public in their views, communicating in private to the Johnson White House that they did not like all the trouble the local CAPs were causing them.

Although open conflict attracted a great deal of attention, quiet negotiation and eventual accommodation were far more common. City hall wanted its people to be involved in CAP decisionmaking, but it was not terribly interested in doing anything that would enhance the CAP's status in city politics. For their part, community activists wanted support and respect from city hall, but they wanted autonomy as well. Out of these conflicting positions came the pulling and tugging of negotiation as each side also saw the need to come to an agreement. City hall could not endlessly withstand the political heat of an agitated community action agency, while CAPs needed to get up and running so that they could show results.

31. J. David Greenstone and Paul E. Peterson, *Race and Authority in Urban Politics: Community Participation and the War on Poverty* (Russell Sage, 1973), p. 100.
32. Levitan, *Great Society's Poor Law*, p. 111.

The OEO did not sit idly by and wait for city governments to work things out with their CAPs. Its corps of field representatives with the power to approve local programs became actively involved in negotiations between local governmental leaders and the CAPs. The field representatives were imbued with the OEO's operating philosophy that local programs should sit atop "three-legged stools." The three legs were officials from city government, established private agencies that had been fighting poverty before the war on poverty was born, and representatives of the poor.[33] This kind of partnership did not offer the autonomy that community activists wanted—though were never promised by the legislation; and it gave less power to city government than it wanted—though more than cities thought they had been dealt by the law.

The ultimate product of these negotiations varied widely from city to city as there turned out to be surprising variety in the shape of the three-legged stools. In particular, the arrangements that resulted ranged considerably in the degree to which they encouraged citizen participation. Working arrangements that were favorable to citizen participation were related less to the political strength of a city's black population than to the strength and effort of reform elements it was allied with.[34] In the end these settlements seemed to be successful political arrangements because, as noted earlier, relatively few cities took advantage of the Green amendment to take control of their CAPs.

The negotiated solutions to maximum feasible participation may have brought the community action program needed stability but did not bring it much acclaim. The war on poverty could not cure poverty, of course, and fell victim to its own overblown rhetoric, to white backlash, and to Republican criticism. (Republican Senate leader Everett Dirksen called the war on poverty "the greatest boondoggle since bread and circuses in the days of the ancient Roman empire.")[35] The OEO would continue into the Nixon years, but reorganizations moved its most popular programs to other departments and agencies and left it with fewer responsibilities and the increasingly unpopular community action program. The emphasis in the Nixon administration was on a negative income tax rather than on social service programs.[36]

---

33. Wofford, "Politics of Local Responsibility," p. 77.
34. Greenstone and Peterson, *Race and Authority in Urban Politics*, pp. 245–46.
35. Selover, "View from Capitol Hill," p. 167.
36. Daniel P. Moynihan, *The Politics of a Guaranteed Income: The Nixon Administration and the Family Assistance Plan* (Vintage, 1973), pp. 211–12.

Looking back at the experience of the community action program as it existed in the 1960s reveals that neither Congress, the OEO, nor local governments ever trusted rank-and-file poor people with authority over their lives. During its years in operation the community action program has never become a grassroots program for the masses. Still, it has not been without its successes.[37] The poor who have participated in CAPs and who still participate in some of the continuing CAP programs received valuable training in the bargaining processes of pluralist politics. This was no small accomplishment; the cumulative number of people who sat on CAP boards or worked directly for OEO is significant. A generation of minority leaders received an apprenticeship in politics sponsored by the federal government.

The community action program itself contributed to the rising influence of blacks in urban politics. In many communities the local CAP was a vehicle that helped to incorporate minority interests in the governmental process. Black leaders used CAP resources to establish themselves in electoral and bureaucratic politics.[38] Since blacks were mobilizing on several fronts at this time, the contribution of the CAPs is easily overlooked. Yet they provided an institutional base for community leaders and gave them access to policymakers. In the end, though, the community action program could never live up to its promise of building widespread participation into urban policymaking. Denounced by critics as an excess of participatory democracy, CAPs were instead just the opposite: restrained exercises in representative democracy.

This Time, the Middle Class

In the wake of the controversy and disappointment over public involvement in the war on poverty, citizen participation did not fade away. On the contrary, it could not have done better if it had been publicly hailed as a brilliant success. In the decade after the Economic Opportunity Act was enacted, more than 150 new citizen participation programs

37. See James J. Vanecko, "Community Mobilization and Institutional Change: The Influence of the CAP in Large Cities," *Social Science Quarterly*, vol. 50 (December 1969), pp. 609–30.

38. Paul E. Peterson and J. David Greenstone, "Racial Change and Citizen Participation: The Mobilization of Low-Income Communities through Community Action," in Robert H. Haveman, ed., *A Decade of Federal Antipoverty Programs: Achievements, Failures, and Lessons* (Academic Press, 1977), p. 273.

were created by the federal government.[39] Why did nothing succeed like failure?

The reason is simple: because citizen participation in the war on poverty included only poor people, policymakers assumed that it had little relevance to programs designed to involve the middle class. Implicitly, members of Congress and agency officials believed that the failure of community action programs resulted from the poor's cynicism, lack of education, and weak political skills. The expectation was that middle-class people would know how to use the programs, and bureaucrats and citizen participants would work together harmoniously. Thus, when legislation was passed creating health system planning agencies, revenue sharing, and product safety standards, citizen participation requirements were incorporated into the statutes. Public involvement programs were made part of such diverse laws as the Coastal Zone Management Act of 1972, the Airport and Airways Development Act of 1970, and the Energy Reorganization Act of 1974.

Citizen participation was not forced upon Congress or agencies by a well-organized lobby that pushed strenuously for such programs. Liberal interest groups may have helped to keep citizen participation on the political agenda, but these organizations made no coordinated effort to work for specific types of public involvement programs. Rather, citizen participation was an idea that survived because it had unusual intellectual appeal and, for a time, virtually no political opposition. Citizen participation programs were a response to the general feeling during the 1960s and 1970s that American democracy was sadly in need of reform. Rising levels of distrust in government, the domestic turmoil over the war in Vietnam, the disorder in the streets of Chicago during the 1968 Democratic convention, and the anger of blacks that had exploded into terrible riots in a number of cities all led toward the inescapable conclusion that the governmental process needed revitalization. Somehow it needed to be more responsive, closer to the people, and more concerned about what ordinary citizens wanted.

Along similar lines, citizen participation was seen as an antidote to the failure of pluralism. The vision of pluralist democracy expounded by Robert Dahl and others fell victim not only to the criticism of doubting

39. Walter A. Rosenbaum, "Public Involvement as Reform and Ritual," in Stuart Langton, ed., *Citizen Participation in America* (Lexington, Mass.: Lexington Books, 1978), p. 84.

political scientists, but also to the reality of popular discontent with American government. For the intellectuals who mused about the state of democracy, steps toward participatory democracy were at least an acknowledgment that America needed a new and compelling vision of its democratic practices. No coherent school of thought called for true participatory democracy, but the rhetoric from the left demanding "power to the people" suggested the direction that a new theory might take.

Citizen participation also appealed to those anxious about what was thought of in the 1960s as the "urban crisis." A major concern was that urban America had lost its sense of community. People managed to live in proximity to each other without being neighbors. Middle-class civic values may have replaced the worst aspects of machine politics, but this modern culture also seemed to leave a void in the political life of American cities. Critics like Paul Goodman argued that, as American cities evolved, they became "slums of engineering" characterized by "empty 'belonging.' "[40] The urban planning of the 1950s was reviled, and urbanologists began calling for collaboration between citizens and city planners.[41] The urban crisis was one of spirit as well as resources. This concern for community, an element of support for the creation of CAPs, became more important as the decade wore on and the problems of the cities took center stage.

With this powerful set of expectations and theories about why citizen participation would work, new programs proliferated. At the national, state, and local levels, administrative agencies were told to become more open and more participatory. Until the Reagan administration changed the tenor of the debate, advocates successfully framed the argument as being between those who wanted more democracy and those who wanted less. More usually won. Even when it came to extraordinarily complex issue areas, advocates in and out of government were able to argue convincingly that the public should participate in the policymaking process. The state of California, for example, created an Office of the Public Advisor within its Energy Commission to encourage citizen participation in the licensing of nuclear power plants. When laboratories doing recom-

40. Paul Goodman, "In Search of Community," *Commentary*, vol. 29 (April 1960), p. 320.

41. See, for example, David R. Godschalk and William E. Mills, "A Collaborative Approach to Planning through Urban Activities," *Journal of the American Institute of Planners*, vol. 32 (March 1966), pp. 86–95.

binant DNA experiments surfaced, so too did roles for local citizens in regulating them.[42]

Nevertheless, the growth in the number of programs stood in sharp contrast to their proponents' satisfaction with them. Participants repeatedly claimed that the actual procedures used to involve them in government were a sham, designed only to fulfill an agency's obligation under its public participation requirement. Much of this criticism centered on the symbolic nature of public hearings, a common technique of citizen participation. A hearing can easily be turned into a "dog and pony show," where officials dutifully present a plan, listen attentively to suggestions and complaints by those who attend, and then go ahead and carry out the plan exactly as they intended to do in the first place.[43] A study of public participation in the Environmental Protection Agency (EPA) concluded that public hearings tended to be symbolic when the proposal presented was a fait accompli developed without any input from the public and considered without evaluation of competing policy alternatives.[44]

The fundamental conflict was that citizens wanted not only to speak their mind at an open hearing, but also to have some control over policy outcomes. When participants did not get their way, they would often conclude that the process was rigged and that administrators had no intention of bending their plans to comply with citizen preferences. One student of public involvement programs described them as "rituals," in which everybody involved merely went through the motions of citizen participation.[45] In fairness, it should be said that some programs went beyond perfunctory hearings to include citizen groups in planning or to foster a process that forged a real consensus among disparate groups. For example, the Army Corps of Engineers' "fishbowl planning" brought about meaningful participation in the development of water projects in different parts of the country.[46] And some states were successful in build-

42. See Sheldon Krimsky, "Beyond Technocracy: New Routes for Citizen Involvement in Social Risk Assessment," in James C. Petersen, ed., Citizen Participation in Science Policy (University of Massachusetts Press, 1984), pp. 43–61.

43. Barry Checkoway, "The Politics of Public Hearings," Journal of Applied Behavioral Science, vol. 17, no. 4 (1981), pp. 566–82.

44. The study was conducted by the National Water Commission, as cited in Walter A. Rosenbaum, "Slaying Beautiful Hypotheses with Ugly Facts: EPA and the Limits of Public Participation," Journal of Voluntary Action Research, vol. 6 (July 1978), p. 166.

45. Rosenbaum, "Public Involvement as Reform and Ritual," p. 81.

46. Daniel A. Mazmanian and Jeanne Nienaber, Can Organizations Change? Environmental Protection, Citizen Participation, and the Corps of Engineers (Brookings, 1979).

ing effective citizen advocacy into the ratemaking process for public utilities.[47] But overall, relatively few administrators believed in participatory democracy. Participation was decoupled from authority over decisionmaking as public involvement opportunities were prevented from encroaching on the autonomy of agency personnel.

The success stories gave hope to participation advocates, and although the exemplary programs were few in number, the push for citizen participation accelerated when Jimmy Carter was elected president in 1976. Liberal proponents had assumed that much of the failure of citizen participation during the Nixon and Ford years was due to political opposition by conservative administrators. Most of these programs had been created to address environmental or consumer protection issues, and liberals could easily conclude that their administrators were more concerned about pleasing traditional Republican business interests than sharing power with advocates of an expanded federal role in these areas.

Although this complaint had some validity, the problems with public involvement went far beyond the ideological opposition of Republican administrators. Little thought seemed to be given to the possibility that the programs were fundamentally flawed rather than sabotaged by the administrations in power. Instead, with a sympathetic president in office, proponents thought the programs could at last be fine-tuned to work the way they were designed to. If expectations were high when Carter was elected, they absolutely soared when he began to make his appointments to relevant agencies. Carter placed more than fifty activists from citizens' groups in leading policymaking positions throughout the government. With people like David Hawkins from the Natural Resources Defense Council as an assistant administrator of the EPA and Peter Schuck from Consumers Union as a deputy assistant secretary at Health, Education, and Welfare (HEW), there could finally be progress in making citizen participation work.

The good intentions of the Carter administration were soon borne out. The administration not only upgraded existing programs, but tried to fundamentally alter the representation of interests within government. It actively pushed a proposal to form a new consumer protection agency. This agency would have performed oversight on the rest of the executive branch, intervening in other departments and agencies when the interests of consumers were being slighted. Washington-based public interest

47. William T. Gormley, Jr., *The Politics of Public Utility Regulation* (University of Pittsburgh Press, 1983).

groups, which had only mildly supported citizen participation, were strongly in favor of the proposal; they envisioned a close working relationship with the consumer protection agency. They believed that they would be able to initiate agency action by bringing wrongdoing to the attention of like-minded colleagues on its staff.

But it was not to be. Already antagonized by an aggressive Federal Trade Commission (FTC) under the leadership of consumer advocate Michael Pertschuk, business lobbies made the fight against the consumer agency something of a holy war. A coalition led by the Chamber of Commerce and the Business Roundtable embarrassed the Carter administration with a stinging defeat of a watered-down proposal in the House in 1978. The administration's strategy in the wake of this legislative rebuke was to strengthen citizen representation in policymaking by developing comprehensive public participation plans for executive branch agencies.[48] Although details of how citizen participation would be implemented were left to the individual agencies, White House guidance of the effort was designed to ensure a coordinated approach to the problem. The result of the administration's renewed efforts came in the form of Executive Order 12160, issued in September 1979. It called for "early and meaningful participation" by consumers in agency policymaking. The president's charge was to "make the government think like a consumer."[49] Each agency was required to have a consumer affairs staff with a senior officer in charge, and each also developed a detailed public participation plan and published it in the Federal Register.

Across the whole of the federal establishment, agencies as diverse as the Interstate Commerce Commission, the Postal Rate Commission, and the Commodity Futures Trading Commission detailed their plans for bringing consumers into the decisionmaking process. Even the Department of Defense complied with the spirit of the president's policy with publication of its plan for "two-way communication" between itself and the public.[50] A little more than a year later, of course, Jimmy Carter was voted out of office and the ambitious executive order did not get much of a chance to succeed. Before government had learned to "think like a consumer," Ronald Reagan told it to think otherwise.

48. Louise G. Trubek, David M. Trubek, and Paul G. Kent, The Executive Order on Consumer Affairs Programs: New Voice for "Consumers" in Federal Agencies? (Madison, Wis.: Center for Public Representation, 1980).

49. U.S. Consumer Affairs Council, Implementing the Consumer's Executive Order (January 1981), p. 1.

50. Federal Register, June 9, 1980, p. 39233.

The Conservative Counterattack

Lacking any concentrated opposition, citizen participation programs managed to grow in number despite their lack of success. When opposition finally did arise, however, the failure of these programs to show demonstrable progress in achieving their abstract goals left them all too vulnerable. The irony of the counterattack against public involvement was that while liberals were faulting citizen participation programs for working poorly, conservatives criticized them for working too well. For those concerned about the health of America's free market economy, citizen participation represented an expansion of already burdensome regulatory procedures. Businesses found themselves having not only to comply with a complex set of rules and regulations to produce or market their products, but also to submit to hearings and agency reviews in which citizens might be able to force them to make costly changes in their plans. The conservative charge against public involvement programs was that they were tools not so much of the "public" but of wealthy liberal elites. They were instruments used to delay, impede, and defeat the efforts of businesspeople who were trying to offer goods and services to interested consumers. If "time is money," then citizen participation was quite costly: business saw it as additional red tape affecting the bottom line.

When the Reagan administration came into office in 1981, citizen participation was quickly classified as part of the liberal agenda that it was elected to undo. Even in those areas where citizen participation programs did not interfere with the free market—nutrition programs, for example—the Reagan administration regarded them with hostility. The administration chose to define these programs as manifestations of big government rather than the means by which people protect themselves against the power of the state.

A variety of tactics were used to dismantle existing citizen participation programs, but the primary weapon was the budget cutting that took place during the administration's first year in office. For those liberals in Congress trying to fight the domestic budget reductions, citizen participation programs were hardly seen as the place to draw the line in the sand. Although they did not agree with the administration that these programs were "fat," liberals were not prepared to argue that they were the real meat of the agencies either. Liberals had considerably more pressing priorities to try to save from the budget cutters. There were great outcries in Congress over the EPA's plans to cut back its enforcement efforts but barely a whimper when its public affairs office was cut to roughly half of the forty-five positions it had during the last year of the Carter administration. When the Consumer Product Safety Commission absorbed its office of public participation into its central administrative structure, no one really paid any attention.

Public participation programs were natural targets for budget cutting because of their typically vague basis in law. Legislation rarely spelled out what would be required of an agency to meet its public involvement mandate. Consequently, the administration chose to interpret these laws in ways that minimized the obligation of agencies to consult with the public. Under the new regime at the Federal Aviation Administration, for example, the citizen participation requirement for airport planning was reduced to this simple standard:

> Prior to submission of the map, the airport operator shall afford interested persons adequate opportunity to submit their views, data and comments concerning the correctness and adequacy of the draft noise exposure map and descriptions of projected aircraft operations.[51]

On the surface this appeared to be a requirement for public involvement, but it did little more than affirm the basic thrust of the 1946 Administrative Procedure Act, which gives interested parties the right to comment on proposed regulations.

The administration defended its actions by arguing that rather than trying to eliminate citizen participation, it was turning responsibility for it over to the states and cities. Its reasoning was that since citizen participation is a form of grassroots democracy, those at the grass roots should decide how much of it is appropriate. If states and cities wanted extensive public involvement in policymaking, they could have it; Washington, however, was not going to require it. The administration's actions on citizen participation appeared to be part of its push for its own "new federalism," under which authority over many allocation decisions and other policy choices previously held by the national government would be left to local or state governing bodies. Yet, in revising the requirements in the various agencies of the government, the administration did nothing to distinguish between those programs that were wholly local in nature (like community development block grant project planning) and those

51. Jeffrey M. Berry, "Maximum Feasible Dismantlement," *Citizen Participation*, vol. 3 (November–December 1981), p. 4.

unconcerned with local preferences (like FTC rulemaking). In truth, the weakening of standards for public involvement had little to do with the new federalism. Instead, these actions were intended to free the country of programs that were seen as tools of antigrowth, antibusiness liberals.

Why did citizen participation for the middle class fail as miserably as citizen participation for the poor? First and foremost, it failed because agency bureaucrats were not interested in sharing their authority with citizens. Moreover, they had little reason to do so. Administrators had the discretion to design programs and to decide what constituted substantive participation. Not surprisingly, they created largely symbolic programs. Bureaucrats do look to outside groups for political support, which is why many lobbying groups enjoy a privileged relationship with the agency that administers the programs they are concerned with. But citizen participants really had very little to offer agencies in return for a role in policymaking. The people at the grass roots who took the time to become involved were just not organized in ways that could have provided an agency with the kind of political support that would have been valuable to it.

A second reason was that Congress never provided any incentives for effective citizen participation. Congress approved of citizen participation, but without any intensity of feeling about such programs for the middle class. The issue was not important enough to warrant serious oversight, and Congress felt little pressure to force agencies to do a better job of administering their public involvement programs. Indeed, when legislators' pet projects were delayed by citizens whose mobilization was aided by a public involvement program, the administering agencies would be scolded by those members of Congress.[52]

Third, as has already been noted, liberal advocacy groups were only superficially supportive of public involvement. Public interest groups, which seemed to be the natural constituency for citizen participation, never made public involvement programs a priority issue. These organizations are quite elitist in operation; they are staff dominated and have relatively weak structures for incorporating rank-and-file input.[53] In deploying their organizational resources, they were entirely rational to emphasize lobbying and litigation, run out of the Washington office, rather than to try to build a strong grassroots network that could actively

52. Rosenbaum, "Public Involvement as Reform and Ritual," p. 91.

53. Jeffrey M. Berry, *Lobbying for the People: The Political Behavior of Public Interest Groups* (Princeton University Press, 1977).

participate in agency rulemaking and project planning at the regional or local level. The organizational maintenance costs of such an operation are extremely high, and the annual budgets of these organizations are modest. It also made sense to deemphasize citizen participation because experience had taught these groups that Washington lobbying was a more effective strategy in influencing public policy.

Fourth, the federal administrative agencies that designed the public involvement programs never developed an adequate solution to the problem of *scale*. For a national program, which citizens were the appropriate constituency to involve? When the Department of Agriculture set up a public involvement plan for the food stamp program during the Carter administration, which of the millions of recipients should have been given the chance to participate? Building an effective and ongoing network of participants on a national scale is a daunting task. Mobilizing people to participate in the administrative process is inherently difficult, but it becomes even more difficult when what goes on in local proceedings is so tenuously bound to rulemaking in Washington. Proposals for local development projects offered individuals more reason to participate, but their episodic nature made them a poor vehicle for building participatory institutions.

Cumulatively, these problems presented seemingly insurmountable barriers to effective citizen participation. But in light of the success that some programs enjoyed, was some type of citizen participation structure capable of overcoming these obstacles? The evaluative research suggests that structure had little to do with success. The creation and maintenance of effective citizen participation programs was not a function of tinkering with the institutional arrangements until the right formula turned up. A comprehensive study of health systems agencies found that the level of citizen participation was not statistically related to the techniques utilized to involve the public.[54] In another study, a research team at Tufts University analyzed evaluation studies of public involvement programs in a wide range of policy areas to see if democratic policymaking could be "*built* into the administrative process by instituting specific citizen participation requirements." Apparently not. Few structural characteristics were correlated with program effectiveness in involving rank-and-file citizens. The authors concluded that where programs worked, it was

54. Barry Checkoway, Thomas W. O'Rourke, and David Bull, "Correlates of Consumer Participation in Health Planning Agencies: Findings and Implications from a National Survey," *Policy Studies Review*, vol. 3 (February 1984), pp. 297–310.

likely to be a function of the commitment of individual administrators to make them work.[55]

Like the community action program, these public involvement programs for the middle class were poorly conceived experiments in participatory democracy. Like the community action program, they never offered a share of real policymaking authority to people at the grass roots. And as with the community action program, citizens were wise to assume that participation in them was not worth their time.

Conclusion

History teaches lessons, and the lesson that policymakers seemed to have learned from the 1960s and 1970s is that citizen participation is unworkable. It is not a lesson about underfunded programs or poorly designed administrative structures. Rather, it is that citizen participation cannot accomplish the lofty goals of democratic theory because of the inescapable realities of American politics. The evaluative research on public involvement programs lends credence to this conclusion. Nothing in this literature demonstrates that particular institutional structures or procedures lead to effective citizen participation.

Yet the real lesson to be learned from the citizen participation programs of this era is not that public involvement is unworkable, but that it cannot be conceived of as an administrative reform. It must first be a *political* reform—a change must take place that enhances the value of effective citizen participation. The rewards to administrators of operating effective programs and the sanctions for failing to do so must be significant. Otherwise symbolic efforts will prevail as administrators act, understandably, to preserve their authority.

Program administrators could easily maintain their autonomy when public involvement was mandated, because legislators and executive branch officials were not ready to dilute representative democracy with doses of participatory democracy. Despite the populistic rhetoric that surfaces from time to time in American politics, distrust of the masses endures. The programs of this era were not built on a belief that rank-and-file citizens, relying on face-to-face interaction, should be given responsibility to make decisions on their own.

55. Jeffrey M. Berry, Kent E. Portney, Mary Beth Bablitch, and Richard Mahoney, "Public Involvement in Administration: The Structural Determinants of Effective Citizen Participation," *Journal of Voluntary Action Research*, vol. 13 (April 1984), pp. 7–23 (emphasis in original).

Despite the legacy of failure, citizen participation retains one power-fully attractive attribute: it represents the democratic ideal in a way that representative democracy never can. It involves people taking responsi-bility for their government, being conscientious citizens, and improving their communities through their own hard work. The idea itself can never be dismissed, no matter how many times efforts to implement it in the political system have failed. Thus critics, who can cite these failures of the past if they wish, must still oppose citizen participation proposals on tactical rather than philosophical grounds.

The power of the idea of participatory democracy led to another legacy of the experiments of the 1960s and 1970s: requirements for citizen participation remain at every level of government. Although they are seriously attenuated at the federal level, at the state and local level some good-faith efforts still provide citizens an opportunity to influence policymaking. Even though most programs have representative structures that allow only some citizens to participate on behalf of the broader public, they may be useful starting points for institutional reforms that expand citizen involvement in government.

Consequently, for those who have not given up hope that public involvement programs can someday be the instrument of participatory democracy, there are two foundations from which to build. First, the idea of citizen participation is part of this country's democratic lore. Second, many programs at all levels of government require some form of citizen participation. These requirements can be utilized as a basis for efforts to enhance citizens' role in public policymaking. And in a handful of places, citizen participation works exceptionally well, offering proof that it is not a hopelessly naive ideal suitable only for the dusty tomes of yesterday's political theorists.

CHAPTER 3

The Potential for Success

BIRMINGHAM, Dayton, Portland, San Antonio, and St. Paul stand in stark contrast to the failures of participation, past and present, in many other cities across the nation. In the mid-1970s each developed major neighborhood-based participation efforts that have transformed the political life of their communities. Through their neighborhood offices and citywide networks, thousands of individual citizens have an impact far beyond that of casting a single vote for a candidate. As one planner in St. Paul noted, "Development decisions that affect the neighborhoods simply aren't made until the issue has been taken up with the District Council first."

As in many other medium-sized cities across the country, some strong neighborhood groups flourished in the cities studied long before the participation systems were put in place. But, as in other cities, the organizations were mostly catch-as-catch-can. They covered only a small portion of the city's whole population (especially in Birmingham and San Antonio), sprang up around a hot issue, and often died down a few years later when the all-volunteer energy ran out. Their members always had to stand on the outside of the public policy process, knocking on the door and trying to get in.

What went on within the groups themselves is not unlike what goes on today in these five cities and comparable communities across the nation—citizens coming together face to face to grapple with the issues as they see them. Rules of operation are informal, people join and leave as their interest peaks and wanes, and generally everybody who attends the meetings has a chance to put in their two cents' worth. What is different about the groups in these five cities is that they are organized in every neighborhood of the city and therefore cover all the population; they have regular two-way channels to and from city hall; they have comparatively extensive support staff, training opportunities, technical assistance, and neighborhood offices; and they are empowered to act on behalf of the residents (and local businesses) in their neighborhood. Ac-

46

cess, support, and a recognized, ongoing mission—these factors add up to impact on local policy.

Profiles of Accomplishment

What made these cities different? Why did they succeed when so many others fell by the wayside?[1] The usual suspects—including demographics, population homogeneity, "reform" governments, and economic stimuli—fail to provide a satisfactory explanation.

For example, income patterns in these cities range from one end of the spectrum to the other. Of the 155 U.S. cities between 100,000 and 1 million in population in 1980, Birmingham and Dayton are among the lowest, ranking 145th and 143d respectively in average family income. St. Paul, on the other hand, is in the highest quartile of family income, ranking 32d in the nation. A similar range exists in levels of education: Portland ranks 39th, Dayton 141st. San Antonio has a relatively young population; Portland has a high proportion of senior citizens. While St. Paul has a minority population of just under 10 percent, Birmingham's population is 55 percent African American, and San Antonio is 54 percent Hispanic.[2]

Nor can the answer be sought in the reform character of governmental structure that existed before the participation system was initiated. St. Paul and Birmingham have strong-mayor forms of government, Dayton and San Antonio have council-manager forms (with San Antonio's mayoralty under Henry Cisneros taking on many aspects of a strong-mayor government), while Portland is a pure commission form. In three of the cities, councillors or commissioners are elected at large; in two of them they are elected by district.

Nor was it economic prosperity that allowed these cities the luxury of pursuing the participation system. In fact, each community faced rather difficult economic circumstances at one stage or another during its initial participatory years. Birmingham suffered severe problems from the decline of the steel industry, Portland from a nearly ten-year depression in the lumber industry, and Dayton from drastic cutbacks by automotive parts producers and a key manufacturer, National Cash Register

1. See, for example, Douglas Yates, *Neighborhood Democracy: The Politics and Impacts of Decentralization* (Lexington, Mass.: Lexington Books, 1973).

2. Bureau of the Census, *State and Metropolitan Area Data Book 1986* (Department of Commerce, 1986), table B: Central Cities, pp. 363-501.

(NCR), whose local employment dropped from 30,000 to 4,000 people (in a city of 180,000) in just ten years.

If none of these factors seems to drive the participation process, where do we look for the cause of the participation systems' success? From a closer examination of the operation of the participation process itself and the factors that led to its development and maintenance over more than fifteen years, a clear pattern emerges.

First, there existed a strong motivation to make participation work. This motivation stemmed from three sources: a demand for substantive participation by citizen groups, a clearly articulated vision by a set of governmental leaders, and strong federal participation mandates. The citizen demand provided the energy to make major systemic change possible. This demand, in turn, was often driven by pent-up frustration over the failure of earlier, less ambitious initiatives to make any difference. In Birmingham, for example, the decades of nearly total disenfranchisement of blacks in all areas of community and governmental life led to an outpouring of demand for a new role for all citizens. In Portland, frustration over lack of progress on environmental issues and an attempt to route a new freeway (never built) through a dozen residential neighborhoods led to a recognition that there must be a better way.

The vision was generated by individual leaders who had a mission.[3] In Dayton, it was the vision of a new city manager who wanted to ensure that the massive failures of policy stemming from a lack of participation in the city where he had previously served would not be repeated. In Portland, it was the vision of a mayor (later to become U.S. transportation secretary and then governor) with an activist political agenda who felt that the preexisting sense of neighborhood was an important resource on which to build. Both political and administrative leaders, particularly those in community development or planning departments, were essential to make the vision a reality. The existence of this commitment set these cities apart from the failures considered in the previous chapter.

The federal mandates of the 1960s served as a catalyst for local change when the community was ready for it. In each case the experience with a program that had served only part of the city, such as model cities, or the direct influence of new mandates under the federal community development block grant program (CDBG) was a key factor in the decision to go ahead with a full-scale participation system. In Birmingham, a

3. On the independent influence of administrators, see Susan E. Clarke, "More Autonomous Policy Orientations: An Analytic Framework," in Clarence N. Stone and Heywood Sanders, eds., *The Politics of Urban Development* (University Press of Kansas, 1987).

detailed proposal for a participation system that would include both blacks and whites had been shelved in the early 1970s by the white-majority city council. But when large amounts of federal money became available under CDBG—with the condition that programs be accompanied by a significant participation program—the council promptly took the participation plan off the shelf and implemented it almost intact. It was the combination of these three ingredients—citizen demand, leadership vision, and outside catalyst—that made possible a participatory reform with major political ramifications.[4]

The second factor in the equation that allowed these participation systems to be more than just a flash in the pan involved the fundamentals of their initial design. In each city, three design elements were key:

—Participation was based on small, natural neighborhoods where regular, face-to-face discussion of the issues was possible by all who would take the time to be involved. The population of these neighborhoods is typically between 2,000 and 5,000 but in each city ranges widely (from 70 to 14,000 in Portland, for example). This range is primarily due to the importance given to natural boundaries and the indigenous determination of those boundaries. Only in St. Paul, where a major debate raged over this question for two years at the program's beginning, was the decision made to go with larger districts having an average population of 16,000. The St. Paul decision created a small enough number of districts (seventeen) that each could work directly with city hall. In Birmingham, Dayton, and Portland, a second tier of organizations was found necessary to achieve this objective.

—The system was conceived of as citywide from the beginning. In contrast to many participation efforts under the Office of Economic Opportunity (OEO), model cities, and CDBG programs that shriveled away upon the withdrawal of federal mandates and funds, each of these cities recognized that limiting participation to only a portion of the city would severely restrict its impact. In Birmingham, Dayton, and St. Paul, the delineation of neighborhoods throughout the city was nearly complete within a few years of the program's beginning. In Portland, neighborhoods joined the system one by one as they saw its value to them, although some were recognized in all sectors of the city from the beginning. In fact, one of the reasons the political support for these systems has been sustainable is that residents in every part of the city have a

---

4. On Birmingham, see Steven H. Haeberle, *Planting the Grassroots: Structuring Citizen Participation* (Praeger, 1989).

stake in the system. This support has enabled each system to weather not only economic bad times, but also drastic federal cutbacks in the programs they relied upon for funding, and in some cases mayors or city council majorities hostile to, or jealous of, neighborhood power.

—The major political innovations necessary to sustain the participation system—developing a systematic flow of information to the neighborhoods; supporting neighborhood outreach and communications; providing specific mechanisms for policy input on key development, planning, and budgeting issues—were present at the outset rather than added piecemeal as the system developed. The results of these innovations demonstrated the value of participation to citizens and government officials alike. Without such clear results, the whole system could have been easily dismissed. The existence of these features in the initial plans for the system do not, of course, mean that the structures have been static. Major changes in neighborhood roles, staffing patterns, the policy areas effectively open to participation, allocations for specific programs and system components, and operational approaches have been made in each city over their systems' lifetimes of more than a decade and a half. Portland, for example, came out only in 1989 with its first set of guidelines for the rights and responsibilities of its recognized neighborhood associations, finally gaining the trust of its fiercely independent neighborhoods. Birmingham has had to substantially reduce the importance of its revenue sharing approach, which allowed neighborhoods to individually allocate a large share of federal funds, as those funds fell severalfold.

The third major factor leading to the success of these programs involves a rather sophisticated political balance. From the beginning, citizen and governmental advocates combined a firm refusal to let partisan politics become part of the participation system with an equally firm insistence that policy issues—and all the "politics" that go along with them—become part and parcel of the system's daily operation. In each city the neighborhood organizations are in the middle of some of the most difficult and controversial issues that the city faces: they are asked to balance business and residential interests; resolve every NIMBY (not in my backyard) siting issue; meet federal and state guidelines; tackle drug abuse and crime; deal with environmental crises; find ways to meet social service and health care demands; balance budgets; review bond issues; and at the same time respond to the usual array of concerns about parking, garbage pickup, stop signs, and noisy neighbors.

Yet in each city a clear understanding exists about the neighborhood's political limitations. The system is designed so that it will not be captured by partisan politics. Because they must represent people from all political parties, supporters of candidates of all stripes, and backers of incumbents as well as their opponents, the neighborhood organizations do not and cannot take stands on political candidates. Neighborhood newsletters, as a condition of their support from the city, cannot become campaign media in an electoral contest. In general, this distinction between issue advocacy and electoral neutrality is well understood and accepted by neighborhood residents. In a few cases where individuals have attempted to make the neighborhood associations into their own political campaign organizations, actions have been taken to reconstitute the associations. Nothing in these requirements, of course, restricts the same individuals who are active in the associations from being active in elections under other organizational frameworks. In fact, more and more candidates for the city councils in these cities have gotten their start in community leadership through the neighborhood associations. Candidates for office go to the associations to impress them of their concern for the neighborhood point of view. Issues of support or neglect of the neighborhoods become deciding factors in their victory or defeat. Only in Birmingham, and only in a few neighborhoods there, does this line seem to be crossed: as one political activist noted about his neighborhood, "There is only a slight pause between the adjournment of the neighborhood association meeting and the calling to order of the Jefferson County Citizens Coalition [the mayor's political campaign organization]."

The final and perhaps most important reason that participation has worked in these cities and has not worked in some others is that each city was able to reach a plateau of strong participation before encountering overwhelming financial or political reversals. Many other cities, for example, failed to establish a broadly based, highly participatory structure before federal mandates changed or supportive politicians left office. Such systems had not productively involved enough of the community to turn to that community for support in troubled times. In the cities we examined, however, the network of community support was developed very early in the participation effort. This process required two to three years of intense negotiation and reformulation of plans in cooperation with virtually every citizen group in the city. But within that period of time, confidence in the seriousness and practicality of the plans grew. Community leaders from all parts of the city recognized that their constituency had a major stake in the process, and a high percentage of the politically active people in the city bought into the system. As a result, the systems not only survived but thrived. More and more local funds have been brought into each system, in spite of tight budgets and even cutbacks in other programs. Only in Birmingham, where heavy dependence on federal funds existed from the beginning and where the participation structure has been more closely tied to city hall, is there a foreseeable threat to the fiscal stability of the participation system.

San Antonio represents an exception to many of the above conclusions and, as will be seen later, to many of the outcomes of strong participation as well. It became part of this study not because of a joint citizen-government participation effort but because of its remarkable Alinsky-style citizen organization, COPS (Communities Organized for Public Service). This organization, begun in the mid-1970s, has come to dominate the politics of the city more than any other single community organization we know of in the country. Like the participation efforts in the other cities of this study, COPS has been able to reach out extensively to citizens in the areas it serves and involve them directly in policy issues that affect their lives.

Yet COPS's success has come largely from sources very different from those of the participation process in this study's other cities. While citizen demands for participation were the energy for their organizing, their initiation was not supported in any way by city government. Instead, COPS was able to fill a power vacuum left by the weakening of the Good Government League, a coalition made up primarily of real estate interests that had dominated city politics for more than twenty-five years.[5] Participation efforts in San Antonio, as in other cities, were substantially aided by federal participation mandates—but through an unusual twist. The city was forced, in effect, to change the method of electing its city council from at-large elections to district-based elections to meet federal mandates against discrimination. As a consequence, COPS was able to influence the positions (and in some cases, behind the scenes, the elections) of a majority of the new councillors. It is extraordinarily well organized along well-defined Catholic church parish lines in about 30 percent of the city but is not organized citywide. As an independent citizen group without government ties, COPS has had no restrictions on its political activities but has generally chosen to remain behind the scenes in electoral contests. In that role it has dramatically changed the way CDBG funds are spent in the community, forced the city to provide long-neglected basic services such as street paving, sewers, and other

5. See David R. Johnson, John A. Booth, and Richard J. Harris, eds., *The Politics of San Antonio: Community, Progress, and Power (University of Nebraska Press, 1983).*

utilities to the Hispanic areas of San Antonio, and refocused attention on a range of issues from housing and flood control to education and human services. Overall, COPS has given Hispanics an enormous impact upon city policymaking, a complete reversal of their exclusion twenty years ago.

The Essence of Strong Democracy

The dramatic changes brought about in each of these cities is strongly linked to an extensive, robust participation structure. It was these structures that led us to consider them as participation models in the first place. What are the elements of the strong participatory structures and what has enabled them to thrive for more than fifteen years? To answer these questions we need to start at the roots of democracy.

One of the most comprehensive attempts to specify the necessary elements of an effective democracy is the treatment presented by Robert Dahl in *A Preface to Democratic Theory*. Dahl carefully elaborates the preconditions for a "polyarchy," his model for a "real world" democracy.[6] While Dahl specifies these conditions in terms of voting, we believe they have as great—and perhaps even greater—validity when applied to a more general decisionmaking process. Listed below are Dahl's eight conditions (slightly reordered) alongside their broader participation equivalents.[7]

Dahl's conditions	*Participation equivalents*
Polyarchy is defined loosely as a political system in which the following conditions exist to a relatively high degree:	Strong democracy is defined as a political system that includes the following conditions to a relatively high degree:
1. Any member who perceives a set of alternatives, at least one of which he regards as preferable to any of the alternatives presently scheduled, can insert his preferred alternative(s) among those scheduled for voting.	1. Any citizen who perceives a set of alternatives, at least one of which he or she regards as preferable to any of the alternatives presently scheduled, can insert his or her preferred alternatives among those scheduled for the participation process.

6. Robert A. Dahl, *A Preface to Democratic Theory* (University of Chicago Press, 1956), pp. 63–89.

7. Dahl, *Preface to Democratic Theory*, p. 84.

2. All individuals possess identical information about the alternatives.

3. Every member of the organization performs the acts we assume to constitute an expression of preference among these scheduled alternatives, e.g., voting.

4. In tabulating these expressions (votes), the weight assigned to the choice of each individual is identical.

5. The alternative with the greatest number of votes is declared the winning choice.

6. Alternatives (leaders or policies) with the greatest number of votes displace any alternatives (leaders or policies) with fewer votes.

7. The orders of elected officials are executed.

8. Either all interelection decisions are subordinate or executory to those arrived at during the election stage, i.e., elections are in a sense controlling; or new decisions during the interelection period are governed by the preceding seven conditions, operating, however, under rather different institutional circumstances; or both.

2. All individuals possess identical information about the alternatives.

3. Every citizen performs the acts we assume to constitute an expression of preference among the scheduled alternatives, for example, takes part in the participation process.

4. In summarizing and evaluating these expressions, the weight assigned to the choice of each individual is identical.

5. The alternative with the greatest support within the participation process is declared the winning choice.

6. Alternative policies that receive the greatest support in the participation process displace any alternatives with lesser support.

7. The chosen policies are implemented.

8. Either all implementation decisions are subordinate or executory to those arrived at during the participation process (that is, the participation process is in a sense controlling); or new decisions during the implementation period are governed by the preceding seven conditions; or both.

Obviously these are very stringent criteria for a model democracy. No participation process can fulfill all of them, and even the best of participation efforts in the real world achieve these criteria to only a moderate degree. The criteria do, however, represent the essence of effective citizen participation. They can be used as a starting point in an attempt to determine how practical participation efforts measure up. In particular, they suggest two broad parameters for this evaluation process, *breadth* and *depth*:

—The *breadth* of a participation effort is the extent to which an opportunity is offered to every community member to participate at every

FIGURE 3-1. Critical Elements of Strong Participation

	Structure	Desired outcome
Breadth	Outreach effort —Open access —Full information flow —Realistic opportunities to participate	Increase numbers of people who participate Improve representativeness of participants Include all citizen concerns on decisionmaking agenda
Depth	Decisionmaking process —Equal consideration of ideas —Direct translation of citizen preferences into policy decisions Effective implementation of participatory decisions	Improve match between policy outcomes and participants' final choices Improve match between policy outcomes and needs of all population segments

stage of the policymaking process. It incorporates the first three points of the framework adapted from Dahl: open access to the agenda, extensive information to citizens about alternatives, and high rates of participation among the population.

—The *depth* of a participation effort is the extent to which the citizens who choose to participate have the opportunity to determine the final policy outcome by means of the participation process. This parameter incorporates the next four criteria based on Dahl's conditions: equal weight given to all citizen preferences, decisions made on the basis of those preferences, translation of those decisions into final policy outcomes, and effective implementation of those policies. The final criterion is simply a statement of the iterative use of the same process to generate additional policy choices as needed during policy implementation.

By focusing on these two parameters, we can evaluate any participation effort. In carrying out this analysis, however, it is also important to be clear about whether its focus is an evaluation of the structure of the participation effort itself or the final outcomes of the process. Figure 3-1 illustrates this distinction.

When the structure of a participation system is the focus of this analysis, an evaluation of the *breadth* of the participation effort translates into the analysis of the outreach effort. How effectively is the opportunity to participate offered to all members of the community? Do citizens receive a regular flow of information about how they can participate and what policy alternatives are being considered? Are the mechanisms of participation accessible to all (including such elementary aspects as time and location for meetings)? Are citizens encouraged to offer new alternatives not on the official agenda? A lack of positive answers to these outreach questions in many participation programs, including those of the 1960s, is often the cause of failure.

Evaluation of *depth* considers the mechanics of the participation process itself. How extensive are the opportunities for face-to-face discussion, consensus formation, and what Benjamin Barber calls "strong democratic talk"?[8] Is the participation process carried through to a concrete decision? Is the participation structure designed to create an implementable policy, and is that implementation process responsive to participation? Participation approaches that fail to meet the outreach criteria often do better on many of these questions of depth, if the assembled group is small enough. They tend to fail here too, however, in one key area—the ability of this small group to be taken seriously in the broader policy development and implementation process.

On the other hand, given a particular participation structure, we can also ask, What are the final outcomes of the process conducted through that structure? To evaluate the breadth of the participation effort with outcomes as the focus, we will want to ask other questions. How many people actually choose to participate? How representative are they of the total population? Are those who choose not to participate supportive of the process and willing to let the process determine final policy outcomes? To evaluate the depth of participation, we will need to know how closely the policy outcomes match the final policy choices of those who participate and of the community at large. Do minority groups and minority opinions gain their share of the policy benefits? Do participants and nonparticipants generally support results of the participation process?

The remainder of this chapter explores the breadth and depth of the participation structures in the five cities of our study, and the following chapter takes up the issue of how these structures change the extent and nature of participation in these communities. Subsequent chapters will be examining the impact of this participation on the critical dimensions of political decisionmaking and community life.

8. Benjamin R. Barber, *Strong Democracy: Participatory Politics for a New Age* (University of California Press, 1984), pp. 173–98.

Breadth of Participation Opportunity

The participation systems in each of the five cities go to extraordinary lengths to contact all their citizens, frequently offering them the opportunity to be involved. This outreach is expensive and difficult to maintain month after month, year after year. But careful attention to open access and a continuous flow of information, along with a commitment to making all citizens aware of the opportunities to participate and the issues at stake, sets these cities apart from politics as usual.

Access of Citizens to the System

The first requirement of any participation system is that citizens have some clear and easy means of access to the decisionmaking process. Of the five cities studied here, the structure for this access was exceptionally well defined in all but San Antonio. In each city, the neighborhood basis for the process allows for face-to-face discussion of the issues and the potential, if not always the practice, for "strong democratic talk."

—In Birmingham, the neighborhoods themselves are the key actors in the process. Since their officers are directly elected at the polls, they immediately gain a certain public legitimacy. And since each neighborhood makes its own decisions about an allocation of public funds (primarily through a CDBG allocation system), the neighborhood association has one clear mission right at the start. But the issue responsibilities run the gamut, from housing and zoning to community education and jobs for youth. Twenty-two formal "communities," typically composed of three to five neighborhoods, are the conduit to the citywide Citizens Advisory Board, a citizen forum on issues affecting the neighborhoods. While purely advisory and not always able to get its way with city council, the board is seen as a means of focused dialogue between citizens and the city.

—Dayton's Priority Boards, on the other hand, are almost agencies in themselves. They are seen by many citizens as quasi-governmental and by many administrators as a formal voice of the neighborhoods. In addition to their role in routing neighborhood concerns to the city and in carrying out the formal functions of an elected community board, the Priority Boards perform a myriad of constituent service functions with individuals in their sector of the city. Their political culture is administrative: most board members see their role as making government agencies do their jobs more effectively. There does exist some ambiguity of roles. The city works both through the Priority Boards and with the neighborhood groups directly. Each has a different representative base: neighborhoods elect their own officers, while citizens elect Priority Board members by precinct and not, in most cases, through the neighborhood groups themselves.

—Most of Portland's neighborhood groups, unlike many in Birmingham and Dayton, have a long history of independence from city hall. From the beginning of the Office of Neighborhood Associations, the individual neighborhoods fought any sign of structure or control by city hall. Only after several years did they accept district coalition offices, which play an intermediary role between the neighborhoods and city hall, even though the staff of these offices are hired by the neighborhoods themselves. Only after fourteen years would neighborhoods accept written guidelines for their operations (on areas such as being open to all residents, reporting minority points of view, and fulfilling their responsibility for disbursements of city funds). The district coalitions, with boards made up entirely of neighborhood association representatives, help support neighborhood outreach and advocacy activities and provide the day-to-day link to city hall. Individual neighborhoods are also encouraged to work directly with city agencies and with the city council, and many additional participation opportunities, such as the citywide Budget Advisory Committees, are open to individuals in the city without regard to neighborhood affiliation.

—St. Paul's District Councils came out of a three-year process of negotiation between the city (especially the mayor, council, and planning department), existing citizen groups, and individual citizens. Each District Council has its own bylaws and election procedures, and many are separately incorporated and raise their own funds. More than in any of the other cities, these councils are the focus of neighborhood-city interaction. Their powers are substantially greater than the very limited sketch provided in the city ordinance describing their creation. If citizens want something done in their neighborhood, if developers have a project, or if agency leaders want to drum up support, they go first to the District Councils. With seventeen neighborhood offices and an impressive array of community center buildings, the structural base of the system is more extensive than in any of the other cities. But it is also stretched more thinly—the chronic complaint concerns the lack of funds to pay a living wage for each council's staff or to maintain the community center network.

—COPS in San Antonio survives not on city funds—in fact, it refuses to accept government money of any kind—but on its intricate network of parish organizations. Each of the twenty-five to thirty active parish groups finds its own way to support itself with varying degrees of assistance from the local church. Substantial annual dues—usually raised in the local church—make up the lion's share of the citywide organization's annual budget. The major constraint on the organization is that their active parish groups cover only about 30 percent of the city's population. The city has made some effort to encourage neighborhood groups in other parts of the city, and several neighborhood-based coalition organizations are active, but in large part COPS's sizable clout comes from a massive mobilization of citizens from its quarter of the city.

In each of the cities, neighborhood boundaries were determined with a great deal of community input. In Birmingham, for example, a door-to-door survey established a consensus of citizen perceptions about neighborhood and community limits. In St. Paul, the district boundaries grew out of a two-year negotiation with citizen committees and existing neighborhood groups. Other "second-tier" boundaries in two cities apparently received somewhat less citizen input. They were determined in Dayton by a conscious effort to include high- and low-income residents in pie-shaped wedges radiating from the central core to the city limits, and in Portland by following the lines of natural geographic features and historical organizational coalitions. Except for several cases of overlapping neighborhood boundaries in Portland and San Antonio, each resident is represented by one and only one neighborhood. Business managers and commercial property owners are also active participants, explicitly recognized by the bylaws of several neighborhoods in Portland and St. Paul.

Generally, a clear means of access through neighborhood-based organizations is a common feature of all five cities. A citizen who wishes to have a voice on issues covered by the system is likely to know where to go. This clear means of access is muddied somewhat, however, in three of the cities. In the non-COPS areas of San Antonio, particularly, a resident is often left without any clear means of access. In Dayton, the second-tier Priority Boards tend to dominate or in some ways compete with the neighborhood level of representation. And in Portland, a proliferation of committees and formal participation opportunities tends to undercut the claim of either neighborhood groups or district coalitions to be *the* voice of the citizens.

Information and Outreach to Citizens

Citizens cannot participate without early and adequate information about the participation process, the times and places they can become involved, and the potential impact of the issues upon their lives.

Of the five cities examined, Birmingham provides the most extensive flow of information to citizens. Every month a newsletter is sent to every household in every neighborhood. City hall provides the staff, the printing, and the postage. Individual neighborhoods provide the message, as long as it is not "political" (meaning that it does not take a position on either a candidate for elected office or a ballot question—a common restriction placed on the neighborhood systems in all but San Antonio).

A second approach to citizen outreach is illustrated by Portland's reliance on independent neighborhoods and district staff. The city gives specific encouragement to the district offices to provide funds for neighborhood outreach to citizens. As part of the annual contract with the district offices, a specific amount of city funds is put aside for the printing and postage of at least one neighborhood newsletter for every household. If the neighborhood can creatively find ways to reduce costs for the publication, with donated printing or volunteer door-to-door distribution instead of mailing, for example, the same city funds can support several publications or newsletter issues.

A third aspect of neighborhood information flow is most fully developed in St. Paul.[9] While all the cities have some mechanism for alerting neighborhood organizations about pending matters of interest, the St. Paul "early notification system" most clearly spells out the nature of what must be sent to the District Councils and when it must be sent to give timely opportunity for response. The material includes meeting notices and agendas from all major city agencies, forty-five-day advance

9. See Richard C. Rich, "Participation and Representation in St. Paul's District Council System," report prepared for the Center for Responsive Government, Washington, 1980; and Richard C. Rich, "Systematic and Individual Effects of Formal Citizen Participation Programs," paper prepared for the 1988 annual meeting of the Southern Political Science Association. On the planning function of the St. Paul neighborhood associations, see William M. Rohe and Lauren B. Gates, *Planning with Neighborhoods* (University of North Carolina, 1985).

notice for liquor licenses, development ads, street vacations, and special assessments; and detailed requirements for rezoning, conditional uses and variances, and building condemnations or demolitions. In fact, the material is so voluminous that several of the District Council staff complained to us of being overwhelmed by the paperwork from the city.

One final approach to information, also developed most fully in St. Paul, is the use of neighborhood newspapers to communicate the activities of the neighborhood organizations. The tradition is well established in St. Paul that every District Council have some access to a neighborhood newspaper of its own. Several run their own monthly tabloid, and others have open access to the pages of commercial ventures. The papers include calendars of events, descriptions of city proposals affecting the neighborhood, and reports of District Council activities. Most of the papers are delivered free to every household in the district. These extensive communication efforts are only possible because the districts are large enough to support the effort with both resources and activities to be reported, and each District Council has its own staff to keep up with the tasks involved.

The ability and commitment to get information into the hands of all citizens in the community on a regular basis is one of the strongest characteristics of the participation systems in each of these cities. On most issues, these efforts seem successful in making information available to citizens in time for them to take appropriate action as each individual chooses. We found little evidence that these city governments withhold substantive information on any plans or proposals affecting specific neighborhoods. And when information does arrive too late, the network of neighborhood or district organizations has the demonstrated capability of obtaining more time to allow for appropriate citizen input.

City Resources Committed to the Process

If an effective opportunity is to be offered to all citizens to participate in city policymaking, the resources must be available to do the job. The primary resource is staffing. In fact, comparisons of citizen participation efforts throughout the country revealed that if only one piece of information were used to rate the strength of a citywide effort, that criterion should be the number of full-time staff members devoted to citizen and neighborhood outreach—or more precisely the number of such staff per 100,000 population of the city.

With the exception of San Antonio, the commitment of these cities to adequate staffing is clear. Birmingham has a community resources staff consisting of a director and eight to twelve full-time organizers to assist neighborhoods in their work. Dayton has a total of twenty-two staff members, most of whom work out of the individual Priority Board offices. Portland has more than twenty staff members, including crime prevention coordinators, between its central Office of Neighborhood Associations (ONA) and the district coalitions. St. Paul has one central participation coordinator and the equivalent of twenty-six staff in the districts, nearly half paid by outside grants and funds raised by the districts themselves.

San Antonio is in a category by itself. The city initiated in 1985 a neighborhood planning office that survived only one year of operation with two full-time employees. The office was killed by opposition from COPS, which argued that it served no useful purpose. COPS itself has only a tiny staff, two or three full-time employees, and out of principle accepts no administrative funds from the city. A key to its operation is the network organized along the lines of the Catholic church's parishes and the corresponding staff in those parishes who have done so much to make COPS effective. Many of the original leaders of the parish organizations were the priests themselves. The parishes are also the source of most of the organization's financial resources.

In each city, then, substantial staff resources are committed by the city or in the case of San Antonio by independent parishes within the city. In addition, a substantial number of planning staff members are frequently available to work with the neighborhood groups. This is clearest in St. Paul where most of the Planning Department seems to be in one way or another associated with planning efforts involving the District Councils. In Portland and Birmingham, specific planning staff are periodically assigned to neighborhood work. Finally, these cities make available substantial nonstaff resources. Funds to pay office rent are available in three of the cities, funds for printing and mailing are available in four, and money for a variety of overhead costs is available to the second-tier organizations in two cities and directly to the District Councils in St. Paul.

The sum of these efforts—providing open access, maintaining an extensive information flow, and establishing a long-term commitment of city resources to the participation process—represents a serious attempt to offer realistic participation opportunities, continuously, to every resident of the city. The results of these efforts are moderately successful:

between 49 percent and 72 percent of the population is aware of the participation system, according to the population surveys conducted as part of this analysis. (These figures exclude San Antonio, where only a portion of the city is covered by COPS.) Yet the outreach effort is clearly not maintained at levels that the best community organizing efforts are able to achieve by knocking on every door in a few target neighborhoods. Overall, only 13 percent to 18 percent of citizens report being personally contacted during the last two years and asked to take part in neighborhood association activities.

Depth of Participation Opportunity

Evaluation of the depth of the participation effort requires a more complex analysis than evaluation of its breadth. As will be developed in later chapters, the ability of participants to influence policy in these cities varies a great deal from one issue area to the next. In neighborhood land use policies, for example, participants clearly have dramatic impact. To a high degree in St. Paul and to a lesser but still significant degree in the other cities, the neighborhood position on neighborhood land use issues is the city policy. When land use issues reach a certain economic scale, however, at the point where the city perceives that its vital interests are at stake, neighborhood influence is no longer as powerful. We saw neighborhood preferences being overturned in the case of a water theme park and racetrack in Birmingham and a major shopping plaza in Portland, for example. In these cases, some of the neighborhood concerns are usually addressed, but overall approval of a development project that has a major economic impact for the whole city remains in the hands of the city council and mayor.

The impact of the participation system on other issues is generally related to the degree to which they are tied to neighborhood turf. Each participation system, however, has built in a range of specific mechanisms that help to balance the interests of all neighborhoods and all participants and that allow average citizens to have substantially more impact on policymaking and policy implementation than they would otherwise be able to muster. Particularly important are mechanisms that insert neighborhood needs directly into the budget process, affect specific neighborhood allocations, and involve capital budgeting for the city as a whole. In addition, provisions for defining the decisionmaking process, assuring access to administrators, and allowing neighborhood control over staff of the participation system significantly affect the depth of the participation process.

Opportunity to Affect Citywide Budget Priorities

One of the most direct measures of the depth of a participation system is its ability to grapple realistically with the city budget. In none of these cities is this opportunity successfully managed with respect to operating budgets, school budgets, or regional agency budgets. But the capital budgets of the cities—and most clearly the portion of capital budgets coming from federal sources—have in some cases been closely integrated with the participation system.

St. Paul provides the shining example in this area. The city's Capital Improvement Budget Committee (CIB) illustrates how a neighborhood-based process can have real clout citywide. The approach is quite simple, and in its simplicity is its power. The CIB is made up solely of representatives nominated by the District Councils and approved by the mayor. The committee originates essentially all capital project proposals for the city, from all sources of funds—local, state, or federal. It works through three major task forces that provide the opportunity for each member to rate each proposal that has been made. These individual ratings are added to create a total ranking for each project. The projects are then discussed in priority order, and the committee determines its recommended allocation. Few changes are made by the mayor or city council once the proposals have come out of the CIB. Overall, as much as 70 percent of the projects funded by the combined capital budgets are those originally initiated by the neighborhoods.

The other four cities have various means to address citywide budget issues, but none is as effective as in St. Paul. Dayton has its own citywide CDBG committee, but effective control is wielded by city staff, not by the Priority Boards or the neighborhoods. In Portland, the Budget Advisory Committees perform this role to some degree, but actual ability to affect budgets varies greatly from one committee to the next. Birmingham has a fixed allocation formula for capital fund distribution to neighborhoods; no direct role for citizens is available to alter the overall pattern of funding. The COPS budget role in San Antonio depends on extremely effective lobbying, using Alinsky-style confrontation tactics in the early years and their reputation for grassroots-based political clout in later years, to line up a majority on the city council on most issues.

Opportunity to Affect
Neighborhood Allocations

Even where there is little opportunity to affect citywide priorities and allocations between neighborhoods, city governments will often allow a neighborhood organization to have a major role in determining how an allocation designated for that neighborhood will be spent. Each of the five cities does this well, except for San Antonio in the non-COPS areas.

The Birmingham system is perhaps the most straightforward. Each neighborhood receives an allocation of capital funds coming into the city, governed by a strict formula based on population and income level. (In recent years all neighborhoods have received a flat minimum because of a dramatic decrease in available funds.) The neighborhood, through its elected officers and its open meetings, determines how those funds will be spent. Major projects are often contracted through normal city procedures. If a neighborhood association is inactive one year, its funds carry over intact to the following year. This system has handled a great deal of funding, sometimes on the order of hundreds of thousands of dollars for a neighborhood with a few thousand people. It has enabled major rehabilitation of many low-income black neighborhoods long neglected by earlier administrations and the building of previously nonexistent infrastructure.

Like Birmingham, San Antonio has seen a tremendous redirection of resources to Latino sections of the city almost completely neglected in earlier eras. Due largely to COPS's lobbying, money for huge flood-prevention efforts and for the first time for paved streets, sewers, and utilities has been applied to many low-income Latino parishes.

The story in the other cities is less dramatic but still impressive. The CIB process in St. Paul gives neighborhoods major powers of project initiation for their own communities along with their role in citywide allocation. In Dayton and Portland, the process of defining neighborhood needs highlights the neighborhoods' priorities. In these two cities, small projects are handled well, but larger projects tend to remain attached to the traditional city development systems with little input from citizen groups.

Ability to Define the Decisionmaking Process

In the field of citizen participation more opportunities for participation are not always better. Multiple avenues for participation in the cities examined here can sometimes lead to serious confusion for citizens. A definite trade-off is involved. On the one hand, different kinds of participation opportunities encourage more and more people to be involved in a way that best fits their own needs and perspectives. On the other hand, competing and vaguely defined options for participation can sometimes lead to uncertainty about where, when, and by whom a decision is to be made. They can also lead to questions about who is truly speaking on behalf of a particular neighborhood or group of citizens.

Portland offers a good example of multiple participation opportunities and uncertainty in representation. Time and time again administrators would emphasize how open this city was compared with other cities they had worked in. They would stress how many different avenues were offered for participation, and how seriously citizen input was taken in each process. Indeed, open channels seemed to exist for individual citizens to meet with administrators; for dozens of special citizen advisory committees to express their views; for neighborhoods to be heard before city council, through the District Coalition Boards, and through the Office of Neighborhood Associations; and for special participation efforts such as the Central City Plan to bring in thousands of responses from targeted outreach efforts. These opportunities have led to a number of positive effects on policymaking in Portland, as will be discussed in chapters 5 and 6. However, relative levels of dissatisfaction and distrust of city government appear to be higher among participants in Portland than in some of the other cities. The citizen interviews revealed considerably more hostility among neighborhoods and between neighborhoods and city hall than elsewhere. And the uncertainty about who is speaking for whom may be one factor that left Portland's neighborhood associations vulnerable to the charge of being "unrepresentative" of their neighborhoods in the heat of a recent battle with the city's largest superstore chain.

The other cities seem to suffer significantly less in this regard. The District Councils in St. Paul clearly speak for residents in their area and form the majority in most citywide citizen bodies. In Dayton, the Priority Boards play a similar role, with some competition from the neighborhood organizations and some concern that they themselves are too much creatures of the city to fully represent local residents. COPS is the unequivocal voice of San Antonio's Hispanic community. And in Birmingham, the neighborhood associations have very little competition in representing residents' interests, with the single exception of an independent support network for the city's lowest income neighborhoods called Neighborhood

Services, Inc. (NSI). The advocacy arm of this organization, Greater Birmingham Ministries, successfully sued the city in the late 1970s to redirect its CDBG funds to these neighborhoods.

While none of these cities, except perhaps Portland, seems to face obvious adverse effects from vagueness in the policymaking process, all could be more specific about where decisions are made, particularly about the interaction between the city council, city agencies, and the participation system. Many of these relationships are workable but are often left as unstated and informal understandings. From the point of view of the average citizen who is not party to these understandings, increased specificity could improve accountability and the sense of opportunity for real policy impact—both preconditions for a strong participation effort.

Strength of Administrator Involvement

The access that citizens have to line administrators during the participation process has a major impact on their ability to affect services and programs. In many cities today, as in most of the OEO programs of the 1960s, administrators are called out to neighborhood meetings when a crisis develops or when important new programs are being developed. But regular, ongoing contact is much more problematic. This situation is quite different in each of the core cities studied here. Two of these cities, in particular, have developed extensive mechanisms for this purpose.

Dayton is clearly the leader in maintaining such contact. Each month, usually as part of a regular Priority Board meeting, an Administrative Council is held; representatives from each major city agency, as many as ten to twelve people, appear before the Priority Board to field any and all questions or complaints from participants. They may report progress of specific projects or answer questions raised in previous sessions. Not all representatives will speak on any given night. The council's operation provides for clear, public resolution of routine matters and establishes a strong link between the agencies and priority board members. It closely fits Dayton's political environment, which demands strong accountability from government officials in every endeavor.

Portland's approach involves Budget Advisory Committees (BACs) for each major department. These committees, made up of neighborhood representatives and other interested citizens, act as a sounding board for administrative initiatives throughout the year, particularly at budget preparation time. They do not allow for widespread contact between citizens and administrators on routine issues but do give a few citizens the opportunity to grapple with agency problems in depth and to bring fresh perspectives to the departments. Recruitment and initial training for the BACs is handled by the central Office of Neighborhood Associations. In addition, the "big BAC," or Bureau Advisory Coordinating Committee, brings together representatives from all the individual BACs to consider citywide administrative policies.

The other core cities in the study rely largely on ad hoc or arm's-length contact between neighborhoods and agency representatives, developing close working relationships only when the neighborhood is carrying out specific projects with a particular agency. Numerous grant programs to neighborhoods, immediate concerns ranging from crime to housing development, or development of new regulatory actions can be catalysts for this kind of contact. In addition, when issues arise neighborhoods frequently request the presence of certain departmental personnel—for example, a police representative, a neighborhood planner, or an inspectional services officer. Written neighborhood needs reports in Portland and Dayton and regular service-oriented public opinion surveys in Dayton provide systematic information to administrators on current neighborhood priorities. Other information programs, such as St. Paul's early notification system, provide communication in the other direction. These approaches seem to work fairly well in these cities to address major neighborhood concerns when they arise. They fail, however, to develop the strong relationships between administrators and citizens that both the Dayton administrative councils and the Portland BACs are able to generate.

Control of Staff

As the operation of the participation system in each city was examined, the importance of staff direction became abundantly clear. Paid staff supply the administrative support and organizational abilities that citizen participants often cannot devote to volunteer work. The staff also provide the cohesion that keeps the organization together year after year, through the ups and downs of volunteer leadership energy and attention. Each city has its own approach to staff allocation, and the choices made determine much about the character of the system.

One approach is simply for the city to hire and manage the staff out of city hall, as in Birmingham. There are no district or neighborhood offices. The consequences of this system are that the staff agenda is rather closely controlled by the city itself. Our interviews in Birmingham revealed that a rigid hierarchy had existed in previous years, with staff members forbidden to bring any issue raised by the neighborhood directly to the operating agency. Instead they were required to go "through channels" involving the Community Resources Division and its parent Community Development Department. While these restrictions no longer exist, the system remains under the close scrutiny of the department.

At the other end of the scale is the hiring and direction of staff for the participation system by independent citizen-based organizations, the approach generally followed by St. Paul, Portland, and San Antonio. In St. Paul, each District Council hires and fires its own staff, subject only to its annual budget, a core of which is provided by the city, with supplementary funds (in some cases in much larger amounts) wherever they can be raised. Portland's six District Coalition Boards have a similar arrangement, although occasionally the staff of the central ONA has played more of a role in this process when a new district board is organized. COPS in San Antonio, of course, remains completely independent from the city in staff and all other respects. In all three cities, the decisions of the neighborhood and district staff are clearly all their own. This tends to lend a vitality to the system and provide for independent perspectives on every issue that arises.

Between these two approaches, Dayton's Priority Boards hire their own staff, but only from a small number of people who go through a personnel process at city hall. The staff, once hired, has a definite tendency to reflect the perspectives of the staff in the Office of Human and Neighborhood Resources, which employs the Superintendent of Neighborhood Affairs. One field visit witnessed the requisitioning of all Priority Board staff by the city for election day work on behalf of a ballot question of vital interest to the city. Many of the neighborhood leaders interviewed saw these staff as representatives of city hall, not of their own organizations. The separate election of Priority Board members by precinct, not by neighborhood boundaries, tends to reinforce this perception. On the other hand, city administrators told us that "most of the time the staff sides with the neighborhoods rather than the city." And Priority Board members indicated that the staff "generally gets done what we want them to get done." Clearly the Dayton staff walk a tightrope between responsiveness to the city and responsiveness to the neighborhoods.

Conclusion

Most democratic theorists place greater value on face-to-face political activity than on individual private political activity. Yet for all the virtues that face-to-face democracy is said to possess, it is used very little in modern democracies. The operative assumption is that it is impractical and unsustainable.

The five cities in this study prove that strong participation efforts can, in fact, be developed and maintained. The systems in these communities have been going strong for more than fifteen years. Each has made extensive, ongoing efforts to provide a realistic opportunity for every citizen to be involved in the political life of the city. Neighborhood structures exist throughout the cities and provide realistic channels for citizens to have a major impact on final policy. These structures and the productive participation that radiates from them have weathered many a political storm.

These cities that have created these participation successes are not different politically, economically, or structurally from cities of the 1960s or today where participation has failed. In fact, the five core cities vary greatly from one another in all these characteristics and are similar to many other cities that lack effective involvement of citizens. The real difference is in commitment to the participation process by both government and citizen leaders. It is a difference reflected in the design of the participation system and the political and administrative arrangements developed to implement the process over a span of two decades.

In each of the core cities, a wide range of structured citizen-government relationships promotes both the breadth and depth of the participation opportunity. These interactions touch upon almost every facet of community life. They are at the core of the community's envisioning and planning, take a major role in reacting to new initiatives and developing broad policy, function effectively in the day-to-day decisions of administrators and elected officials, help shape the city budget, and take their share of the blame when things go wrong.

On balance, the participation structures in these cities dramatically change the pattern of political opportunities for all citizens—opportunities that provide an effective means for them to shape the issues affecting their lives. Who takes advantage of these opportunities, and how, is the subject of the next chapter.

CHAPTER 4

More Participation?

THE CITY-SPONSORED citizen participation systems described in chapter 3 are impressive in the amount of authority and autonomy they give to the neighborhoods. The neighborhood associations have considerable power and citizens have every reason to take them seriously. Where the neighborhood organizations are strong, residents find it relatively easy to participate in them. As demonstrated in later chapters, both participants and nonparticipants evaluate their neighborhood councils very positively. In short, many of the structures for participatory democracy are in place in these cities.

The structures themselves, however, are not proof of strong democracy. People must animate these structures with talk and action. But how many people? Neither classical nor modern political theory tells us. A reasoned judgment suggests that it should be more than a few and that it does not have to be everybody.[1] Political scientists who have studied political behavior have established no widely accepted baseline that reveals whether activity beyond voting is going up or down.[2] What is generally agreed upon is that there are far too few people taking part in the political process, both inside and outside the voting booth.

This chapter explores the potential for reforming political structures within a community to increase the number of people who participate and the level of their participation. In theory, political structures may act in two ways to increase participation: first, by expanding the range of opportunities available for citizens to participate and, second, by making that participation more meaningful. But do they work this way

1. Bertrand de Jouvenel, "The Chairman's Problem," *American Political Science Review*, vol. 55 (June 1961), pp. 368–72; and Jack H. Nagel, *Participation* (Prentice-Hall, 1987), pp. 84–99.

2. At least one major piece of research has suggested that activity other than voting has remained rather constant or has perhaps increased slightly since the late 1960s. Norman H. Nie and others, "Participation in America: Continuity and Change," paper prepared for the 1989 annual meeting of the Midwest Political Science Association.

in practice? If cities create more opportunities for face-to-face interaction, do more people participate? If participants are able to have more impact through their participation, will they spend more time and effort working on community problems?

Given the strength of the forces that shape political behavior, particularly social class, it is not at all clear that opportunities for strong democracy can be expected to bring people out of their homes and into neighborhood assemblies. Theorists who first argued for participatory democracy did not do so on the grounds that it would expand suffrage. Rather, face-to-face interaction was valued because it offered greater legitimacy to the actions of government, educated citizens about the affairs of state, and instilled the virtues of citizenship and individuals' sense of responsibility for their communities and their states.[3] The emphasis on expanding participation through face-to-face interaction has come from contemporary theorists, like Benjamin Barber, who see communal activity as a way of rebuilding democracy.[4]

As a means of expanding participation, the structures of strong democracy have much going in their favor and much going against them. On the positive side, they can lower the barriers that normally keep people away from the political process. They can make people aware that opportunities exist to tackle problems in their community and bring those opportunities literally to the doorstep of prospective participants. They can provide mechanisms for participation that match the time, money, and skills available to each community constituency. And they can provide the training and guidance to assist wary or unsophisticated citizens through a complex issue.

That strong democracy can make participation worthwhile for the average citizen also argues for a positive influence on participation levels. To the extent that citizens are rational actors, they may be expected to balance the costs and benefits of their participation. Participation that has no effect can provide no benefits to outweigh its costs in time and energy. But if the structures of strong democracy can increase the benefits or decrease the costs stemming from an individual's participation, the rational actor's choice for participation will become more attractive. The end result, according to this line of reasoning, is that if strong democracy

3. Arnold S. Kaufman, "Human Nature and Participatory Democracy," in Carl J. Friedrich, ed., *NOMOS III: Responsibility* (New York: Liberal Arts Press, 1960), pp. 266–89.

4. Benjamin R. Barber, *Strong Democracy: Participatory Politics for a New Age* (University of California Press, 1984).

structures offer citizens the chance to significantly influence the decisions that affect the quality of life in their communities, more citizens will participate more often.

On the negative side of the strong democracy ledger are the increased costs of face-to-face political exchanges for the individual. Meetings where people make decisions about the distribution of goods and services in their community are fraught with the possibility of conflict. Face-to-face democracy assumes active participation and some form of "democratic talk"; going to meetings and observing is not as highly valued as actively participating. The "hallmarks" of strong democracy, writes Barber, are "involvement, commitment, obligation, and service—common deliberation, common decision, and common work."[5] These expectations are extraordinarily demanding of citizens.

In her sympathetic study of citizen participation, Jane Mansbridge found that open and egalitarian settings for face-to-face democracy are still intimidating to many citizens. She concludes that "face-to-face assembly lets those who have no trouble speaking in public defend their interests; it does not give the average citizen comparable protection."[6] "Rather than creating community," face-to-face meetings "may frighten away the very people" they are trying to enlist as participants. Such meetings are difficult because they usually increase the level of "emotional tension."[7]

Consequently, this argument concludes that strong democracy structures may do little to increase participation in local politics. Perhaps only those whose self-confidence already allows them to engage in face-to-face politics will take advantage of neighborhood associations and other similar organizations. If this is true, participatory structures may neither attract more people nor increase people's involvement in community problem solving.

Measuring Community Participation

The neighborhood associations and participation opportunities in the five core cities, when working as designed, clearly meet the structural requirements of strong democracy. Qualitative data (elite interviews, focus groups, and observation of meetings) reveal little doubt that most

5. Barber, *Strong Democracy*, p. 133.
6. Jane J. Mansbridge, *Beyond Adversary Democracy* (Basic Books, 1980), p. 274.
7. Jane J. Mansbridge, "The Limits of Friendship," in J. Roland Pennock and John W. Chapman, eds., *NOMOS XVI: Participation in Politics* (New York: Lieber-Atherton, 1975), p. 261.

of these organizations embody the principles discussed in the previous chapter. Participants are given real responsibility and their individual participation can influence outcomes; the intense experience of participating presents an opportunity for personal growth. People with opposing views cannot be avoided; disagreements are therefore discussed and working relationships often develop. The neighborhood associations are easily accessible, accompanied by abundant outreach activities designed to bring in new participants. In short, these organizations are structured in such a way that strong democracy is possible.

How can we judge whether or not these extensive structures work to bring more people into the community problem-solving process? Ideally, such a judgment would be based on a comparison of the rates of participation in the same cities before and after the introduction of the participation processes and development of neighborhood organizations. Since the participation systems in these cities have been in place for more than fifteen years, this kind of measurement is not possible. The next best approach would be to compare participation rates in these cities with similar cities that lack a strong participation system. It is this approach that we take here, with the obvious caveat that no two cities are exactly the same; the best that can be done is to find cities that are comparable on certain key characteristics.

The control group used for comparison purposes consists of ten cities described more fully in the Methodological Appendix. Each of the five cities in the core study was matched to two cities similar in their demographic characteristics. These matches are for Birmingham, Louisville and Savannah; for Dayton, Buffalo and Norfolk; for Portland, Colorado Springs and Minneapolis; for San Antonio, El Paso and Tucson; and for St. Paul, Omaha and Wichita. The population survey in these ten control group cities contained many of the same questions that were asked in the surveys of each core city. Therefore, a wide range of direct comparisons of participation rates and participation consequences in all fifteen communities is possible.

The first task in this attempt to understand the impact of strong democratic structures on participation rates is to compare the broad levels of community participation in each city. We developed an index of community participation (ICP), capturing a variety of participation activities.[8]

8. The idea underlying this index is much like that developed by Cole, except that the measure used here relies on actual individual-level participation information. See Richard L. Cole, *Citizen Participation and the Urban Policy Process* (Lexington, Mass.: Lexington Books, 1974), especially chap. 2.

The index applies to each individual in the survey. It is designed to distinguish those who are inactive from those who are active in community problem solving and to provide an overall measure of their level of activity.

Since the main interest here is on activity that incorporates face-to-face interaction, the scale is built on activity in both ad hoc groups and formal organizations.[9] Various types of local citizen groups and neighborhood associations offer citizens the opportunity for face-to-face discussion while potentially confronting them with a wide range of attitudes and opinions on specific issues. Thus a major line of questioning began by asking respondents in the city samples if they had "ever actually been active in any community or citizen groups or neighborhood organizations."[10]

Those who answered affirmatively were asked what group or groups they participated in, what specific kinds of activities they took part in, and how often they took part in these activities over the previous two-year period. The resulting open-ended responses were coded, and each group mentioned was evaluated to determine what type of group it was and whether participation in this group could be considered a form of community participation. If the identified group was open to a broad array of citizens, was involved with efforts to influence public policy, and had participants who typically engaged in face-to-face contact, involvement in this group was taken as clear evidence of community participation activity.

Further questioning yielded information about how frequently they participated in these organizations. This information was used to rank participants at the top three levels of the community participation scale according to whether they reported participating more than once a month, once a month, or less than once a month, on average over the previous two-year period.

9. Including all of these forms of political participation in a single index is justified because there is evidence that they all form a single dimension or continuum of participation. A factor analysis including all these types of participation revealed that they all loaded heavily on a single unrotated dimension, and that the factor could not be rotated.

10. The "have you ever actually been involved" question may seem problematic because of the lack of a clear reference to a time frame, especially if respondents answered based on participation that predated the systems of participation. Because the systems have been in place for a significant period of time, this did not appear to present a serious problem. Even though people's memories may be fallible, there is no reason to believe they would be more so in one city than in another.

Ranked below this kind of participation was activity involving "working with others" to help solve some neighborhood or community problem.[11] Based on previous analysis of this type of activity, it seems likely that "working with others" probably offers some potential for strong participation by virtue of its close association with other forms of communal and cooperative activities. But lacking more specific information about what was actually done in working with others, knowing that the respondent did not report participating in local citizen groups or neighborhood associations, and having no information about how frequently the respondent worked with others meant that this type of activity had to be placed at a lower level on the scale of community participation.

Respondents who participated in other kinds of activities, such as helping to form a new group, contacting local public officials, or taking part in a variety of other kinds of organizations (including neighborhood crime watch, social groups, service and church-based organizations, and electoral campaigns), are considered to have taken part in activities potentially characterized as having only a small degree of strong community participation.[12] These endeavors are not likely to incorporate significant amounts of face-to-face political interaction with those who might hold opposing views or to be involved in a significant level of community problem solving. Consequently, this category is placed near the bottom of the scale, above only respondents who reported being totally inactive. For reasons that are discussed in more depth later, group-forming behavior is also included in this category of community participation.

These five indicators of strong democratic participation were used to create a single index of community participation for each individual respondent. The scores of this index range from 0, indicating no apparent involvement in community participation activities, to 5, indicating very frequent involvement in such activities. The extent to which respondents in both the five cities and the ten-city control group engage in community participation activities can be analyzed by examining the relative frequency of each level of this index. Table 4-1 displays this distribution

11. The survey question focusing on "working with others" was used extensively by Verba and Nie to help define their "cooperative" and "communal" activity forms of participation. Sidney Verba and Norman Nie, *Participation in America: Political Democracy and Social Equality* (Harper and Row, 1972), pp. 56–81.

12. Earlier analysis by Verba and Nie confirms that these elements, composed mostly of "particularized contacting" activities, are virtually unassociated with the more cooperative and communal participation acts that we argue are characteristic of strong community participation. *Participation in America*, p. 75.

TABLE 4-1. The Extent of Strong Participation in Fifteen Cities

Level of strong participation[a]	Type or frequency of activity	Number	Percent
0	Respondent participated in none of the activities.	2,212	33.4
1	Respondent participated in crime watch, electoral campaign, contacting local officials, helping to form a new group, or other activities involving some small degree of interpersonal interaction.	1,451	21.9
2	Respondent worked with others to help solve some community or neighborhood problem.	1,563	23.6
3	Respondent participated in a specific citizen group or neighborhood association less than once a month.	658	9.9
4	Respondent participated in a specific citizen group or neighborhood association about once a month.	343	5.2
5	Respondent participated in a specific citizen group or neighborhood association more than once a month.	399	6.0
	Total	6,626	100.0

a. Ranked by the index of community participation (ICP).

for respondents from all fifteen cities combined. The results show that one-third of the people essentially take part in no community participation. A substantial group of people, nearly 46 percent, take part in low levels of community participation (levels 1 and 2). However, very few people go beyond this second level. Only a little over 21 percent of the respondents reported taking part in the three higher levels of community participation. Further analysis shows that about 16.6 percent of the people in the four cities with citywide participation programs have been active in a neighborhood association during the previous two years.

The distribution of respondents across levels of the ICP is consistent with other research on political participation; it is perhaps not surprising that so few people seem to engage in higher levels of community participation.[13] The next step, however, is to compare the communities in the

13. See Verba and Nie, *Participation in America*, pp. 95–101; Lester W. Milbrath, *Political Participation: How and Why Do People Get Involved in Politics?* (Rand McNally, 1965), pp. 110–41; Nagel, *Participation*, pp. 58–59; and M. Margaret Conway, *Political Participation in the United States* (Washington: CQ Press, 1985), pp. 19–26.

TABLE 4-2. Fifteen Cities and Their Average ICP Scores[a]

City and community participation category	Average ICP score	Number of cases
High		
Norfolk, Va.	1.82	163
Minneapolis, Minn.	1.79	153
Portland, Ore.	1.72	1,142
St. Paul, Minn.	1.63	1,090
Louisville, Ken.	1.60	148
Buffalo, N.Y.	1.59	157
Moderate		
Tucson, Ariz.	1.55	158
Omaha, Neb.	1.52	148
Colorado Springs, Colo.	1.50	155
El Paso, Texas	1.50	161
Birmingham, Ala.	1.49	743
Savannah, Ga.	1.45	148
Dayton, Ohio	1.42	993
Wichita, Kan.	1.39	155
Low		
San Antonio, Texas	1.10	1,112
Average for all 15 cities	1.50	6,626
Average excluding San Antonio	1.58	5,514

a. The five cities studied in depth are shown in boldface.

study. To do this, we computed an average ICP score for each of the fifteen cities (see table 4-2).

Two important facts are apparent in table 4-2. First, demographic characteristics would not seem to explain why some cities have higher community participation than others. Cities that are at the low end of income and education measures, such as Norfolk and Louisville, rank near the top of the ICP scale, and others that rank high on income and education, such as Wichita and Colorado Springs, do not score well in community participation. Second, the five cities of the core study do not necessarily stand out from the other cities. It would appear that some other characteristics of these cities that go deeper than either socioeconomic status or strong participation structures lead to their position on the ICP scale. These may involve long-range historical factors, local economic conditions and structures, or broad population characteristics that are beyond the scope of this study.

The findings reported in the table can be used to sharpen the comparisons between the five core cities and the remaining ten cities by creating more compelling control groups. With the exception of San Antonio, the ICP scores form a fairly smooth and monotonic continuum. San Antonio possesses a substantially lower level of community participation than the next closest city, Wichita. In recognition of this, San Antonio will remain separate, essentially composing its own "low community participation" group. The remaining fourteen cities can then be divided into two groups based on each city's relative position above or below the overall average ICP score for these fourteen cities. Thus one group (high ICP cities) consists of the six cities above the fourteen-city average of 1.58 (Norfolk, Minneapolis, Portland, Louisville, St. Paul, and Buffalo) and the other group (moderate ICP cities) consists of the eight cities below the fourteen-city average (Tucson, Omaha, Colorado Springs, El Paso, Birmingham, Savannah, Dayton, and Wichita).[14] Within each of these groups, the cities with structured participation—Portland, St. Paul, Birmingham, and Dayton—can be distinguished from their unstructured counterparts. San Antonio stands apart because structured participation exists in only part of the city.

Before proceeding with in-depth analysis, we need to address one further issue, concerning how representative the fifteen studied cities are of some larger population of cities. The ten cities composing the comparison group may not be very representative of all 170 cities in the United States that have populations between 100,000 and 1 million. As described earlier, the five core study cities were selected precisely because

14. Grouping the cities together in this fashion makes statistical sense. First, each of these three groups of cities is different from each other group in statistically significant terms with respect to their average ICP scores. The overall F-ratio for this three-group comparison is 32.07 with 4 and 6,621 degrees of freedom, significant at the 0.0000 level. Tukey's HSD test indicates that each group is significantly different from each other group at the 0.05 level or beyond. Second, Portland and St. Paul, the two cities in group 1 that are studied in depth, are not statistically different from the other cities in this first group. The F-ratio for this two-group comparison is 0.148 with 1 and 2,851 degrees of freedom, significant at the 0.70 level (not statistically significant), indicating that Portland and St. Paul together are not significantly different from the other high community participation cities with respect to the ICP. And Birmingham and Dayton, the two cities in group 2 that are studied in depth, are not statistically different from the other cities in this second group. Third, Portland and St. Paul (the group 1 cities studied in depth) together are statistically different from Birmingham and Dayton, and each of these pairs of cities is statistically different from San Antonio (the group 3 city). The overall F-ratio for this three-group comparison is 63.88 with 2 and 6,623 degrees of freedom, significant at the 0.0000 level. Tukey's HSD test indicates that each of these groups is different from each other group at the 0.05 level or beyond.

of the depth and breadth of their participation systems. And the ten comparison cities were selected not by some formal random selection procedure that allowed every U.S. city an equal chance of being selected but by trying to match them on demographic characteristics to the five core cities.

Although the selection procedure yields cities similar in demographics, this does not ensure that the comparison cities are in any way representative of some larger number of U.S. cities. To allow the results to be generalized to other cities, it is necessary to assess whether these cities seem, in fact, to be adequately representative. Data from the National Opinion Research Center's 1987 General Social Survey (GSS) provide an additional baseline for such an assessment. The GSS survey included a replication of some of the questions on political behavior used by Sidney Verba and Norman Nie in their 1967 survey of participation in America.[15] Although only some of the questions used to form the ICP scale were included in the GSS,[16] comparisons between this national sample and the city samples should reveal any biases in the populations interviewed for this study. After controlling for socioeconomic status and city size,[17] we found no consistent or statistically significant differences in political participation.[18] People in the fifteen cities, taken together, do

15. Verba and Nie, *Participation in America.*

16. Three questions overlap studies. The first question asked respondents whether they had worked with others to help solve some local or neighborhood problem. A second question asked if people had contacted local public officials about some need or problem and captures, in part, whether residents communicate with public officials through channels other than elections. A third question asked respondents if they have "ever taken part in forming a new group or a new organization to try to solve some community problem."

17. The GSS data were compared using both the entire sample and the subsample composed of respondents who lived just in cities of comparable size to those studied here. In neither case was there a statistically significant difference.

18. The third participation question shared by the GSS and this project's surveys reveals results that are somewhat discrepant. The data from the fifteen-city surveys for the "forming a group" question are fairly consistent with the GSS data for low and high socioeconomic groups, but for middle-SES people, the GSS samples show considerably more participation. In the GSS, 21.2 percent of middle-SES people reported helping to form a new group, and this is almost double the fifteen-city rate of 12.6 percent, the latter showing almost no variation from city to city. These differences cannot be explained on the basis of any population or structural characteristic. Based on the rather inconsistent responses to this question across surveys, we can only speculate that perhaps this question is subject to some confusion or misinterpretation by respondents. Some may answer "yes," they helped form a group, when perhaps they mean only a coffee-klatch or get-together with friends to commiserate one day about the decay of the community. If multiple interpretations are being given to the question, its placement in relation to other questions

not exhibit levels of political participation different from those in the national samples.

Comparisons with the baselines from the ten-city survey and the GSS offer persuasive evidence that the overall rates of participation in the five core cities are unexceptional. The level of strong participation activity is not linked to the presence of structures of strong democracy. Nor is the overall rate of participation predicted by the socioeconomic characteristics of the cities. This is significant because one of the purposes of the citywide systems of citizen participation is to bring the inactive out of their homes and into the political life of their neighborhoods. Clearly, this has not necessarily happened to any greater extent in the five cities than elsewhere.

Biases in Participation

Before examining the broad range of patterns in face-to-face political participation, we need to address the issue of the role of socioeconomic status (SES) and race or ethnicity. SES and race constitute personal characteristics that have been found in other research to be strongly correlated with political participation.

Previous studies have established a clear linkage between SES and political participation, finding that political participants are disproportionately likely to be of higher income and socioeconomic status. This relationship is often referred to as the "standard socioeconomic model" of participation. Moreover, analyses of different forms of political participation generally reveal that the more demanding the act of participation is in terms of required commitment of time and energy, the more likely that type of participation will be disproportionately engaged in by higher SES people. Jack Nagel succinctly summarizes this relationship: "The more intensive the form of participation, the greater the tendency of participants to overrepresent high-status members of the population."[19]

The forms of face-to-face community participation investigated here certainly are among these more intensive activities. Working with others to help solve a community problem, some types of contacting local

on the survey may skew the results toward one or the other meaning. As already noted, the ICP scale places little importance on answers to this question.

19. Nagel, *Participation*, p. 58.

officials about a problem, helping to form a new group, and being active in neighborhood associations all require some degree of personal commitment of time and resources, characteristics commonly used to distinguish intensive political acts.[20] In general, then, community participation would be expected to exhibit significant biases with respect to socioeconomic status. Lower SES people should be considerably underrepresented, at least in a numeric sense, among community participants, and higher SES people should be very much overrepresented.

Even if this pattern is borne out, however, it is also important to establish whether the cities with more structured community participation exhibit greater SES biases in terms of who participates. Do the structures of participation simply provide more points of access to higher SES people who would tend to participate anyway? Or do the structures, with their extensive outreach activities and enhanced participation opportunities, work to stimulate participation by people who might not otherwise participate? Clearly, since it was established earlier that the total number of people participating is not increased by such structures, increasing the propensity of lower SES people to participate could only occur if there is a corresponding decrease in participation by some other group of people.

These questions can be examined fairly directly with the assistance of the survey research conducted in the fifteen cities. There are many ways of measuring the SES of participants and of estimating the degree of under- or overrepresentativeness of people at a given SES level. Here the focus is on a composite measure of SES, a three-category variable that combines family income and the respondent's level of schooling.[21]

The level of representativeness is measured here in a strictly numeric sense, comparing the proportion of participants from a given SES or racial group with that found in the general population.[22] If people of lower SES constitute 20 percent of community participants and 30

20. Nagel, *Participation*, pp. 5–6.

21. The SES variable used here and throughout the book is a simple composite measure based on family income and personal educational attainment. Low SES is defined as people who had low incomes (between $0 and $15,000) or low levels of schooling (less than a high school education). Middle SES is defined as having either middle income (between $15,000 and $30,000) or middle education (at least a high school diploma and some college or schooling beyond high school). High SES is defined as high income (over $30,000) and high education (a college degree or beyond).

22. "The general population" refers to the population aged eighteen years and older, as reflected in the overall frequency distribution from each city's population survey.

percent of the population, then it can be said that these people are underrepresented among community participants by 10 percentage points. This arithmetic difference is used as the first of two indexes of representativeness where a positive number means that the subgroup of people is overrepresented and a negative number reflects under-representation. A number around zero reflects proportionate representation. This difference number is then used to calculate a second index of representativeness by taking the difference as a percentage of the proportion of the population in the SES or racial group. This index of representativeness is precisely the same as that used by Verba and Nie.[23]

Socioeconomic Status and Community Participation

Community participants do, indeed, appear to be disproportionately from upper SES backgrounds. The distribution of community participants by their SES level, compared with the overall distribution of SES in the cities, is shown in table 4-3. This comparison is summarized in two indexes of representativeness. In all five types of cities, lower SES people are significantly underrepresented and upper SES people are significantly overrepresented among community participants.

Cities with more structured community participation do not possess significantly more socioeconomic biases among participants than their unstructured counterparts. The indexes of representativeness suggest that while the more structured cities slightly underrepresent low-SES people compared with the less structured cities (differences of −14.6 vs. −10.8 and −12.4 vs. −10.1), they also slightly underrepresent higher SES people (differences of 15.4 vs. 19.3 and 10.1 vs. 14.5). If there is a socioeconomic group of people that is better represented through community participation in the structured cities than the unstructured cities, it is the middle class. The middle class is not overrepresented in the structured cities; it is simply better represented than its counterparts in the unstructured cities. San Antonio stands out among the groups of cities as having the greatest SES biases, exhibiting the greatest underrepresentation of lower SES people. Thus, despite the efforts of COPS, people who engage in face-to-face political activity in San Antonio are much more likely than

23. Verba and Nie, *Participation in America*, p. 96.

TABLE 4-3. Community Participation and Socioeconomic Status[a]

City participation level and respondent's SES	Community participants (percent)[a]	Percent of population	Indexes of representativeness	
			Difference	Percent
High community participation				
Structured cities[b]				
Low SES	20.7	35.3	−14.6	−41.4
Middle SES	40.5	41.3	−0.8	−1.9
High SES	38.8	23.4	15.4	65.8
N	570	2,231	. . .	. . .
Unstructured cities[c]				
Low SES	24.7	35.5	−10.8	−30.4
Middle SES	32.3	40.8	−8.5	−20.8
High SES	43.0	23.7	19.3	81.4
N	158	608	. . .	. . .
Moderate community participation				
Structured cities[d]				
Low SES	27.9	40.3	−12.4	−30.8
Middle SES	49.2	46.9	2.4	4.9
High SES	22.9	12.8	10.1	78.9
N	341	1,734	. . .	. . .
Unstructured cities[e]				
Low SES	23.7	33.8	−10.1	−29.9
Middle SES	39.0	43.4	− 4.4	−10.1
High SES	37.3	22.8	14.5	63.6
N	169	907	. . .	. . .
Low community participation[f]				
Low SES	22.0	49.1	−27.1	−55.2
Middle SES	41.6	32.3	9.3	28.8
High SES	36.4	18.6	17.8	95.7
N	154	1,112	. . .	. . .

a. Respondents in the top three categories of the index of community participation (ICP).
b. Portland and St. Paul.
c. Norfolk, Minneapolis, Louisville, and Buffalo.
d. Birmingham and Dayton.
e. Tucson, Omaha, Colorado Springs, El Paso, Savannah, and Wichita.
f. San Antonio.

their counterparts in the other cities to be from higher socioeconomic status backgrounds.[24]

24. The same general pattern is borne out with respect to other indicators of SES, including differences between homeowners and renters. In each of the five groups of cities, community participants are more representative of people who own their homes than people who rent their places of residence. But perhaps equally important, the cities with structured participation do not show any greater tendency toward this type of bias than cities without such structure. Again, only San Antonio stands out as having substantially greater participation bias in favor of homeowners.

Minority Status and Community Participation

A related issue involves the level of access provided for people of color and minority status. Existing research on the relationship between race and political participation suggests that African Americans and Hispanics tend to participate less than people of nonminority status, although whether there are differences depends to a large extent on the type of political participation being studied.[25] Moreover, racial differences in participation either become very small, disappear entirely, or even favor minorities, once SES is controlled.[26] In other words, lower SES African Americans and Hispanics participate at approximately the same rates as (or only slightly higher or lower rates than) lower SES nonminority people.[27]

These general findings raise some specific questions relevant to the operation of citywide systems of neighborhood associations. Simply stated, does community participation disadvantage African American or Hispanic people? Does structured community participation create disadvantages for African Americans and Hispanics by creating greater obstacles for their participation, or does it help to overcome some of the apparent disadvantages of face-to-face participation? Does the existence of citywide community participation systems help to overcome the "standard socioeconomic model"?

Analysis of community participation for African Americans and Hispanics produces a two-sided picture. (Respondents are shown by race or

25. For example, Verba and Nie found that personally contacting public officials differs from other forms of political participation. See *Participation in America*, chap. 10.

26. Marvin E. Olsen, "Social and Political Participation of Blacks," *American Sociological Review*, vol. 35 (August 1970), pp. 682–97; Anthony M. Orum, "A Reappraisal of the Social and Political Participation of Negroes," *American Journal of Sociology*, vol. 72 (July 1966), pp. 32–46; J. Allen Williams, Jr., Nicholas Babchuk, and David R. Johnson, "Voluntary Associations and Minority Status: A Comparative Analysis of Anglo, Black, and Mexican Americans," *American Sociological Review*, vol. 38 (October 1973), pp. 637–46; J. Miller McPherson, "Correlates of Social Participation: A Comparison of Ethnic Community and Compensatory Theories," *Sociological Quarterly*, vol. 18 (Spring 1977), pp. 197–208; Nicholas L. Danigelis, "Black Political Participation in the United States: Some Recent Evidence," *American Sociological Review*, vol. 43 (October 1978), pp. 756–71; Richard D. Shingles, "Black Consciousness and Political Participation: The Missing Link," *American Political Science Review*, vol. 75 (March 1981), pp. 76–91; Thomas Guterbock and Bruce London, "Race, Political Orientation, and Participation: An Empirical Test of Four Competing Theories," *American Sociological Review*, vol. 48 (August 1983), pp. 439–53; and Verba and Nie, *Participation in America*, pp. 149–73.

27. Our research confirms that, among all fifteen cities combined, African-American respondents participate at higher rates than whites when socioeconomic status is controlled.

TABLE 4-4. Community Participation among Low-SES Residents,
by Minority Status

Low-SES residents and minority status	Community participants (percent)[a]	Percent of population	Indexes of representativeness	
			Difference	Percent
African Americans				
Portland and St. Paul	9.3	1.9	7.4	389.5
Portland–St. Paul comparison cities[b]	23.9	7.4	16.5	222.9
Birmingham and Dayton	19.6	15.0	4.6	30.7
Birmingham–Dayton comparison cities[c]	25.0	3.9	21.1	541.0
San Antonio	7.8	4.6	3.2	69.6
Hispanics				
Portland and St. Paul	0.0	0.8	–0.8	–100.0
Portland–St. Paul comparison cities[b]	25.0	1.3	23.7	1823.1
Birmingham and Dayton	0.0	0.2	–0.2	–100.0
Birmingham–Dayton comparison cities[c]	10.7	6.0	+4.7	78.3
San Antonio	4.8	31.7	–26.9	–84.9
Nonminorities				
Portland and St. Paul	15.7	32.3	–16.6	–51.4
Portland–St. Paul comparison cities[b]	16.0	26.0	–10.0	–38.5
Birmingham and Dayton	9.2	19.5	–10.3	–52.8
Birmingham–Dayton comparison cities[c]	11.6	23.2	–11.4	–49.6
San Antonio	9.2	12.8	–3.6	–28.1

a. Respondents in the top three categories of the ICP.
b. Norfolk, Minneapolis, Louisville, and Buffalo.
c. Tucson, Omaha, Colorado Springs, El Paso, Savannah, and Wichita.

ethnicity in table 4-4.) On one side, when judged by the straight difference
index of representativeness, it would appear that for both groups the
cities with structured participation do a better job of attracting minorities
in numbers close to those found in the overall population. For example,
in Birmingham and Dayton about 19.6 percent of low-SES African
Americans are community participants,[28] while about 15 percent of the
population is low-SES African American. The comparison cities, whose
community participation is less structured, actually tend to overrepresent

28. Community participants are the respondents in the top three categories of the
index of community participation.

minority populations. In the Birmingham-Dayton comparison cities, about 3.9 percent of the population is low-SES African American, but 25 percent of low-SES African Americans are community participants.

On the other side, low-SES Hispanics in the structured community participation cities (despite their very small numbers in the populations) appear to have virtually no community participation. Even in San Antonio, despite the operation of COPS within the Mexican-American sections of the city, these efforts have not been able to stimulate enough face-to-face political participation among low-SES residents to even approach their level in the population.

There are two ways of interpreting these findings, especially with respect to the African-American population. On one hand, the unstructured community participation cities appear to attract a higher proportion of low-SES African-American and Hispanic people into community participation activities to the point where they far exceed their numbers in the population. On the other hand, the structured community participation cities have low-SES African-American and Hispanic community participants in rough proportion to their numbers in the population, perhaps suggesting a more balanced representation. Overall, the structured community participation cities do not appear to do a universally better job of representing low-SES minority populations.

The Underclass Hypothesis

The idea that social class has become a more important determinant of political participation than race gained new acceptance with the appearance of sociologist William Julius Wilson's works.[29] Wilson suggests that one of the greatest urban problems is the existence of an "underclass" of truly disadvantaged people "who lack training skills and either experience long-term unemployment or are not members of the labor force, individuals who are engaged in street crime and other forms of aberrant behavior, and families that experience long-term spells of poverty and/or welfare dependency."[30] He argues that underclass neighborhoods, where high concentrations of very poor minority people live, are unique not simply because they have such concentrated poverty, but also

29. William Julius Wilson, *The Declining Significance of Race*, 2d ed. (University of Chicago Press, 1980); and Wilson, *The Truly Disadvantaged: The Inner City, the Underclass and Public Policy* (University of Chicago Press, 1987).
30. Wilson, *The Truly Disadvantaged*, p. 8.

because residents live in social and political isolation. The idea that people who live in neighborhoods with high concentrations of poverty have unusual rates of deviant or antisocial behavior can be referred to as the "underclass hypothesis."[31]

If the underclass hypothesis captures a description of urban political behavior, then poor people in poor neighborhoods should be much less likely to engage in community participation activities. Although it is not clear whether the cities studied here are the kinds of cities Wilson has in mind when he writes of the truly disadvantaged,[32] these cities can be used to examine whether their poorest residents seem to be able to overcome serious political isolation. If the systems of citywide participation play no role in helping to overcome the powerful influences associated with the underclass, then poor people who live in concentrated areas of poverty should participate much less than others, including poor people who do not live in poor neighborhoods. On the other hand, if the systems of neighborhood associations are able to help decrease political isolation, then poor people who live in poor neighborhoods should participate no less frequently than other poor people.

In order to investigate this, we need to distinguish the poor from the nonpoor, and poor neighborhoods from nonpoor neighborhoods. Poor people are defined as respondents who reported that their family income was less than $5,000 a year. This standard is somewhat stricter than the official government poverty index.[33] Defining poor neighborhoods requires the adoption of a threshold level of neighborhood poverty. Wilson suggests that a neighborhood with between 20 and 40 percent of the population living in poverty constitutes a poor neighborhood, and a neighborhood with more than a 40 percent poverty rate is extremely poor.

31. This hypothesis is investigated in more depth in Jeffrey M. Berry, Kent E. Portney, and Ken Thomson, "The Political Behavior of Poor People," in Christopher Jencks and Paul E. Peterson, eds., *The Urban Underclass* (Brookings, 1991), pp. 357–74; and "The Political Behavior of Poor People," paper prepared for the Conference on the Truly Disadvantaged, Social Science Research Council and Center for Urban Affairs and Policy Research, Evanston, Illinois, October 1989.

32. Paul E. Peterson, "The Urban Underclass and the Poverty Paradox," in Jencks and Peterson, eds., *The Urban Underclass*, pp. 21–22; and William Julius Wilson, "Another Look at the Truly Disadvantaged," *Political Science Quarterly*, vol. 106 (Winter 1991–1992), pp. 651–52.

33. During the time of these interviews, the official poverty line for a two-person family was slightly over $5,000 and of course was higher for larger families. The $5,000 level was used because the survey questions elicited income information by categories, and this is the category that most closely matched the official poverty line.

We can examine this underclass hypothesis by applying these definitions to four of the five cities studied here.[34] Since virtually no neighborhoods in these cities have a poverty level of 40 percent or more, this analysis will focus on those neighborhoods that satisfy the 20 percent threshold. Sixty-nine poor neighborhoods met this criterion.[35]

As shown in table 4-5, the poor who live in poor neighborhoods in these four cities do not exhibit less face-to-face political participation than other poor people. Indeed, with respect to all of the forms of political participation examined here, the overwhelming tendency is for poor people who live in poor neighborhoods to participate more. The poor in poor neighborhoods do participate slightly less and certainly not significantly less when it comes to being active in neighborhood associations. But the fact that over a quarter of the poor people who live in poor neighborhoods reported participating in their neighborhood associations is probably testament to the level of opportunity offered by these organizations. In short, the poor people who live in these cities' poorest neighborhoods do not seem to exhibit isolation of the sort described by Wilson.

The Forms of Community Participation

The scores for the fifteen cities on the ICP scale demonstrate that overall levels of community participation in the five cities with strong participation structures do not differ markedly from other American cities. Analyses of representational biases reveal that cities with strong participation structures neither encourage nor discourage community participation by low-SES people more than do cities without such structures. Can it therefore be concluded that these participation structures make no difference in participation activity? Or do they change the pattern of participation in some way, within the same levels of overall community participation?

Because the impact of SES upon participation is so strong, SES must be used as a control variable throughout analysis of these questions. From this point on, most of the analysis will be presented in a form that takes into account the SES status of each respondent. The most common

34. San Antonio is not included in this analysis for two reasons. First, it was not possible to clearly delineate neighborhood boundaries. Second, the system of community participation is not citywide.

35. Of these sixty-nine neighborhoods, thirty-nine are in Birmingham, twelve are in Dayton, fifteen are in Portland, and three are in St. Paul.

TABLE 4-5. Local Political Activity and the Underclass Hypothesis

	Participant's class and neighborhood							
	Poor in poor neighborhoods		Poor in nonpoor neighborhoods		Nonpoor in poor neighborhoods		Nonpoor in nonpoor neighborhoods	
Level of participation	Number	Percent yes	Number	Percent yes	Number	Percent yes	Number	Percent yes	Chi square
Have you ever personally gone to see, or spoken to, or written to, some member of the local community about some need or problem?	91	29.7	197	17.8	665	37.6	2,673	40.3	42.6**
Have you ever taken part in forming a new group or a new organization to try to solve some community problem?	84	13.1	188	9.6	646	12.5	2,605	12.2	1.33
Have you ever worked with others in this community to try to solve some community problem?	86	31.4	190	26.3	647	41.6	2,627	42.3	22.0**
Have you ever actually been active in any community or citizen groups or neighborhood organizations?	88	26.1	193	31.1	661	38.4	2,665	44.3	28.8**
Have you personally taken part in the activities of your Neighborhood Association [District Council; Priority Board] in the last two years?	88	13.2	72	8.3	550	19.4	1,360	20.5	7.5**

**Significant at the 0.01 level.
*Significant at the 0.05 level.

approach used in this analysis is to divide the full samples into three parts, by high-, middle-, and low-SES categories, and examine each sub-sample separately.[36]

We used this form of analysis to study the patterns of six major kinds of participation measured by the surveys (see table 4-6, which separates cities into the five groups based on their average ICP scores). The pattern of results one might expect among these five groups, as discussed earlier, is confirmed by the overall averages of community participation (not shown in the table). The ICP averages (means) for the core study cities and their comparison cities are virtually identical: 1.45 for Birmingham–Dayton and 1.49 for their comparison cities, and 1.67 for Portland–St. Paul and 1.70 for their comparison cities. San Antonio trails substantially behind with its 1.10 ICP average.

The nearly identical averages for each of these pairs of city groups, however, mask some very important differences. The patterns of partic-ipation for the specific "weak participation activities" and "strong par-ticipation activities" are quite different from those implied by the averages. For each of the weak participation activities, at each SES level, the core study cities tend to have lower participation rates than their respective comparison cities. For example, 20.8 percent of low-SES re-spondents from Birmingham and Dayton take part in social service group activities, and 29 percent of the low-SES respondents in the Birmingham–Dayton comparison group take part in such activities.

For each of the strong participation activities, however, at each SES level the five core study cities tend to have higher participation rates than their comparison cities. For example, 4.6 percent of the respondents in Birmingham and Dayton contacted neighborhood or issue groups, while only 1.3 percent of the comparison group engaged in this type of con-tacting behavior. Overall, all but three of the eighteen comparisons (row by row) are significant at the 0.05 level or better, and all but three of those are significant beyond the 0.01 level.

The differences in strong contacting activity are particularly dramatic. Normally, a positive response to the question "Have you ever personally gone to see, spoken to, or written to, some member of the local commu-nity about some need or problem?" would mean, as found in the survey's follow-up question about with whom the contact was made, that the person had contacted the mayor's office, a city councillor, or possibly a

---

36. The analysis controls for SES by simply dividing the sample into three subsamples based on the SES variable described earlier.

TABLE 4-6. Patterns of Participation Activity, by SES[a]

Percent of population unless otherwise indicated

Level of participation and SES status	Low community participation city[b]	Moderate community participation cities		High community participation cities		N	Chi square
		Unstructured[c]	Structured[d]	Unstructured[e]	Structured[f]		
Weak participation activities							
Involvement in social and service groups							
Low SES	6.2	29.0	20.8	19.8	24.9	2,589	93.5**
Middle SES	16.8	32.7	19.5	30.9	29.8	2,394	45.9**
High SES	17.9	36.8	21.9	20.8	22.5	1,312	25.2**
Contacting public officials							
Low SES	13.2	20.5	23.2	27.8	26.5	2,596	39.3**
Middle SES	34.0	38.4	32.8	43.9	38.7	2,395	11.8**
High SES	47.3	55.0	45.0	66.9	53.4	1,314	20.2**
Helping group to form							
Low SES	5.7	9.7	9.7	10.9	6.7	2,532	12.3*
Middle SES	11.8	12.1	12.8	13.7	12.7	2,337	0.6
High SES	13.1	20.1	17.9	16.8	19.6	1,285	5.0

Strong participation activities

Involvement in neighborhood and issue groups							
Low SES	6.2	13.2	14.3	18.0	14.9	2,589	30.8**
Middle SES	17.9	16.5	22.5	20.7	26.0	2,394	18.8**
High SES	27.1	30.6	36.0	47.2	42.2	1,312	24.8**
Contacting neighborhood or issue group							
Low SES	1.1	1.3	4.6	2.3	2.0	2,596	20.7**
Middle SES	1.7	0.8	7.7	0.8	3.0	2,395	48.8**
High SES	1.4	1.0	7.9	0.0	4.2	1,314	26.0**
Working with group to solve community problem							
Low SES	15.0	31.6	33.8	33.0	32.8	2545	67.9**
Middle SES	34.9	39.8	42.6	42.6	45.2	2,343	11.7*
High SES	45.1	54.0	54.3	53.6	55.3	1,277	6.4

**Significant at the o.o1 level.
*Significant at the o.o5 level.
a. The numbers in boldface indicate the sets that should be higher than the sets they are being compared with according to the theory of structural participation described in the text. The low community participation city has no explicit comparison set, but may be evaluated in terms of its distance from the moderate community participation cities.
b. San Antonio.
c. Birmingham–Dayton comparison cities (Tucson, Omaha, Colorado Springs, El Paso, Savannah, and Wichita).
d. Birmingham and Dayton.
e. Portland–St. Paul comparison cities (Norfolk, Minneapolis, Louisville, and Buffalo).
f. Portland and St. Paul.

legislator or agency official. This is often referred to as "particularized contacting" behavior.[37] In the cities with strong participation structures, however, a significant number of people contact their neighborhood association or another citizen organization first. This was true for 4.6 percent to 7.9 percent of the respondents in Birmingham and Dayton, in contrast to 1.3 percent to 1.0 percent in their comparison cities. When considered in terms of those who say they have contacted someone, rather than in terms of all respondents, the figures (not shown in the table) seem even more dramatic: in Birmingham and Dayton, more than 20 percent of the contacts people made were to neighborhood or similar citizen groups, compared to less than 2 percent of the contacts in the comparison cities. Clearly the neighborhood organizations in these cities are performing a function that is simply not available in most other cities.

In each city, the system of neighborhood associations accomplishes this function in a way that reflects the specific character and history of political activity in that community. In Birmingham, for example, opportunities for political impact were practically nonexistent for African Americans before the 1970s. With the growth of the neighborhood associations and their links to the city through community coalitions, the citywide Citizens Advisory Board, and the full-time neighborhood resource officers working out of city hall, a direct and powerful avenue for "particularized contacting" and influence on city decisions was opened. In this context, it is not surprising that many of Birmingham's citizens see the neighborhood groups and their elected officers as the best way to make their voices heard.

In St. Paul, on the other hand, a wide variety of active citizen advocacy groups existed long before the District Council system was developed. The councils tended to tie these groups together and provide a specific link to policy influence on issues that affected the neighborhoods. Here, the direct decisionmaking role the councils have on these issues leads people to take their concerns to them. In all the cities, the neighborhood groups are sufficiently accessible and powerful to provide an attractive basis for solving community problems.

In sum, people in the cities with strong participation structures exhibit substantially different patterns of participation than do people in the comparison cities without such structures. While the overall levels of community participation are similar to the levels in the comparison cities, those activities that incorporate more of the elements of strong democ-

37. Verba and Nie, *Participation in America*, pp. 66–69.

racy tend to predominate, and those that incorporate fewer such elements tend to receive less attention from community residents. A more detailed look at the neighborhood-based participation structures in the five core cities further strengthens this conclusion.

Community Participation and Neighborhood Associations

Up to this point, it has been assumed that, at least within one city, all neighborhood associations are created equal. Yet there is good reason to believe this is not the case. The strength of neighborhood organization and the strong participation structures that go along with it vary a great deal within every city. Because each survey conducted for this project was stratified by neighborhood, these participation questions can be examined in relation to the specific neighborhood context. In addition to the survey results, independent information was obtained that allowed an estimate of the strength of the leadership, outreach efforts, and participatory activities of more than 250 neighborhood associations. These estimates are based in large part on factual data provided by the staff of neighborhood support organizations. They are also based on information from others in the community who have had contact with a range of neighborhood organizations in the city and could therefore give comparative evaluations.

These data are used to create a neighborhood participation rating as a reflection of the strength of neighborhood associations. This rating, in turn, facilitates analysis of the relationship between the strength of neighborhood organization and the level of community participation. The results are shown in table 4-7.

Using this rating of neighborhood strength, the pattern of community participation is strong and clear for low- and middle-SES residents. People who live in neighborhoods with strong organizations tend to participate more, and people who live in neighborhoods with weaker associations tend to participate less. On the other hand, there is no pattern of association between neighborhood strength and community participation for high-SES participants. Apparently those who are generally more likely to engage in community participation—higher SES citizens—are the least affected by the added impetus and resources of neighborhood associations.

Neighborhood strength is thus an important factor influencing the decision of citizens to participate actively in their communities. It is

TABLE 4-7. Neighborhood Strength and High Community
Participation, by SES

Percent in top two levels of ICP

Socioeconomic status	Neighborhood organization strength			N	Chi square[a]
	Low	Moderate	High		
Low SES	5.9	6.5	11.4	1,391	13.0**
Middle SES	10.4	15.0	16.5	1,317	10.6*
High SES	22.7	22.5	21.6	720	0.1

a. A separate chi-square test was performed for each SES level. Each chi-square value is based on a 3 × 3 table (three categories of the index of community participation—low, moderate, and high—by three categories of neighborhood strength).

**Significant at the 0.01 level.

*Significant at the 0.05 level.

particularly important in boosting the participation of low- and middle-SES residents. While on a citywide basis strong participation structures seem to change the pattern of community participation but fail to change its overall levels, strong participation structures at the neighborhood level seem able to accomplish both objectives.

The reason for this is clear. Stronger neighborhood associations, by definition, mean more extensive door-to-door outreach efforts, more frequent neighborhood events, more information going out to neighborhood residents, and more volunteers spending more time to make all of this happen. A more active neighborhood group creates more opportunities to participate than does a weaker group. And the increased opportunity to participate leads to increased participation.

In some cases the participation in the neighborhood group simply shifts the location in which an individual spends his or her time in community participation—the already active person spends more time with the neighborhood group and less time with a civic group in which he or she had been active before. It is also true that in a neighborhood where many people are already active civic participants, those people are likely to form a stronger neighborhood group than in areas where civic activity is unusual. But in many other situations, people who had not been active before, at least not in any group dealing with social or political issues, become active in the neighborhood association because they are repeatedly offered the opportunity to participate and have an impact on public policy and community life. Nevertheless, substantial numbers of people, nearly 50 percent of those in even the strongest neighborhoods in the most participatory cities, simply do not participate in strong participation activities. For the other 50 percent, however, both political culture and participation structure can make a major difference in the role they play in the political system.

Conclusion

Would-be reformers of all political stripes have argued that the key to reviving American democracy is to give people meaningful control over decisions that affect their lives. People are said to abstain from voting and other forms of political behavior because they feel that ultimately what they do will make little difference. The data from the five cities are sobering testimony to the difficulty of stimulating political participation. Although the neighborhood associations in these cities vary substantially in how well they function, for the most part they offer highly meaningful channels of participation. In small neighborhood groups, individuals have the opportunity to significantly influence decisions that affect the quality of life in their neighborhoods. Yet the number of citizens involved in community participation activities is not greater in the core study cities than in the cities with which they were matched that have no citywide systems of participation.

Compared with most American cities, these neighborhood associations represent a substantial decentralization of political power. Why is it that this devolution of political authority has not brought people out of political isolation? Most likely, the reason is that participatory democracy demands too much from citizens to be broadly appealing. People are not unwilling to devote time to their communities. As emphasized in chapter 1, Americans are extraordinarily generous with the time they volunteer to civic activities. But face-to-face democracy can be intimidating. Even though these systems of citizen participation are centered in the neighborhood, where people may know many other participants, the give-and-take of small group politics remains an unattractive way to spend an evening for the vast majority of people.

At the same time, structured, citywide systems of community participation can be developed without creating any more bias in the participants it attracts than face-to-face participation as practiced without any citywide structure. Four of the five cities with structured participation exhibit no more socioeconomic, residential, or racial bias among face-to-face participants than the comparable cities without such structure. However, the structured systems are not able to overcome the very significant socioeconomic biases that are inherently associated with intensive participation. Structured participation systems do no worse than unstructured systems in attracting participants across a broad socioeconomic spectrum, but they do no better either.

The data offer some hope, however, that structures of strong democracy can positively affect participation in city politics. Some important patterns emerge from analysis of the surveys in the five cities by neighborhood. When neighborhoods are ranked by the organizational strength of their neighborhood associations, those neighborhoods with the most solid organizations seem to have more strong democracy activity. This relationship is limited to low- and middle-SES residents, but this is hardly a disquieting finding given the relatively high level of participation by those with high incomes. The magnitude of this effect in the five cities is not enough to produce overall levels of participation that stand out from baseline comparisons, but the relationship in low- and middle-SES neighborhoods is clear and significant. If the weaker neighborhood associations can be strengthened in these cities, some modest improvement in the overall rates of participation is likely.

The surveys also demonstrate that the structures of strong democracy are linked to the types of political activity that go on in a neighborhood. When neighborhood associations are available to residents, many of those who are politically active will take advantage of them to press a complaint or make a request. People in the five core cities who are willing to engage in face-to-face democracy tend to regard the neighborhood associations as important players in city politics.

Do neighborhood participation structures produce strong democracy? The answer is maybe yes and maybe no. To the extent that strong democracy requires an expansion of participation to the chronically disenfranchised and politically inactive, the answer is no. The chronically inactive do not tend to be any more involved in the cities with strong democracy structures. To the extent that strong democracy requires that people engage in fundamentally different kinds of participatory activities, the answer is yes. Clearly, the cities with strong democracy structures present active people with very different ways of expressing themselves and of participating in public affairs. Strong democracy structures channel participants' energies into communal and cooperative activities rather than activities that are fundamentally isolating. Whether participation in these activities makes these people better or happier citizens, produces local government that is more responsive, or makes governance easier or more difficult will be investigated in the chapters to come.

Part Two —————————————————————————
Does Government Respond?

CHAPTER 5

Controlling the Public Agenda

ONE OF THE ATTRIBUTES of democratic societies is that governments are expected to be responsive to the will of the people. This is a
simple and noble idea. But how do we know if the government's actions
are true to the wishes of the governed? And how do we know if citizen
participation makes any difference in the decisions government makes?

These are central issues in democratic theory, but there is no agreed-
upon way of measuring whether government actions match the "will of
the people." Recognizing that any one approach can be problematic, we
use a number of different approaches to determine if government is
responsive to the people's "will" in the five core cities. This effort begins
by breaking the problem down into three component parts, each representing a stage in the policymaking process. In this chapter we look at
the first two stages, both of which are part of agenda building. Government can be said to be responsive to its constituents if their concerns are
placed on the agenda of problems with which the government is concerned. A related question is whether a political system has biases in
problem definition and agenda setting that work to favor the concerns
of some sectors of society over those of others.

Entry of an issue onto the agenda does not ensure that government
will actually respond in the manner that the people wish. Thus we must
look at another aspect of policymaking to see how government officials
react to the issues before them. An issue may be placed on the agenda
by a determined minority but may be discounted by most in government
as a problem that has a low priority or as one that cannot be solved. To
test whether or not there is a match between the priorities of citizens
and the priorities of government, political scientists have utilized measures of attitudinal concurrence between elites and ordinary citizens. In
an era of scarce resources, whose priorities get attention?

We look at responsiveness in the later stages of the policymaking
process in chapter 6. Even if those in government agree with citizens
about the issues that deserve the most attention, there is no assurance

that they will devise policies that meet the preferences of the people. Consequently, it is important to look at actual policy outcomes, to examine the winners and losers of policy conflicts and issues to see if government decisions are in line with public opinion.

The question of policy outcomes is examined from another perspective in chapter 7. Given the complexity of both contemporary issues and the incrementalism and compromise that often characterize our political process, it is difficult for ordinary citizens to know in any objective sense who won and who lost in most public policy matters. However, their *perception* of who won and lost affects their sense of whether government is fair and open to all. A government that is perceived to be fair is likely to be one that people believe is going to listen to them and respond to their preferences. Moreover, such perceptions affect individuals' calculus as to whether or not it is worth their while to become involved in politics.

A crucial question overlaying all of these aspects of responsiveness is what difference does participation make? Is government more responsive to citizens who are highly active political participants? Do the neighborhood associations in the five core cities make a significant difference in the way city hall responds to the demands made upon it?

Public Problems, Political Issues

The world is full of problems, but government deals with only some of them at any one time. People were homeless before homelessness became a visible, disturbing political issue. At some point, however, the homeless on the street became government's responsibility. The study of agenda building is the study of how public problems become defined as political issues. An agenda is simply the set of issues that a government is considering at any one time. A new policy does not have to be formulated for an issue to be on the agenda; government merely has to give serious thought to taking some action.

The study of agenda setting is relatively recent in origin and there is only a small, though highly informative, literature on the subject. Various studies have focused on the transformation of individual problems into political issues,[1] the catalytic agents that bring problems into view,[2] the systematic comparison of how different problems reach the

---

1. See, for example, Barbara J. Nelson, *Making an Issue of Child Abuse: Political Agenda Setting for Social Problems* (University of Chicago Press, 1984).

2. Roger W. Cobb and Charles D. Elder, *Participation in Politics: The Dynamics of Agenda Building*, 2d ed. (Johns Hopkins University Press, 1983).

agenda,[3] and the biases that prevent certain problems from ever getting on the agenda.[4]

Two generalizations from the literature are of particular interest here. The first is that agenda setting is fundamentally biased in favor of those who possess the most resources. This has been demonstrated from a variety of perspectives. One approach has shown that individuals and interest groups with great resources, principally those from the business world, have substantially better access to policymakers. Thus their problems are much more likely to reach the governmental agenda than those of others.[5] Another manifestation of this bias is that certain problems do not become issues at all because of the way citizens have been socialized. Some social or political concerns become defined as so vitally important that competing claims upon government are never effectively raised. John Gaventa develops this line of thinking in his study of exploited Appalachian coal miners. Gaventa argues that political power is also the process "by which social legitimations are developed."[6] People's definition of themselves and their role in society may be manipulated in such a way as to depoliticize them.

The second generalization we want to explore is that agenda setting is a haphazard process, with random factors explaining the entrance of many issues onto the political agenda. In his study of health and transportation issues, John Kingdon failed to find a systematic process by which problems become defined as governmental responsibilities. Instead, unpredictable events and trends create windows of opportunity through which problems get on the agenda.[7]

None of the contemporary analysts of policy initiation makes the case that agenda building embodies principles of democratic government. Do

3. John W. Kingdon, *Agendas, Alternatives, and Public Policies* (Little, Brown, 1984); Nelson W. Polsby, *Political Innovation in America: The Politics of Policy Initiation* (Yale University Press, 1984); and Frank R. Baumgartner and Bryan D. Jones, "Interest Groups and Agenda Setting in America," paper prepared for the Conference on Organized Interests and Democracy, Cortona, Italy, May 1990.

4. John Gaventa, *Power and Powerlessness: Quiescence and Rebellion in an Appalachian Valley* (University of Illinois Press, 1980); and Jeffrey M. Berry and Kevin Hula, "Interest Groups and Systemic Bias," paper prepared for the 1991 annual meeting of the American Political Science Association.

5. Clarence N. Stone, *Economic Growth and Neighborhood Discontent: System Bias in the Urban Renewal Program of Atlanta* (University of North Carolina Press, 1976).

6. Gaventa, *Power and Powerlessness*, p. 15. See also Peter Bachrach and Morton S. Baratz, "Two Faces of Power," *American Political Science Review*, vol. 56 (December 1962), pp. 947–52.

7. Kingdon, *Agendas, Alternatives, and Public Policies*.

our five cities confirm the conventional wisdom? Cities cannot be fully responsive if some constituencies have a much easier time getting government to consider their problems than others do. Likewise, if policy initiation has a high degree of randomness, agendas cannot be said to reflect the responsiveness of government to the concerns of citizens. What must be established here is whether the entrance of new issues onto the agenda is structured by systemic bias, random developments, or a reasonably equal competition between all significant sectors of each of our cities. Furthermore, we want to know what difference citizen participation makes. It is entirely plausible that the local governments are highly supportive of what the neighborhood associations do in their communities, but at the same time they limit the impact of those organizations by tightly controlling the agenda of citywide issues dealt with by city hall.

The research methodology utilized here was designed to overcome the chief limitation of the literature on agenda setting: the building of generalizations on a small number of cases. Yet scholars have concentrated on looking at one or at most a handful of cases, for good reason. It is not easy to establish how an issue reaches the agenda. As Nelson Polsby puts it, policy does not "appear out of the sea like Botticelli's Venus—dimpled, rosy, and complete on a clamshell."[8] There are no available data bases, and gathering the necessary information on each individual issue is time-consuming. Consequently, scholars have depended on detailed case analysis as their primary research tool.

The large number of elite interviews done in the five cities offered an opportunity to develop a sizable set of cases detailing how problems reach the political agenda. A major portion of each standardized elite interview with city councillors, administrators, and citizen group leaders was devoted to eliciting information about a single issue. After each respondent identified a set of issues he or she had worked on, the interviewer asked that person to give a "fairly detailed chronology" of one of those issues. We selected the particular issue on the basis of a number of criteria. Preference was given to the issue the person was most involved with to maximize the detail we received and to increase our confidence in the accuracy of the story we were given. Frequently, the issue they spent the most time on was something that was really "their baby," an issue they had been with from the beginning. We steered respondents away from internal issues, such as departmental reorganizations or prob-

8. Polsby, *Political Innovation in America*, p. 5.

lems of interest group maintenance.[9] The interviewers probed respondents to fill in sketchy parts of their story, to amplify intriguing points, to evaluate the contribution of the citizen participation process if they had not done so already, or to expand their discussion of other relevant areas of the research.[10]

This approach, unfortunately, has some shortcomings. Respondents frequently exaggerate their own role or that of their organization. In return for the economy of having people tell us about an issue instead of doing historical research ourselves, we get the participants' biases concerning who and what was most important in the development of each issue. Nevertheless, the accounts we have are quite detailed, and we believe the broad contours of the stories we heard are reliable enough for the relatively simple statistical work that was conducted. (Part of our confidence is based on hearing some of the cases from multiple sources. The basics of each story were similar enough to establish the reliability of this method).[11]

Ideally, these case histories would constitute a random sample of all issues that reached the agenda in the period immediately preceding the interviewing. But it is impossible to establish a random sample since there are no clear boundaries to the universe.[12] Still, since interview subjects covered the range of policy areas that cities are responsible for, the sample contains case histories that are reasonably representative of all the recent, new policy initiatives during the time of the fieldwork. For the purposes of understanding agenda building, the real problem is not that the sample lacks randomness but that it does not contain problems that failed to reach the agenda. That is, the sample is composed of only those problems

9. Respondents were also steered away from policies that seemed to be modest, incremental changes from existing policy. The resulting issues that were discussed cannot, however, be described as clear *innovations*. In the five cities we found very few policies that represented broad new directions in public policy. The issues analyzed here can best be characterized as significant changes in a city's existing policy but also as approaches that have very likely been tried elsewhere.

10. For a similar methodology based on issue narratives, see Frank R. Baumgartner, *Conflict and Rhetoric in French Policymaking* (University of Pittsburgh Press, 1989).

11. In those instances where we had duplicate issue narratives, we examined the discrepancies—almost always minor in number—and made an effort to reconcile the differences. Where the accounts were clearly at odds and we had detailed versions of each, we coded the answer as "don't know." If one answer was highly detailed and the other sketchy or contradictory, we coded the response in line with the detailed response. Virtually none of these cases with divergent responses involved the variables reported in the statistics here.

12. Polsby, *Political Innovation in America*, p. 6.

TABLE 5-1. Sources of Policy Initiation

Percent unless otherwise indicated

Issue or policy area	Neigh- bor- hood asso- ciation	Local govern- ment	Other govern- ment	Business	Citizen group	Multiple initi- ators	Don't know
				Initiators of policy proposals			
Crime	10.0	3.1	0.0	0.0	0.0	29.4	25.0
Neighborhood empowerment	10.0	9.4	0.0	0.0	13.3	0.0	0.0
Environment	20.0	3.1	45.5	0.0	6.7	17.6	25.0
City services	0.0	9.4	9.1	6.3	0.0	11.8	0.0
Economic development	20.0	31.3	9.1	81.3	13.3	11.8	50.0
Public works	0.0	9.4	9.1	6.3	6.7	5.9	0.0
Health, poverty	0.0	15.6	27.3	6.3	26.7	17.6	0.0
Other[a]	40.0	18.8	0.0	0.0	33.3	5.9	0.0
N	10	32	11	16	15	17	4
N as percent of all issues initiated	9.5	30.5	10.5	15.2	14.3	16.2	3.8

a. Includes public nuisances, declining living conditions, race relations, high taxes, youth issues, and education.

that succeeded in gaining enough attention to be placed on the city's agenda. This is characteristic of research on agenda setting. Studying "nonissues" is a bit like studying the voice of the dog that did not bark.[13]

Despite the use of follow-up questions to try to complete the respondents' issue narratives, many completed interviews were missing some information and had to be excluded from the statistical analysis. In the end, 105 cases met all the coding criteria. After the five cities were combined, the first step was to ask who was responsible for initiating new agenda items. Local government is the most prolific initiator (30.5 percent), but the general pattern is one of considerable dispersion (see table 5-1).

13. An effort was made to overcome this inherent problem in research on agenda setting by asking respondents to identify issues on the "back burner." The hope was to track the progress of problems that people were trying to get on the agenda. Too often, though, the issues mentioned had received enough attention to qualify as being on the agenda. They simply had not yet led to a new policy's being enacted. Asking people to identify problems that government has not recognized seems to require a level of thought and abstraction that makes it very difficult to elicit usable responses.

Despite the elaborate set of city-sponsored citizen participation structures in place, the neighborhood associations score relatively low as agenda setters, initiating approximately 10 percent of all issues. The vast majority of new issues in the five cities are generated by conventional sources. Citizen groups, whose overall potential is surely diminished by the activism and resources that are channeled through neighborhood associations, still manage to initiate more issues than the citizen participation structures. In Portland, a small group of environmentalists banded together and eventually got the city to pass a solar access ordinance. The policy prohibits construction of any new homes or buildings that cast an undue amount of shade onto single-family dwellings, thus protecting their access to the sun. In San Antonio, the Homeowners Taxpayers Association, led by C. A. Stubbs, made a particularly impressive effort to restrict the city's spending. It got a spending cap placed on the ballot and a heated campaign ensued. The group, which was not well funded, depended heavily on Stubbs's radio talk show appearances and other free exposure. Mayor Henry Cisneros led a concerted city hall effort against the proposal and the spending cap was voted down.

The Structure of Neighborhood Advocacy

This first analysis of the interviews suggests that the citizen participation structures of the five cities have not done much to empower the neighborhoods in the agenda-building process. There was certainly no expectation that local government or private interest groups would become feeble initiators in a system containing active and resourceful neighborhood associations. Still, why is it that the neighborhood associations seem to be relatively weak policy initiators? More broadly, does this test of who catalyzes attention on individual issues fairly gauge the impact of the neighborhood associations on the nature of these cities' agendas?

The variations in the way the city-sponsored programs are organized does not seem to make much difference in their impact on policy initiation. All of the city-sponsored systems were unimpressive in their agenda-setting capacity. That Dayton aggregates its neighborhoods into seven Priority Boards while Birmingham has nearly one hundred neighborhood associations seems to matter little. What does matter is that all the systems work to give the neighborhoods a great deal of autonomy. Also critically important is that the decentralization of the citizen participation structures is not balanced by mechanisms that work to coalesce the resources of all the neighborhoods into an effective single voice for "the people."

The Logic of Noncollective Action

A beginning point in analyzing how the neighborhood associations operate within the constraints and opportunities of city politics is to understand that they are just one element in a highly complex web of relationships. Cities are often the implementing agent for policies that are made at the state or federal level. Divided authority may give cities the right to initiate projects and programs but then subject them to layers of review by funding sources. Douglas Yates goes so far as to argue that "urban policy making takes place in a political and administrative system that is fragmented to the point of chaos."[14]

Nevertheless, it is autonomy that the neighborhood residents seem to value most. In Portland the neighborhood associations were so protective of their independence that they fought city hall for fourteen years to keep it from writing a set of guidelines that defined the rights and responsibilities of such organizations. In the focus groups with neighborhood association activists, only a modest amount of criticism was voiced about the lack of cooperation between neighborhood organizations. But when neighborhood leaders talked about their frustrations with city hall, they spoke of the need for more power and autonomy at the individual neighborhood level.[15] Increasing the fragmented nature of city politics by enhancing neighborhood autonomy is not seen as a problem. In none of the cities was there widespread interest in creating a strong organization to aggregate the political resources of the neighborhood associations.

One reason there is little interest in mobilizing the collective strength of the neighborhood associations is that they compete for resources.[16] Within a city, individual neighborhood associations watch what other neighborhood associations are getting. Some neighborhoods—usually low-income neighborhoods—qualify for certain kinds of funding and

14. Douglas Yates, *The Ungovernable City: The Politics of Urban Problems and Policy Making* (MIT Press, 1977), p. 34.

15. One reason the neighborhood associations place such a premium on autonomy is that they are wary of their dependence on city government for the staff resources that are so vital to their success. That tie makes them ever more vigilant of protecting the autonomy they have. See Marilyn Gittell, *Limits to Citizen Participation: The Decline of Community Organizations* (Beverly Hills: Sage, 1980), pp. 241–51.

16. John Clayton Thomas, *Between Citizen and City: Neighborhood Organizations and Urban Politics in Cincinnati* (University Press of Kansas, 1986), pp. 122–41.

those that fall within or near the eligibility guidelines are vigilant in monitoring funding awards. This problem is most evident in Birmingham, where one neighborhood, Five Points South, became both a symbol of neighborhood revival and an object of intense jealousy. A poor but not dirt-poor neighborhood, it qualified as a Neighborhood Strategy Area and was thus eligible for a large allocation of community development block grant (CDBG) money. It eventually received substantial support, and forceful leadership by the Five Points South neighborhood association was instrumental in effectively targeting these funds. Other Birmingham neighborhood associations saw political ties rather than real need as the reason behind Five Points South's success in obtaining government support. The problem with Five Points South's large funding package, said one administrator, is that "now everybody wants one." Much of the battle for resources was settled in Birmingham through an allocation formula that remained essentially constant for most of the history of the neighborhood system. This formula, based on population and income of each of the city's neighborhoods, gives to each neighborhood for development projects it selects a share of CDBG and other funds that come into the city. In the heyday of CDBG, some neighborhoods of several hundred or a few thousand people were able to directly determine the allocation of up to $100,000 in development funds each year.

Without stronger mechanisms for collective advocacy, the neighborhood associations will likely remain comparatively weak initiators of new programs and policies. Neighborhood associations are consumed with handling their current tasks; as voluntary organizations with access to only a small staff of city-paid community organizers, they do not have slack resources. They do well in reviewing zoning requests and development proposals, responding to policy proposals sent out by city hall for their consideration, and articulating the complaints of residents about the problems that concern them. Developing detailed policy or development proposals is quite another thing. The neighborhood associations are at a considerable disadvantage in comparison with administrative agencies or private businesses. When neighborhood associations play a primary role in policy initiation, it is likely to come through the articulation of grievances that are subsequently shaped into policy proposals by city agencies. This happened in Dayton when some neighborhood associations became upset because the city was tearing down abandoned houses in their area without first consulting them about alternative uses for the houses. They asked their Priority Board to see what it could do. The city subsequently agreed to provide neighborhoods with a list of houses it would like to demolish and promised that it would not tear any down without the neighborhood association's permission. This is certainly a valid form of agenda building, but it is a limited one.

Gradualism, Anticipation, and Planning

The argument so far has dwelt on the role of the neighborhood associations in putting new items onto the political agenda. Before proceeding in the analysis, however, we must ask a rather basic question: what qualifies as a *new* item? This is not a simple matter. Since policymaking is typically an incremental process, policy changes are usually gradual extensions or modifications of previous policies. When new concerns arise, the inclination of government is not to start from scratch but to try to adapt whatever relevant efforts it is making to the problem at hand.[17] Some issues are so dramatically new, though, that they stretch the concept of incrementalism beyond all utility. When the federal government committed itself to a national space program, antecedents of such an effort were slim. The project clearly constituted a new undertaking; it was not simply an extension on a bigger scale of what the government was doing already.[18]

Research on agenda setting has focused on those issues that tend toward the nonincremental. Consequently, the emphasis has been on identifying sharp breaks with past practice that stand out because of events, crises, and dramatic changes in the political climate.[19] Yet a seemingly "new" issue can arrive on the agenda as part of an evolutionary progression that began with other related problems. Often a recombination of earlier debates and alternatives brings forth an issue that had not been actively discussed before. The issue of an arms embargo against South Africa emerged after an extended "softening" period during which other proposals aimed at the apartheid regime received attention.[20]

17. Charles E. Lindblom, "The Science of Muddling Through," *Public Administration Review*, vol. 19 (Spring 1959), pp. 79–88.

18. Paul Schulman writes, "Nonincremental, indivisible policy pursuits are beset by organizational thresholds or 'critical mass' points closely associated with their initiation and subsequent development." "Nonincremental Policy Making: Notes Toward an Alternative Paradigm," *American Political Science Review*, vol. 69 (December 1975), pp. 1355.

19. Polsby, *Political Innovation in America*, p. 10.

20. Robert F. Durant and Paul F. Diehl, "Agendas, Alternatives, and Public Policy: Lessons from the Foreign Policy Arena," paper prepared for the 1989 annual meeting of the Western Political Science Association.

Agenda building in city politics should be considered in this broader light. If the notion of agenda building is expanded to include issues that may have emerged more gradually, is the record of the neighborhood associations any better? This leads to a second question: are the neighborhood associations effective at keeping things off the agenda? Is this kind of power, which pluralist critics claim is possessed by business, more broadly held within the community? Finally, the planning process that so absorbs local administrative agencies should be examined. In many areas of city policymaking, planning and zoning decisions create agenda "boundaries" and lead both policy entrepreneurs and business developers toward some types of projects and away from others. Within this context, does the citizen participation process place significant constraints on what can be initiated by others?

Unfortunately, no direct data-collecting effort was aimed at comparing new issues that were clear breaks with the past with those that emerged in a more gradual evolution. Interview respondents were not asked to distinguish between the two, and thus the figures already cited also contain cases that fit this second category. Consequently, the series of questions asked in the elite survey may not have fully tapped the impact of the neighborhood associations on the gradual, evolutionary emergence of new issues.

What we can look at, though, is the institutionalized role that the neighborhood associations play in transmitting the demands, preferences, and complaints of their constituents to various administrative agencies. In St. Paul, the Capital Improvement Budget Committee allocates its funds strictly on the basis of formal requests made by the District Councils. Shifts in the pattern of requests can create new policies even though the neighborhoods have made no collective demand on city hall. For example, capital funding requests by individual neighborhoods to build a community center soon produced community centers throughout the city. Support for the maintenance of the centers has become a recurring part of the city budget, and efforts to scale back city support of them have been bitterly resisted by the neighborhoods. Both Dayton and Portland have neighborhood needs programs that rely on the neighborhood associations to channel complaints from citizens to a central office that, in turn, sends them on to the relevant administrative agency. Each individual complaint or request is recorded in a computer system and responses to them are tracked. The responses from the agency—which may be, for example, that they will be able to carry out that project on a certain date, that they will consider the issue and work with the requesting neighborhood on the possibility of the project, or that resources do not allow work on that project this year—are not only sent to the requesting neighborhood but also compiled in a document available to any interested citizen. Since the mayor and other leading officials in each city study the patterns of the complaints and responses, the neighborhood needs programs cannot help but "soften up" the policymaking process for new initiatives to address problems that are not being satisfactorily dealt with.

If neighborhood associations are capable of gradually pushing the city in new directions, are they also capable of pushing the city *away* from other potential initiatives? Neighborhood associations are not necessary to create a power of anticipated reactions for a city's neighborhoods.[21] In all cities government officials and businessmen anticipate what will fly and what will not. The question is whether neighborhood associations significantly enhance the power of anticipated reactions for their residents. Neighborhood associations play such an instrumental role in the approval of any public project or private development within their boundaries that there is little doubt that they increase this kind of power. Would-be policy initiators know that residents do not have to overcome inertia to organize to stop something they disapprove of. Each community is already organized and has the power to seriously wound, if not kill, what it does not like.

The anticipation of what will pass muster at the neighborhood level is augmented by agency rules and norms designed to keep administrators from trying to escape or minimize neighborhood review. Agencies do this not simply because of a philosophical commitment to citizen participation, but because they want to avoid unnecessary delay.[22] The Port Authority of St. Paul, which has the job of putting together packages of land and financial incentives to promote business development, surely prefers not to have to deal with the neighborhoods, which only ask for things that make the Port Authority's land use deals more problematic. Since avoiding neighborhood clearance is not possible in St. Paul, the Port Authority relies on its early notification system to alert neighborhood associations to proposals that are in the works. Knowing that it will have to take developers before a District Council and then will have

21. For an overview of this notion, see Jack H. Nagel, *The Descriptive Analysis of Power* (Yale University Press, 1975), pp. 16–19.
22. In chapter 8 we analyze the relationship between neighborhood association activity and delay in the policymaking process.

to ask for its formal approval makes the Port Authority highly sensitive to neighborhood opinion. If they do not get the District Council's approval, continuing the proposed project would be senseless. Said one Port Authority official, "We've never gone ahead with a project that's been initially disapproved by a District Council."

The influence of the neighborhood associations over the agenda-building process is also magnified by the planning processes within the cities. The neighborhood associations become the vehicle for ensuring that citizens have a say in setting priorities for the city and for its neighborhoods. In Portland, for example, neighborhood plans commissioned by the city are done by the neighborhood associations. Most of them have land use committees and some even have a land use specialist on their staff. These neighborhood plans specify what kind of development is acceptable in each area of the community. The fifteen citywide committees working on the Central City Plan drew the names of many of its community participants from lists provided by the neighborhood associations. Each administrative agency has a Budget Advisory Committee (BAC) that draws much of its membership from names sent downtown by the neighborhood associations. The BACs tackle a wide range of issues from the geographic distribution of expenditures in a development agency to the need for a new computer system in a personnel office. In many cases, citizens on these committees respond to specific questions and issues raised by agency personnel, but in other cases the citizens themselves are raising previously unrecognized concerns and developing initiatives for change that would otherwise never have been raised. The Office of Neighborhood Associations provides ongoing training and support to ensure that citizens can tackle these demanding jobs. The BACs are not focused on the neighborhoods, but they provide an unusual opportunity for citizens to become directly involved in the nitty-gritty of city policymaking. Whenever the city of Portland does any planning, it is *participatory* planning. The neighborhood associations are always involved, and in neighborhood-level zoning decisions they are dominant. All development proposals are made within a set of constraints established by plans in which neighborhood associations have participated.

Although the neighborhood associations are infrequently direct initiators of new agenda items, they play an important secondary role in creating a policymaking environment that will be hospitable to some kinds of proposals and unkind to others. They incrementally alter agendas, force initiators to anticipate their preferences, and play a vital role in the planning process at both the neighborhood and citywide levels.

More than anything else, the neighborhood associations give an institutionalized voice to residents at the early stages of the policymaking process when ideas are being formulated into proposals.

Garbage Cans in City Politics

The analysis so far has treated agenda setting as a systematic process subject to the normal struggle for influence among competing factions. Political scientist John Kingdon argues, however, that agenda building is not a predictable, systematic process. Drawing on research by Michael D. Cohen, James G. March, and Johan P. Olsen, Kingdon likens the agenda-building process to their "garbage can" model of organizational decisionmaking. Cohen, March, and Olsen portray bureaucracies as "organized anarchies" with uncertain preferences, changing participation in decisionmaking and a trial-and-error approach to problem solving.[23] In their view an organization "is a collection of choices looking for problems, issues and feelings looking for decision situations in which they might be aired, solutions looking for issues to which they might be the answer, and decision makers looking for work."[24]

Kingdon found that in Washington "advocates develop their proposals and then wait for problems to come along to which they can attach their solutions."[25] These solutions thus sit on the shelf unless a confluence of favorable factors gives them new relevance. This happens when "the separate streams come together at critical times. A problem is recognized, a solution is available, the political climate makes the time right for change, and the constraints do not prohibit action."[26] When all this happens, a "policy window" is said to open.

To find out if city politics fits the garbage can model of agenda building, we paid particular attention in the interviews to the accounts of the circumstances surrounding the entrance of a new issue onto the agenda. Follow-up questions were used liberally to pin down where the idea for the program described came from. After reviewing all the information elicited from the issue narrative, we coded each case as to whether the new solution had been taken off the shelf. Was the initiative pre-

---

23. Michael D. Cohen, James G. March, and Johan P. Olsen, "A Garbage Can Model of Organizational Choice," *Administrative Science Quarterly*, vol. 17 (March 1972), p. 1.
24. Cohen, March, and Olsen, "A Garbage Can Model," p. 2.
25. Kingdon, *Agendas, Alternatives, and Public Policies*, pp. 93–94.
26. Kingdon, *Agendas, Alternatives, and Public Policies*, p. 93.

TABLE 5-2. Sources of Policy Solutions

Source	Percent of all policy initiations
Existing solution adapted to new problem	6.7
Solution developed in immediate context of problem	75.2
Don't know, could not determine	18.1
Total	100.0

viously prepared in some other context and then attached to the subsequent problem? Although a determination could not always be made, the overwhelming majority of cases did not fit the garbage can model (see table 5-2). In 75 percent of the cases the solution evolved out of the immediate problem at hand. Only about 7 percent of the time was the new proposal a reincarnation of a solution identified in a earlier and different context. One of these few garbage can cases was in Dayton, where the Chamber of Commerce and other business interests had tried unsuccessfully to get the need for downtown office space on the city's agenda. When a proposal for a new performing arts center emerged, some of the same people were able to gain attention for the office space problem by floating a proposal that would include a new office building within the same complex. They used the open window to their advantage, although the arts complex proposal was killed and the new office building was a casualty of the battle.

Much more common was the case of a window opening without being coupled to a particular solution. In Dayton, for example, allegations of police corruption opened up a policy window. This handed an opportunity to the city manager, but he demurred, and merely formed a committee to look into what might be done. There was no police reform package on the shelf—or at least none that he chose to try to link to the other developments that came together then. Consequently, the emergent problem was not defined by a solution that had found its opportunity. Because of the broad representation on the committee, including members of some Priority Boards, there was no suspicion that the committee was formed only for the purpose of legitimizing a solution already arrived at. Perhaps the city manager's office did not want to cross swords with the police department and chose not to take advantage of the open policy window. Whatever the motives in the particular case, this type of response was observed over and over again. Open windows resulted in committees that conducted real searches for solutions rather than being coupled with a solution already on the shelf.

Why is it that the garbage can model works so poorly in explaining agenda building in city politics? There are, of course, substantial differences in the methodology of this and the Kingdon study. Yet our findings are so completely opposite to Kingdon's that it would be difficult to explain away the divergent conclusions as strictly a function of methodological approach. Rather, the explanation seems to be rooted in the fundamental differences between national politics and local politics.

First, there are vast disparities in the scale and complexity of the institutional actors. In the health field, for example, Kingdon's sample of issues included national health insurance, medicaid, medicare, and hospital cost containment.[27] New initiatives in these areas have enormous impact on many well-organized sectors of society. Interest groups effectively represent almost all sides in each of these issues. The White House is involved, along with massive federal bureaucracies. Members of Congress are by nature cautious and will want to make sure that a new law is not going to hurt them back home. Moving the federal government off the dime is no easy job. In short, Kingdon's argument that all the factors have to come together at the right time and under the right circumstances for a new initiative to get on the agenda is logically compelling. In contrast, at the local level there are bureaucracies of modest size, a small interest group universe, and city councils that are generally weak players in the policymaking system. Would-be policy initiators face a much smaller inertia problem.

Second, the resources available at the national level allow policy entrepreneurs to float interesting but politically problematic proposals merely with the hope of attracting some attention. Constraints at the local level make this difficult. The larger Washington lobbies have research staffs that can develop highly specific proposals and take them to sympathetic legislators. Members of Congress have substantial staffs, and senior members have access to additional staff on their committees. A member will be well served by highly entrepreneurial staffers who search for emerging policy problems with which their boss can become identified.[28] It is entirely rational behavior for a legislator to commission a study by a specialized support staff such as the Government Accounting Office, have his staff use that report as the basis for drafting legislation, and then introduce that legislation with the full knowledge that the

27. Kingdon, *Agendas, Alternatives, and Public Policies*, p. 230.
28. David E. Price, *Who Makes the Laws? Creativity and Power in Senate Committees* (Cambridge, Mass.: Schenkman, 1972).

proposal is not likely to go anywhere for years. In congressional politics, a prolonged softening-up period is considered a normal part of the legislative process for new and controversial proposals. Because the president's time frame is more limited, the administration places more emphasis on solving immediate problems than in getting the ball rolling for something that may happen in the future. Whatever priorities the president chooses, however, he and his White House staff have the entire federal bureaucracy at their disposal to help them formulate detailed new policy proposals.

A local government is like a third-world country in comparison to the federal government in terms of resoures available. City councils do not have a significant staff apparatus to back them up. City councillors have the incentive to float ideas to gain the gratitude of their constituencies or to get their names in the paper, but what they offer as a proposal is not likely to be well researched or highly detailed. The small bureaucracies of local governments do not have enough staffers to devote people to developing policy proposals that are not immediately necessary. Many lobbies active in city politics depend largely on volunteers. Those with paid staff are likely to have only one or two professionals who do not have the luxury of working on back burner issues. In sum, urban political systems do not have the extra resources to use to develop proposals that are not going to be actively considered right away.

Third, the incentive structures for local and federal politicians are different. Presidents and members of Congress must be preoccupied with the formulation of new policies and programs. Their reelection campaigns are built on proposals they have made and enactments they have supported. Administrative management of the federal government is not likely to be a significant issue. But on the local level, delivery of services may be the central concern come election time. For top city officials, making sure the garbage workers do not go out on strike and the snow is removed promptly may be more important than coming up with new proposals on health or welfare.[29]

Fourth, in local politics the policy window for economic development is always open. Some scholars have argued that the principal purpose of local government is to further the economic prosperity of the city.[30] To accomplish this, top policymakers must be concerned about attracting

29. Yates, *The Ungovernable City*, pp. 17–41.

30. Paul E. Peterson, *City Limits* (University of Chicago Press, 1981); and Stephen L. Elkin, *City and Regime in the American Republic* (University of Chicago Press, 1987.)

new development projects and new industries, while making sure that existing businesses are kept happy and willing to remain within the boundaries of the city. Any developer or businessman with a credible and significant proposal can gain immediate attention from local government. When developers proposed a new racetrack in Birmingham, it was instantaneously on the city agenda. No softening-up period was necessary. Economic development projects go to the head of the line— they do not have to fight for space on the agenda. Despite the fact that national administrations are always deeply concerned about the state of the economy, the situation is not really analogous. Not every serious proposal for nurturing the nation's prosperity is going to reach the agenda.

Agendas, Responsiveness, and Public Opinion

The elite interviews provide a fairly clear picture of the policy initiation process in these five cities, but by themselves they do not help us understand the responsiveness of the local policy agenda to the needs and desires of the general citizenry. By combining the results of these elite interviews with the surveys of the general populations, we can begin building a systematic picture of the extent to which public officials in these five cities seem to be in tune with their citizens. The reflection of the public agenda in the attitudes of public officials provides some insight into how "responsive" the public agenda is to the people of the respective cities.

Almost all recent attempts to examine democratic policymaking seem to agree that there must be a linkage between the attitudes of citizens and the policies pursued by government before the policies can be said to be responsive.[31] In general, the theory of policy responsiveness involves more than the simple correspondence between people's demands and public policy outcomes. Some of the earlier scholarship on public policy responsiveness, discussed in chapter 6, simply compared measures of population need with expenditures on categories of spending that roughly met that need. More recent analyses of responsiveness issues have tried to refine the concept and measurement by taking into consideration some of the many mitigating factors that earlier analyses omitted.

---

31. Sidney Verba and Norman H. Nie, *Participation in America: Political Democracy and Social Inequality* (Harper and Row, 1972), pp. 299–302.

One way the idea of policy responsiveness has been refined is by including attitudinal components. These components reveal what citizens say they want and what public officials say they are doing, something the earlier analyses could only assume.[32] These attitudinal components suggest that for public policy to be responsive, public officials must first concur with citizens on what the important issues are and how the government should respond. In other words, for government to be responsive to citizens, citizens must form opinions about what problems ought to be addressed by government, these opinions must be communicated to public officials, public officials must hear these messages, and officials must adopt these opinions as their own.[33] Only when this set of linkages has been established can public officials then make decisions that conform to what the people really want or need.

Sidney Verba and Norman Nie and Susan Hansen were the first to examine the empirical correspondence between citizens' and officials' problem and issue perceptions within the context of policy responsiveness.[34] They did this within the framework of "attitudinal concurrence." These analyses of attitudinal concurrence were based on surveys of 1,438 citizens and 306 public officials spread across some sixty-four randomly selected communities with populations of 60,000 or more. In each of the communities a random selection of citizens was asked, "What is the most important problem facing this community?" The community officials were asked, "What does the average person around here think are their problems and needs?" and "Are there some community problems that you have been particularly active in trying to solve?" The answers to these open-ended questions were coded and used to compute a concurrence score for each of the sixty-four communities.

The open-ended questions produced a list of about twenty-five major problems. For each problem mentioned, the number of citizens who

32. For some, as will be discussed in chapter 6, only the citizen side of this is important. To these people, what public officials say they are doing is of much less consequence than what they actually do in terms of decisionmaking. See Paul Schumaker, *Critical Pluralism, Democratic Performance, and Community Power* (University Press of Kansas, 1991), especially chap. 12.

33. See Robert A. Dahl, *A Preface to Democratic Theory* (University of Chicago Press, 1956); and Dahl, *Who Governs? Democracy and Power in an American City* (Yale University Press, 1961).

34. Verba and Nie, *Participation in America*; and Susan B. Hansen, "Participation, Political Structure, and Concurrence," *Americal Political Science Review*, vol. 69 (December 1975), pp. 1181–99.

mentioned the problem was multiplied by 1 if any leader mentioned the same problem, and 0 if no leader mentioned it. Then these products were summed across all mentioned problems. This sum was then divided by the number of citizens interviewed in the community. This yielded for each community a single concurrence score representing the level of agreement between citizens and leaders on the important problems in that community. Although these analysts never addressed this connection, the effort is clearly intended to indicate the correspondence between citizens' statements of what their local governments ought to be doing and what is actually on the agenda of public officials.

Hansen argued that the structure of politics in the local community (by which she means voting, electoral competition, political party activity, the level of citizen participation in local organizations, and the form of selection of local leaders) has a major influence on concurrence. The results of her analysis suggest that more participatory communities tend to exhibit greater levels of concurrence, although the political structure of the community also seems to be related to concurrence, albeit less strongly. Political participation, then, is associated with a tendency for the problems identified by the general citizenry to be firmly entrenched in the agendas of local officials. Hansen notes that the patterns suggest a dynamic in which the level of participation produces leaders who are more attuned to the needs of citizens and whose attitudes are influenced by the shape of citizens' attitudes. Despite this pattern, Hansen stopped short of inferring a causal connection with concurrence because of the possibility that concurrence was due to manipulation of public opinion by elites. Yet this is by far the best evidence to date on the relationship between political participation and attitudinal concurrence.

The procedures used to estimate the level of leader-citizen concurrence in these earlier studies may have been appropriate given the task at hand, but because of the very small numbers of citizens and officials interviewed in any one city, the results are not likely to reflect very accurately the actual extent of concurrence. In this study we interviewed a large number of citizens and officials, providing much more reliable assessments of what is and what people think ought to be on the public agenda.

Estimating Attitudinal Concurrence

The main concern here is with the overall level of concurrence between citizens and public officials as an indicator of the extent to which citizens' issues make it onto the public agenda. If community participation structures constitute superior vehicles for the translation of the public mood to policymakers, then the cities with stronger participation structures and more community participation (St. Paul and Portland) should exhibit higher levels of concurrence than Dayton, Birmingham, and San Antonio.

But the level of concurrence is certainly not the only concern of this study. Such a broad picture does not account for various biases that may influence the way the agenda is set. For example, participation programs could conceivably bias the political system in favor of the few people who take the time and make the effort to participate. Presumably, such a biased system would be created if participants are disproportionately able to get their issues on the public agenda and if these issues are different from what nonparticipants would like to see on the agenda. Are the people who frequently participate in the five cities better able than nonparticipants to get the public agenda to reflect their views? Or are the issues that are important to public officials usually the same as the issues that are important to the broad range of citizens?

On the other side of the coin, biases may exist with respect to minority residents of the city. To what extent are racial or ethnic minorities' issues captured by the public agenda? If the systems of neighborhood associations are able to provide egalitarian access to public officials, then the public agenda should not disfavor racial or ethnic minorities. At the same time, if such systems are able to avoid the pitfalls of earlier participation efforts, then the public agenda should not be seriously skewed in favor of minorities to the expense of nonminorities.

Estimating attitudinal concurrence in a city is no simple task. If one were to ask, as we did, a relatively large number of citizens and nearly all major public officials what are the most important problems the city needs to address, it is not at all clear what kind of a match between citizens and officials would reflect the highest level of concurrence. If 40 percent of the citizens in a given city said that crime was the most serious problem, what percentage of public officials would have to give the same answer to indicate a high level of concurrence on this particular issue? What overall pattern of match between citizens and leaders across all issues in the city would reflect the highest level of concurrence? Answers to these questions are not straightforward; they become even more complicated when one must assess multiple answers from each respondent.

So as to not artificially constrain citizens or public officials in their articulation of problems, we recorded multiple responses. Each person could identify more than one important problem. Consequently, the responses of citizens and officials can be compared in a number of different ways, including comparing the percentage of citizens who mentioned a specific problem with the percentage of officials, the percentage of responses given by citizens to the percentage of responses given by officials, or some mixture of these two. The difficulty can be summarized this way. If 40 percent of the citizens said that crime was the most important problem, and 40 percent of *officials* also pointed to crime, would this be reflective of more concurrence than if 40 percent of the *answers* given by officials related to crime? Again, the answer is not clear.

Perhaps the main reason it is difficult to specify what constitutes a high level of concurrence is that concurrence is a multidimensional concept, and no single index or measure is likely to tap all of its dimensions. At a minimum, it is clear that concurrence can be assessed in a number of very different ways. Consequently, we decided not to rely on any single measure but to examine concurrence through several different indicators. These include:

—An assessment of the level of agreement between citizens and public officials, between citizens and subgroups of citizens, and between subgroups of citizens and public officials, on *citywide* issues or problems the general citizenry mentioned most frequently. This is accomplished by computing "concurrence scores," as explained below.

—An evaluation of the *priority* given to the citywide issues based on their ranking in terms of the frequency of mention by citizens, subgroups of citizens, and public officials. This is done by computing a Spearman's rank-order correlation coefficient (rho) for each city.

—An assessment of agreement between citizens, subgroups of citizens, and officials with respect to whether each of some fourteen problems are identified by citizens as being important issues or problems *in their respective neighborhoods*. This is accomplished by computing concurrence scores.

Assessments of concurrence between citizens and officials with respect to citywide problems are based on answers to open-ended questions. Citizens were asked, "What would you say is the most important single problem in the city at this time?" Most respondents provided two answers to this question, so both were coded. Public officials were asked with respect to citywide issues, "What would you say are the three or four most important problems in the city at this time?" Up to five responses were actually coded for public officials. The raw answers to these questions were coded separately for each city. Subsequently, they were evaluated and, after a series of steps, collapsed into some twenty response categories standardized across cities. General public and elite responses were then recoded using the same coding scheme.

These citywide problems were then used to compute an initial set of concurrence scores, one for each city. The ten issues most frequently mentioned by citizens were listed along with their respective percentages. Then the corresponding percentages of officials or subgroups of citizens, referred to as the comparison group, were listed for each of the citizens' issues.[35] If the citizens' percentage exceeded that of the comparison group, the comparison group could be said to underreflect citizen views. Thus the citizens' percentage was subtracted from the comparison group's percentage, yielding a negative number. If the citizens' percentage was less than that of the comparison group, then the comparison group could be said to adequately reflect the views of the citizens. Public officials, therefore, are not "penalized" directly for overstating a problem that is important to citizens. The negative values were then summed across all issues, and this sum was standardized by taking it as a percentage of the total percentage of citizens identifying these issues. The concurrence score was then computed as 100 plus the standardized value multiplied by 100. If public officials always responded at least at the level of citizens, the resulting concurrence score would be 100. If no public officials said that citizens' issues are important, the resulting score would be zero.

An example taken from the top three problems in Birmingham illustrates this calculation. The three top issues for citizens in Birmingham, in terms of frequency of mention, were crime (24.6 percent), poor economy or loss of jobs, unemployment, and so forth (19.4 percent), and poor city administration (13.3 percent). Comparing these percentages with those from city councillors revealed that no councillors mentioned crime, 70 percent mentioned the state of the economy, and 10 percent mentioned poor city administration. The computation is: $(0 - 24.6) + (10 - 13.3) = -27.9 \div 57.3$ (the total percentage of citizens responding to the three problems). This yields a standardized value of -0.487. The concurrence score is then computed as $100 + (-0.487 \times 100)$, or 51.3. By computing these scores for each city, we can try to assess which cities' public agendas seem to correspond more to general public opinion.

35. When the comparison is between all citizens and a subgroup of citizens, this comparison consists of percentages based on responses. When the comparison is between citizens or subgroups of citizens and public officials, public officials' percentages are based on respondents.

This concurrence score does not measure how well the overall priorities of public officials match those of citizens. Specifically, it does not reveal whether the officials seem to give the same priority ordering to the problems of the city as do citizens. To capture the priority rankings, all twenty citizen problems (as well as the top ten issues taken separately) were rank-ordered for citizens and officials, and then Spearman's rho was calculated.[36] The higher the rho value, the closer are the two groups' lists of issue priorities. When calculated for each city, rho values provide another assessment of how well the ranking of priorities on the public agenda seems to correspond with that of the public and allow comparisons among cities.

The third indicator of concurrence is based on neighborhood rather than citywide problems or issues. To what extent do the neighborhood problems that people identify appear among the issues thought to be important by officials? Do public officials incorporate the problems of specific neighborhoods into the public agenda? To begin answering these questions, we asked citizens whether some fourteen different issues or problems constituted problems in their neighborhoods. Public officials were asked whether any of those issues was a problem anywhere in the city, and if so, where. Public officials' responses were coded to reflect whether each specific issue was considered a citywide problem, a problem in some but not all neighborhoods, or a problem in no neighborhoods.

The answers to these questions are used in two ways. First, concurrence scores were computed based on the difference between the percentage of the general public identifying a neighborhood problem and the percentage of public officials acknowledging the same problem. If an issue was reported as a neighborhood problem for over half of the general public, the percentage used in the calculation for public officials was the percentage saying the problem was a "citywide problem." If an issue was reported as a problem for between 25 and 50 percent of the general population, the percentage of public officials saying the issue was a problem for "some or many, but not all" neighborhoods was used. And if less than 25 percent of the population said that an issue was a problem

36. In order to assign rankings to the responses, we used a technique in which all issues within about 10 percentage points were given the same ranking. This was done because using the "raw" rankings based on actual percentages produced an extremely large number of "tied rankings" for public officials due to the relatively small number of respondents. Having a larger number of tied rankings for one group of respondents but not for the other made interpretation of the rank-order correlations difficult.

in their neighborhoods, the percentage of officials saying that the issue was "not a problem" was used.

As was the case with the earlier concurrence score, only the negative values, where officials underreflect the public's views, were considered. Then the negative values were averaged across all fourteen issues (the value for each city is reported separately), and this value was standardized to the average percentage that the general public identified all fourteen issues as problems. The neighborhood issue concurrence score was then computed as 100 minus the standardized negative percentage. The resulting score potentially ranges from between 100 (a situation in which public officials never underreflect the views of the general public) to zero, (public officials never agreed with the views of citizens). Thus numbers closer to 100 represent greater concurrence of public officials with citizens across all fourteen issues, and numbers closer to zero represent less concurrence.

Concurrence on Citywide Issues

If the nature of community participation plays a major role in communicating citizens' concerns and priorities to public officials, we would expect Portland and St. Paul to stand out among the five cities. Overall, however, there is no clear-cut pattern suggesting that public officials in Portland and St. Paul are more in tune with the general public than officials in San Antonio, Dayton, or Birmingham. The concurrence scores based on citywide issues, found in table 5-3, reveal that city administrators in Birmingham and San Antonio tend to better reflect the issues of citizens, with Portland and St. Paul somewhat behind. However, city councillors in St. Paul and Portland are apparently more in tune with the general citizenry. These results suggest that higher levels of community participation do not appear to make city administrators more likely to place citizens' issues on their agendas but do seem to affect city councillors' issue agendas. Councillors in the cities with higher community participation are much more attuned to citizens' concerns than councillors in the other cities.

The relatively high position of Portland is borne out by the rank-order correlations (capturing priority rankings), also found in table 5-3, although St. Paul does not fare as well. Overall, administrators' priorities with respect to all twenty issues are most similar to citizens' priorities in Birmingham, San Antonio, and Portland and less so in Dayton and St.

TABLE 5-3. Concurrence Scores and Rank-Order Correlations for Citywide Issues

Cities	Top ten citywide issues			All citywide issues		
	Admini-strators	Councillors	Both	Admini-strators	Councillors	Both
	Concurrence scores					
San Antonio	81.2	71.4	83.9	78.1	67.4	80.7
Dayton	64.3	43.4	65.0	56.3	37.9	56.9
Birmingham	95.7	53.1	92.5	87.5	57.8	84.6
St. Paul	63.5	78.3	78.7	61.1	71.0	75.0
Portland	67.5	77.6	76.6	63.1	72.5	74.5
	Rank-order correlations					
San Antonio	0.455	0.727	0.454	0.765	0.709	0.753
Dayton	0.252	0.144	0.200	0.359	0.485	0.341
Birmingham	0.615	−0.160	0.630	0.790	0.556	0.786
St. Paul	0.058	−0.161	−0.109	0.279	0.557	0.441
Portland	0.615	0.576	0.576	0.620	0.540	0.608

Paul. Councillors' priorities on all issues most closely match those of the general public in San Antonio. Citizens' and councillors' priorities match about equally in St. Paul, Birmingham, and Portland. The main reason for the difference between the results from the concurrence scores and the rank-order correlations is that the concurrence scores take into account only issues that officials consider to be less important than citizens. In terms of priority rankings of issues, however, Portland and St. Paul do not stand out among the five cities as having greater agreement between public officials and the general citizenry. Although concurrence between citizens and city councillors increases as the level of community participation increases, the lack of a consistent pattern for administrators suggests that something other than the operation of systems of community participation may influence the agenda on citywide issues. In other words, cities with more community participation have citizens who are more successful at getting their concerns across to administrators, and this success is not improved by the existence of systems of neighborhood associations.

Concurrence on Neighborhood Issues

Perhaps the more important question, given the neighborhood basis for the structure of community participation, is how Portland and St.

TABLE 5-4. Concurrence Scores for Fourteen Neighborhood Issues

City	Concurrence scores		Average negative differences	
	Administrators	Councillors	Administrators	Councillors
San Antonio	91.1	86.5	-3.4	-5.2
Dayton	56.3	57.9	-17.3	-16.7
Birmingham	62.2	57.7	-15.6	-17.4
St. Paul	70.5	67.7	-9.4	-10.3
Portland	91.5	71.7	-2.7	-9.2

Paul compare with the other cities in concurrence on neighborhood is-sues. Here there is a clear and consistent pattern. The concurrence scores based on fourteen neighborhood issues, shown in table 5-4, reveal that, ignoring San Antonio for the moment, there is a monotonic increase moving from Dayton and Birmingham to St. Paul and Portland. This pattern is essentially the same for administrators and councillors.

The specific results comparing concurrence on citywide versus neigh-borhood issues for Birmingham may be important for another reason. As noted in chapter 3, it is the only city whose participation system is centrally managed from city hall. Although the relatively high scores for Birmingham on most of the measures of correspondence between citizens and administrators for citywide issues could in some way be attributed to the operation of what some have called Mayor Richard Arrington's "political machine," the high scores do not carry over to neighborhood issues. It seems plausible that the centrally managed participation system is much more attuned to citywide issues and as a trade-off is not partic-ularly effective at communicating neighborhood problems to city admin-istrators. Thus Birmingham's administrators might be expected to exhibit a higher level of concurrence than other cities on citywide issues and yet an unexceptional level of concurrence on neighborhood issues.

Nevertheless, with the exception of San Antonio, greater community participation seems to improve considerably the ability of people to communicate neighborhood problems and issues to public officials and to get these problems on the public agenda. But is the relatively high position of San Antonio due to the operation of community participation (largely through COPS), or is some alternative process at work? To answer this question, concurrence scores are computed just for the resi-dents of the COPS areas of San Antonio. These scores, shown in table 5-5, reveal that the neighborhood problems of COPS-area residents, whether they participate in the COPS organization or not, are much less likely to be among the issues mentioned by public officials than the

TABLE 5-5. Concurrence Scores for Areas of San Antonio

	Administrators			Councillors		
Area	All citizens	Frequent participants	Non-participants	All citizens	Frequent participants	Non-participants
Covered by COPS	57.9	34.5	49.0	57.2	52.7	52.4
Covered by other neighborhood organizations	87.2	85.6	91.5	79.1	79.9	82.8
With no neighborhood organizations	86.5	70.0	73.4	95.5	80.2	90.1

problems of residents of other areas of the city. In short, it would not appear that COPS produces the higher than expected concurrence scores for San Antonio. Indeed, these concurrence scores for non-COPS areas may well be a partial product of a backlash due to the perception that the highly visible COPS organizations are getting more than their share of attention from public officials.

Concurrence and Community Participants

To what extent do the systems of neighborhood associations disproportionately communicate the concerns of those who participate rather than the concerns of a broad spectrum of the population? To answer this question, concurrence scores and rank-order correlations were calculated between public officials and those who participate at the highest three levels of the index of community participation (ICP). If the systems are biased in favor of those who participate, two patterns should be observed. First, the cities with the most community participation (St. Paul and Portland) should have higher concurrence scores than the other cities; second, concurrence scores for community participants should be higher than the scores for the general population.

The results of this analysis, as reflected in table 5-6, suggest that neither of these patterns is borne out. On citywide issues, the concurrence scores for administrators and community participants are actually lower in St. Paul and Portland than elsewhere. City councillors, on the other hand, do seem to be more attuned to the issues of concern for community participants in St. Paul and Portland than elsewhere. When the community participants' scores are compared with those from the general public (tables 5-3 and 5-4), patterns of bias would be evident if there were more concurrence for participants than for the general public. On citywide issues, however, there is a remarkable degree of similarity. There is no evidence that community participants do any better than the population as a whole at getting their issues on the agenda of public officials.

On neighborhood issues, there is evidence of slight bias in favor of community participants in only one city. Although Portland exhibits the greatest concurrence for community participants with both administrators and councillors, these numbers are actually slightly lower than for the general population (table 5-4). Only in St. Paul are the concurrence scores for community participants higher than for their counterparts in the general population. In short, the systems of neighborhood associations do not appear to introduce agenda-setting biases in favor of participants on citywide issues, and only in St. Paul do they seem to provide a disproportionate ability for community participants to get their neighborhood concerns on the city's agenda.

Concurrence and African Americans

The results from San Antonio raise a related but more general question concerning the ability of the chronically disenfranchised to affect the public agenda. How well do the systems of neighborhood associations communicate to public officials the needs and opinions of people who are chronically left out of city policymaking? Answers to this question can take many forms, but here the focus is on the extent to which black residents of the five cities seem to be able to get the public agenda to respond to their demands.[37] Chapter 4 made clear that the cities with more structured community participation create neither disproportionate participatory barriers nor disproportionately favorable forums for African Americans. But how well do the public agendas of these cities seem to reflect the views of people of color? The more participatory cities were shown above to have public agendas more reflective of their populations' views on neighborhood but not necessarily on citywide issues. Do they also seem to have agendas that are more reflective of the expressed priorities of the black population?

37. Other ethnic or racial minorities may be of equal importance to the broader issue of responsiveness to people of color, but the public opinion surveys do not provide adequate samples to investigate these.

TABLE 5-6. Concurrence Scores and Rank-Order Correlations for Community Participants' Citywide and Neighborhood Issues

| | Top ten citywide issues | | | | Fourteen neighborhood issues | | | |
| | Concurrence scores | | Rank-order correlations | | Concurrence scores | | Average difference | |
City	Administrators	Councillors	Administrators	Councillors	Administrators	Councillors	Administrators	Councillors
San Antonio	83.4	74.8	0.503	0.703	78.4	73.0	−8.8	−11.0
Dayton	69.9	52.3	0.579	0.615	56.1	32.8	−19.0	−29.1
Birmingham	96.1	58.2	0.442	0.167	59.6	48.7	−17.4	−22.1
St. Paul	65.3	79.4	0.294	0.249	73.3	72.8	−9.4	−9.6
Portland	68.5	78.3	0.748	0.821	90.8	75.0	−3.0	−8.2

TABLE 5-7. Concurrence Scores and Rank-Order Correlations for African Americans' Citywide and Neighborhood Issues

| | Top ten citywide issues | | | | Fourteen neighborhood issues | | | |
| | Concurrence scores | | Rank-order correlations | | Concurrence scores | | Average difference | |
City	Administrators	Councillors	Administrators	Councillors	Administrators	Councillors	Administrators	Councillors
San Antonio	81.7	72.1	0.267	0.485	63.0	62.4	−16.6	−16.9
Dayton	66.6	47.1	0.421	0.082	55.3	47.4	−19.2	−22.6
Birmingham	95.9	55.2	0.812	0.542	49.4	42.4	−24.0	−27.4
St. Paul	62.1	77.5	0.152	0.644	79.0	89.8	−5.4	−2.6
Portland	69.8	79.2	0.297	0.333	49.8	47.1	−24.3	−25.5

To answer this question, concurrence scores and rank-order correlations were computed between the views expressed by each city's African-American population and its public officials. This was done for both the top ten citywide issues (based on the open-ended questions) and the neighborhood issues (based on the fourteen specific neighborhood issue questions).[38]

On the citywide issues, city councillors' issue agendas are generally more aligned with blacks' in the higher community participation cities, as reflected in table 5-7. This pattern is clear from the concurrence scores, where St. Paul and Portland councillors appear fairly closely attuned to the citywide issues of the African-American population. San Antonio is again a consistent exception, although city councillors in Birmingham also appear to rank their citywide issue priorities somewhat more like the black population than might be expected just on the basis of the level of community participation. When these results are compared with those for the entire population, as shown in table 5-3, there is remarkably little difference. Especially in terms of the concurrence scores, African Americans appear to have about the same ability to get their issues on the public agenda as the rest of the population.

City administrators show a very different pattern with respect to citywide issues. Birmingham administrators stand out as being extremely closely aligned with the black population on both the concurrence and rank-order correlation measures. This is undoubtedly due to the relatively large size of the black population in Birmingham. Indeed, at least with respect to the rank-order correlation, administrators tend to be more closely aligned with the black population as the size of this population increases. Although the size of minority population has been shown elsewhere to have little relationship to an ability to achieve electoral incorporation,[39] the size of the black population does seem to affect the extent to which the local public agenda is responsive, at least on citywide issues.

With respect to neighborhood issues, however, only one city, St. Paul, stands out in table 5-7 as being more reflective of the black population.[40]

38. The computation of these scores and correlations is identical to that described earlier.

39. Rufus Browning, Dale Rogers Marshall, and David Tabb, *Protest Is Not Enough: The Struggle of Blacks and Hispanics for Equality in Urban Politics* (University of California Press, 1984).

40. In terms of statistically significant differences, blacks and whites differ on two of the fourteen neighborhood issues, and on one of these (street maintenance), whites actually

Although St. Paul has the smallest black population among the five cities, its public officials are consistently more attuned to the issues that are important to that population. African Americans in Portland, the city with the highest level of community participation, are apparently not better able to get the public agenda to be responsive than their counterparts in cities with less community participation. Perhaps surprisingly, Birmingham's concurrence on neighborhood issues appears unexceptional. Neither administrators nor councilors appear to be especially well attuned to the neighborhood problems of the African-American population. When these results are compared with those for the entire population shown in table 5-4, the results are fairly consistent. The concurrence scores suggest that the public agenda is somewhat less responsive to blacks than to the population as a whole in San Antonio and Portland.

Just as was the case in the analysis of the entire population, the more centrally operated participation system in Birmingham seems better able to help African-American citizens influence the agenda of public administrators on citywide issues than on neighborhood issues. But African Americans' citywide issues are also more likely to be on the agenda than their neighborhood issues in Portland and San Antonio, cities that do not have centralized participation systems. The public agendas in the cities with more community participation do not particularly do a better job of reflecting what their black populations think is important, and they certainly do not do any worse.

Conclusion

This first step toward assessing the responsiveness of government in the five cities has produced a rather mixed picture of the effectiveness of the neighborhood associations. The decentralized structure of the citizen participation systems weakens the capacity of the neighborhood associations to initiate new issues onto the agenda. The neighborhood organizations are not coalesced into effective aggregate units that could speak on behalf of an alliance of communities. Neighborhood associations jealously guard their autonomy and have little inclination to share the resources necessary to create such cooperative organizations. Their resource bases are not insignificant, but they are already overwhelmed

---

are more likely to say it is a problem. The number of issues on which blacks and whites differ significantly in the other four cities ranges from seven in Dayton to ten in Birmingham.

with the tasks they have and it is difficult for them to take on such labor-intensive activities as developing new programs or designing proposed development projects.

At the same time, the neighborhood associations are highly influential in creating boundaries for their city's agenda. They incrementally affect priorities through the communication and project selection mechanisms set up by various city administrative agencies. The fact that they provide a way of dealing with the collective action problem—getting people to volunteer time to a political organization—means that developers know there will be a reaction to their proposals by an organization with many procedural and substantive weapons at its disposal. Finally, all city planning processes affecting land use are heavily influenced by the citizen participation structures. The very existence of the neighborhood associations gives people a vehicle to define their priorities as to what ought to be on the city's agenda.[41]

The results of the citizen surveys, when compared with those of the elite interviews, reinforce this picture. The neighborhood-based systems with higher levels of community participation do not do a particularly good job of getting citywide issues on the public agenda of city administrators, although they do a better job of influencing the agenda of city councillors. It is also clear that the people who participate in the neighborhood associations are not disproportionately able to set the public agenda. Yet the strongest pattern reveals that, with the exception of San Antonio, councillors and administrators tend to be more attuned to the general public's neighborhood issues in the cities with higher levels of community participation. At the same time, however, community participants themselves are not particularly better able than the general citizenry to get their neighborhood issues on the agenda in cities with higher levels of community participation. Thus the systems of neighborhood associations do appear to be effective mechanisms for citizens to communicate their neighborhood needs to public officials, and they do this without creating excessive biases favoring only those who choose to participate.

Cities with higher levels of community participation do not necessarily provide African Americans an enhanced ability to get issues on the

41. Even if people are not active in the neighborhood associations, the strong sense of neighborhood identification that these organizations foster will help them to define community problems. See Matthew A. Crenson, *Neighborhood Politics* (Harvard University Press, 1983), p. 124.

agenda. On citywide issues, city councillors show a slight tendency to be more in line with the black population as the level of community participation increases. For administrators, what seems to matter more than community participation is the relative size of the black population. On neighborhood issues, while one of the higher community participation cities (St. Paul) seems to have a public agenda (for administrators and councillors) that corresponds to that of the African-American population, the city with the highest level of community participation (Portland) does not.

San Antonio is a persistent exception to most of the patterns. Despite having relatively low community participation, the agendas of San Antonio's councillors and administrators are highly reflective of the views of the general citizenry. This responsiveness does not appear to be caused by policymakers' being particularly attuned to COPS participants or neighborhoods. And there is evidence that, with respect to neighborhood issues, this relatively high responsiveness occurs despite the fact that policymakers' agendas are not very reflective of the views of the African-American population.

All of this suggests that the operation of the systems of neighborhood associations, rather than competing with the existing systems of democratic electoral politics, actually strengthens the link between citizens and elected officials. Moreover, it appears to do so in a way that fosters a more equal distribution of influence. While the councillors in the cities with greater community participation are more attuned to the issues articulated by citizens, there is no evidence that the opinions of narrowly organized or special interests are disproportionately favored.

None of these results addresses the question of the impact of community participation structures on actual policy outcomes or decisions. These results simply suggest that community participation has a particular type of impact on the agenda of city officials. When the participation systems do succeed in changing the policy agenda, does that translate into actual changes in public policies and decisions? Chapter 6 addresses this question by extending this discussion to the issue of policy decisions and outcomes.

CHAPTER 6

Shaping Policy Outcomes

TODAY AMERICANS FEEL more than ever that government is unresponsive to their needs and demands. Large numbers of people seem to believe that government responds more to special interests than to their personal interests or their conception of the public interest. But does this mean that governments are, in fact, unresponsive to what people want?

We investigated the extent to which citizens' views actually become part of the public agenda in chapter 5. As suggested in that chapter, however, agenda setting tells only part of the story. Indeed, the agenda is important to most people only if it bears some relation to what governments actually do in terms of policy decisions, programs, or services. Citizens' priority issues could be squarely on the agenda of public officials while the apparatus of government pursues programs or policies that do not reflect the actual preferences of the people. This chapter, then, turns its attention to the issue of policy outcomes—who wins when it comes time to decide the day-to-day business of city government. Thus the issues here are how responsive are the policies of cities to their citizens, and are there ways that city policies can be made more responsive? Specifically, is there any evidence that community participation structures improve local government's ability to be responsive to the expressed needs and preferences of citizens? Answering these and related questions can be quite complicated and requires that the concept of policy responsiveness be developed more precisely.

The Idea of Policy Responsiveness

Because policy responsiveness means different things to different people, we need to be clear about what responsiveness means in the context of urban politics. Much of the existing literature on policy responsiveness is based on some form of rigorous empirical research, so it is important to explain how different concepts of responsiveness have been measured.

This analysis will clarify the reasons specific measures of policy responsiveness have been developed in this study.

The idea of public policy responsiveness is most often traced to the work of V. O. Key, Jr.,[1] and was developed by others, including Thomas R. Dye,[2] and Richard Dawson and James Robinson.[3] Most of the earlier research was concerned with understanding why some governments are more responsive to disadvantaged people than others. In the language of Key, researchers wanted to determine why some states or city governments were more concerned than others with providing benefits to "have nots." The initial hypothesis, deriving from a belief in the propriety of democratic political processes and institutions, was that governments with the greatest competition for political office would have political leaders who were more attuned to the needs of the poor.

The idea was that states or cities in which elected officials won their offices by narrow margins would feel some electoral insecurity and therefore would be more interested in satisfying their constituents as a way of bolstering their chances of future reelection. They would then pursue policies responsive to the needs of people, including the specific needs of the poor. Thus the researchers expected to find an association between the closeness of elections and the level of spending for public welfare. These hypotheses, however, were soundly refuted in the works of Dye, who demonstrated that economic development (the level of economic resources), not interparty competition or some other political system trait, was the chief determinant of how responsive state and local governments were to the poor.

Since the time of these earlier analyses, research on policy responsiveness has moved away from comparative state and local analysis and concomitantly from reliance on measures of aggregate public spending on benefits, such as per capita welfare expenditures. The main reason for this evolution is a recognition that the broad measures may not capture the actual dynamics of policy responsiveness and that expenditures by themselves may mask very important variations in how local governments treat their constituents. For example, two city governments with comparable welfare populations that spend identical amounts of

1. V. O. Key, Jr., *American State Politics: An Introduction* (Knopf, 1956).
2. Thomas R. Dye, *Politics, Economics, and the Public: Policy Outcomes in the American States* (Rand McNally, 1966).
3. Richard E. Dawson and James A. Robinson, "Inter-Party Competition, Economic Variables, and Welfare Policies in the American States," *Journal of Politics*, vol. 25 (May 1963), pp. 265–89.

money per capita on welfare may spend that money in totally different ways. One government may spend it to provide direct social services for the needy, while another may spend it to support a bureaucracy that provides little in the way of direct services. More recent research on policy responsiveness has developed alternative measures of the expression of "need" by citizens and has tried to improve the measurement of government policies.[4]

Reliance on such expenditure indicators also has been criticized because it fails to capture what people want out of government. Two governments with similar welfare populations, spending identical amounts of money on welfare functions, may actually face very different sets of demands from their welfare populations. The idea of policy responsiveness, as generally accepted in the last twenty years, asserts that government policy, to be considered responsive, must bear some relation to what people want. Therefore, scholars must measure the expressed attitudes of people in specific communities as part of their evaluations of policy responsiveness.

Even if welfare recipients in two cities make the same demands on their respective governments, these demands might be placed into entirely different mixtures of demands from other, sometimes competing, groups of people. For example, in one city public officials might be able to improve the quality of services for the poor without serious political opposition, while in the other such efforts might be blocked by a particularly active association of homeowners. The political challenge for public officials in these two cities would be quite different. For this reason, simple correlations between cities' political system characteristics and public expenditures cannot capture the full dimensions of policy responsiveness. How policymakers handle their reactions to various demands has been addressed through development of the idea of "policy responsiveness balance."

Still unchanged is a recognition in the research that evaluating the policy responsiveness of governments must be rooted in policy outcomes. Although public expenditures may not be very precise measures of policy outcomes, the research effort is still well intended. For a government to be considered responsive to its citizens or to segments of its constituency, analysis must center on some actions of that government. In this chapter

4. Rufus P. Browning, Dale Rogers Marshall, and David H. Tabb, *Protest Is Not Enough: The Struggle of Blacks and Hispanics for Equality in Urban Politics* (University of California Press, 1984).

we focus on the decisions of policymakers on issues and conflicts arising in the community.

Policy Responsiveness Balance

Policy responsiveness balance is concerned with the distribution of responsiveness across different segments of the population within given jurisdictions. This concept goes directly to the heart of who wins *and* who loses in public policy decisions. It is not enough to establish that officials *agree* with citizens, as investigated in chapter 5. Nor is it enough for officials to respond to most citizens or a majority of citizens. Policy balance attempts to capture the notion that more responsive policies are those that are able to meet some people's needs or demands without sacrificing the needs of others. In the aggregate, where trade-offs are inevitable, people whose needs are not met in one service area may have their needs met in other areas. Clearly, the concept suggests that more responsive cities do not always have the same people winning or losing on every issue.

Policy balance has been addressed by focusing on the extent of "policy bias" or "responsiveness bias" reflected in the actions of local government. Paul Schumaker and Russell Getter's studies, perhaps the best example of this genre of analysis, tie citizens' preferences to actual policy outcomes as represented by spending levels for different city service functions.[5] By aggregating the preferences of citizens with specific characteristics (such as income level, education, and race) and matching spending on specific services to these preferences, one can infer the extent to which some people get more from local government than others. The idea, then, is to study to what degree patterns of responsiveness bias exist and the factors that correlate with those patterns. Schumaker and Getter's analyses were designed to compare the levels of responsiveness bias in fifty-one medium- to large-sized cities.

5. Russell W. Getter and Paul Schumaker, "Contextual Bases of Responsiveness to Citizen Preferences and Group Demands," *Policy and Politics*, vol. 6 (March 1978), pp. 249–78; Paul Schumaker and Russell W. Getter, "Structural Sources of Unequal Responsiveness to Group Demands in American Cities," *Western Political Quarterly*, vol. 36 (March 1983), pp. 7–29; Paul Schumaker and Russell W. Getter, "Responsiveness Bias in 51 American Communities," *American Journal of Political Science*, vol. 21 (May 1977), pp. 247–81; Paul Schumaker, "Citizen Preferences and Policy Responsiveness," in T. N. Clark, ed., *Urban Policy Analysis: Directions for Future Research*, vol. 21: *Urban Affairs Annual Review* (Beverly Hills: Sage, 1981); and Paul Schumaker, *Critical Pluralism, Democratic Performance, and Community Power* (University Press of Kansas, 1991).

Their results suggest a relationship between the level of political participation and the type of responsiveness bias. As will be discussed in more detail shortly, they found that the channeling of political participation through well-organized interest groups tends to increase the responsiveness bias in favor of advantaged people.[6]

Existing empirical studies of responsiveness bias are not without their problems. As with the earlier studies of policy responsiveness, studies of responsiveness bias rely on broad categories of public expenditures as measures of benefits to specific groups. Analyses by Schumaker and Getter suffer from the additional problem that citizen preferences are never measured directly but rather are estimated or inferred from demographic characteristics and nationwide attitudinal data. These problems, perhaps endemic to broad studies of large numbers of cities, have been overcome in Schumaker's more recent analysis of policy responsiveness in Lawrence, Kansas.[7] To date, however, despite the obvious need to develop direct measures of citizen demands, no comparative analyses of cities have been reported using more rigorous methods of measuring demands or preferences.

Our survey data from the five cities can be utilized to overcome many of the shortcomings of earlier research. Before the analysis turns to examining popular preferences and policy outcomes, the question of bias should be addressed in more detail. Why should we expect that policy outcomes do not equally favor all major segments of the community?

Nearly all the studies of policy imbalance suggest some common sources of bias. Policy imbalance tends to result from the nature of the political system operating in the local community, the opportunities for access to the system by different groups of people, and the structural characteristics of the community's political system. For example, one characteristic of our political system is that in many communities citizens must rely on well-organized interest groups to articulate their demands. This type of mechanism tends to introduce imbalance into the system because people have different abilities to organize or become active in existing interest groups. Thus, as Schumaker and Getter note,

> It is not group activity *per se* which results in responsiveness bias; rather it is the unrepresentative nature of the composition and demands of the most well-organized, permanent, and active groups in the community which results in responsiveness bias.[8]

6. Schumaker and Getter, "Responsiveness Bias," pp. 271–72.
7. Schumaker, *Critical Pluralism.*
8. Schumaker and Getter, "Responsiveness Bias," p. 272.

Because well-organized local interest groups tend to be disproportionately composed of advantaged people, the resulting "communications
with city hall [cause] officials to attain a nonrepresentative view of the
overall structure of citizens' policy preferences."[9]

Although responsiveness bias could be produced by any well-organized group, business tends to be among the best organized and most
permanent interests in city politics. Business has the slack resources and
an organizational infrastructure that makes it relatively easy to aggregate
its interests and press its demands upon government. The way local
governments respond to business, therefore, is the starting point for
analysis of policy responsiveness and bias.

The Power of Business

The ease with which business can get its problems onto the agenda,
as described in chapter 5, implies that it usually gets its way in local
politics. If the primary purpose of cities is to expand their economic base,
they must be attractive sites for enterprise. A city with the reputation of
being unconcerned about the interests of business is a city flirting with
danger. However, a city cannot be attractive to business solely by offering
the right kind of tax abatements or development packages to new businesses. Leaders of the business community want to feel that they have a
special relationship with those at city hall. They want to know that the
door is always open.[10]

If local government is so concerned about economic development that
it gives business an open policy window, it stands to reason that it would
also give business much of what it wants in terms of policy outcomes.
Yet even though city officials clearly have a great deal to gain from
pleasing business, the constraints on government may be much different
later in the policymaking process. Too often business is assumed to be
powerful because of its ample resources. But as James Q. Wilson warns,

> One cannot *assume* that the disproportionate possession of certain
> resources (money, organization, status) leads to the disproportionate
> exercise of political power. Everything depends on whether a resource
> can be converted into power, and at what rate and at what price.

9. Schumaker and Getter, "Structural Sources of Unequal Responsiveness," p. 9.
10. See Clarence N. Stone, *Regime Politics: Governing Atlanta, 1946–1988* (University
Press of Kansas, 1989).

TABLE 6-I. Whose Issues Get Resolved?

Percent unless otherwise indicated

Winner in resolution of issue	Initiator of policy proposals						
	Neigh-bor-hood asso-ciation	Local govern-ment	Other govern-ment	Business	Citizen group	Multiple initi-ators	Don't know
Ongoing, not yet resolved	20.0	12.5	27.3	18.8	13.3	35.3	50.0
Initiator	50.0	50.0	36.4	31.3	66.7	41.2	50.0
Opposition	0.0	15.6	18.2	18.8	13.3	5.9	0.0
Compromise	10.0	12.5	9.1	31.3	6.7	11.8	0.0
Other	20.0	9.4	9.1	0.0	0.0	5.9	0.0
N	10	32	11	16	15	17	4

That, in turn, can only be learned by finding out who wins and who loses. [11]

To find out who wins and who loses, each of the narrative case histories elicited in the elite interviews and investigated in chapter 5 was coded to indicate the final outcome of the controversy. In table 6-I the initiators of the issues are cross-tabulated with the eventual "winners," the parties in whose favor the final decision was made. These data clearly show that the power to get issues onto the agenda is quite different from the power to influence subsequent policymaking. Business turns out to be the least successful of all initiators in winning the policy conflicts generated at its initiative. In only about one-third of the issues it initiated was business the winner. Although the subsample is small, it is interesting to note that the neighborhood associations had an unusually good ratio, winning half the issues they initiated and losing none.

Further evidence that the power of the neighborhood associations is much greater than their role in agenda setting might suggest comes from looking at who stood in opposition to the initiators (see table 6-2). In 50 percent of the cases where business got an issue onto the agenda, the neighborhood associations were the primary opponents. Citizen groups were the opponents 19 percent of the time, and local government was business's opponent on only 6 percent of the issues. In short, local gov-

11. James Q. Wilson, "Democracy and the Corporation," in Robert Hessen, ed., *Does Big Business Rule America?* (Washington: Ethics and Public Policy Center, 1981), p. 37 (emphasis in original).

TABLE 6-2. Primary Source of Opposition

Percent unless otherwise indicated

Source of opposition	Neighborhood association	Local government	Other government	Business	Citizen group	Multiple initiators	Don't know
			Initiator of policy proposals				
Neighborhood association	0.0	18.8	9.1	50.0	0.0	0.0	0.0
Local government	30.0	12.5	18.2	6.3	53.3	41.2	25.0
Other government	20.0	0.0	18.2	0.0	0.0	5.9	0.0
Business	10.0	9.4	9.1	6.3	6.7	17.7	25.0
Citizen group	10.0	12.5	18.2	18.8	0.0	5.9	0.0
Lack of resources	30.0	40.6	18.2	12.5	26.7	29.4	25.0
Public opinion	0.0	6.3	9.1	6.3	13.3	0.0	25.0
N	10	32	11	16	15	17	4

ernment continues to show its sympathy toward business as the policymaking process continues, but the opposition to economic and development initiatives from other quarters is significant enough to stop business from getting its way much of the time. When business loses or is forced into a compromise that favors neither side, the neighborhood associations are the most likely adversary.

The Demand for Development

An important qualification to these data is that not all business-related issues are created equal. On the most critical development issues, the development side almost always wins. During the time the field research was conducted, eight major development projects stood out from the rest because of the scope of the physical change they would bring to the surrounding neighborhoods and the impact they would have on the local economies. These eight were the World Trade Center in St. Paul; a performing arts complex in Dayton; a Fred Meyer megastore in Portland; a water theme park, a racetrack, and airport expansion in Birmingham; and Sea World and the Alamodome in San Antonio. In all cases but the Dayton arts center, the developments won approval.

The level of opposition in these cases varied widely. In Dayton, an arts complex may still be built one day, but the proposal that was defeated stirred a considerable amount of anger. It was developed by business leaders without widespread citizen participation. During the controversy a city planner said,

> This one is completely and privately driven by the corporate folks. They announced a plan over a year ago and presented it as a *fait accompli.* "We're going to come in and give you Lincoln Center, a plaza that will be great for downtown. But in the meantime, we have to tear down all the historical buildings."

The corporate patrons not only showed disregard for the historic buildings on the site, they angered veterans by responding callously to their questions about Memorial Hall, an existing performance structure. They also failed to anticipate the problems they would create for one of downtown's largest employers, a savings and loan that was on the same block as the planned construction. But most of all, the plan was resented because it was developed in secret. In a city where administrators have to routinely go before Priority Boards to discuss policy actions they are contemplating, this closed process rankled both citizens and, off the record, many city administrators. Said one high-ranking official at city hall, "I believe that the process can make all the difference. Had it started out as a grassroots thing or at least as an open process . . . I think we'd be on a completely different track."

When the Fred Meyer chain proposed to build a huge combination grocery store and department store complex adjacent to a residential section of Portland, that area's neighborhood association fought the proposal tooth and nail. In San Antonio, COPS lost in its referendum campaign against the Alamodome stadium. Sea World had a much easier time there. In Birmingham, some homeowners were against the Birmingham Turf Club racetrack, but opposition from the neighborhood associations in the affected areas was surprisingly mild. The water theme park faced somewhat more concerted resistance from the neighborhood associations immediately adjacent to the site, but the city granted approval nonetheless. In the case of the airport expansion, which was also approved, opposition was largely confined to the homeowners whose residences were to be relocated. Finally, the World Trade Center, which was avidly sought by St. Paul's city government in a statewide selection process, faced no opposition at all and had the enthusiastic backing of the District Council for the downtown area.

Although the citizen participation systems responded to these developments in diverse ways, local governments were consistent in their behavior. When a large number of jobs and sizable tax revenues are at stake, city hall will use the resources at its command to see that the proposals come to fruition. Indeed, because of the scale and complexity of the kind of projects discussed above, government is usually a co-initiator along with the private developer. For projects with a significant economic impact, local governments will go head-to-head in opposition to neighborhood associations, though they will first try to work out compromises that do not threaten the integrity of the projects.

Even cities that value citizen participation and take its procedural requirements seriously cannot be unconcerned about their economic future. Cities must balance the welfare of all against the preferences of a small group of neighborhoods that may be adversely affected by a development. Opponents of these projects were all disappointed when the city ruled against them, but only in the case of the Fred Meyer store in Portland did a neighborhood association react that it had been dealt with unfairly and that the citizen participation system had not really worked. (Dispassionate observers would not likely reach the same conclusion. The views of this particular neighborhood association were taken seriously at city hall.) One of the ironies of well-functioning citizen participation structures is that they give legitimacy to decisions that go against a neighborhood. The rest of the city will likely assume that the affected community got a fair hearing because of the participation requirements, making it more difficult for that neighborhood to gain public support in its fight to reverse a decision.

On other important but smaller projects and proposals, business is quite vulnerable. Again, on projects it initiates alone, business is the *least* successful of all sectors of the community. Two reasons explain why business influence on a broad range of issues is relatively unimpressive. First, the role of business in the five cities' power structures has changed considerably over the past several decades. In two of the cities, San Antonio and Birmingham, minorities have taken firm control of city government. The white business establishments there have found themselves playing by a new set of rules. In all of the cities, many of the companies that were long the backbone of the local economy have disappeared or withered to a shell of their former selves. Birmingham, once the steel capital of the South, lost U.S. Steel, and the massive blast furnaces stood as a monument to the city's past until a small group of entrepreneurs founded Birmingham Steel in its place. National Cash Register (NCR) once was a force to be reckoned with in Dayton, but the company has exported most of the jobs it had there to overseas plants.

Mergers and acquisitions have thinned the list of corporations that call Portland home. The new high-tech firms that are headquartered in the Portland area have not shown much inclination to become involved in city politics.

Mirroring these changes has been the collapse or decline of the organizations that were major vehicles of business influence in the five cities.[12] For example, the Good Government League in San Antonio and the Area Progress Council in Dayton were once the embodiment of the local power elite. Now they are only remembrances of things past. In Portland, the decline in influence of the downtown businesses led to the creation of a group, the Association for Portland Progress, that has tried to restore business clout. In Birmingham, the power of the white establishment began its decline after it successfully maneuvered Bull Connor out of office. (As public safety commissioner, Connor, an unrepentant racist, had sullied Birmingham's reputation with his hostility toward the civil rights movement.) Those who claim that America is ruled by a power elite would argue that this decline makes little difference. The interchangeability of members of the ruling class who go back and forth between political office and business is said to ensure that policy will follow class interests.[13] This is not a convincing notion for our five cities. At the time of the fieldwork, three of the mayors were members of minority groups, another's previous occupation was tavern owner, and the other was from a middle-class background. The city councils incorporate more members who are self-consciously "neighborhood people" than those who are identified as "business people." Even though top officials in these local governments are highly concerned about business preferences, the level of organization by business is still an important factor in determining its influence in the rough and tumble of city politics.[14]

The second reason that business often fails to get its way grows out of the first. As big business declined in these cities, newly formed neigh-

12. Business on the national level demonstrated an opposite trend. The challenges to business's influence in Washington politics led to greater organization by industry. See Jeffrey M. Berry, *The Interest Group Society*, 2d ed. (Scott, Foresman/Little, Brown, 1989); and David Vogel, *Fluctuating Fortunes: The Political Power of Business in America* (Basic Books, 1989).

13. See C. Wright Mills, *The Power Elite* (Oxford University Press, 1956).

14. The mechanisms that promote elite rule are examined in Thomas R. Dye, *Who's Running America: Institutional Leadership in the United States*, 5th ed. (Prentice-Hall, 1990); and Michael Useem, *The Inner Circle: Large Corporations and the Rise of Business Political Activity in the U.S. and U.K.* (Oxford University Press, 1984).

borhood associations found it easier to gain a prominent role in city politics. There was not a complete power vacuum by any means, but competing organizations had considerable opportunity to step in and demand to be part of the policymaking process.[15] This was not a natural or inevitable transfer of power. The changes that affected big business in these five cities—especially the decline of industrial companies and the growth of minority populations—are common to large cities across the country. Yet citizen participation did not take hold in all these other cities. The cities studied here are rare cases where significant resources have been devoted to the neighborhood associations and where adminstrators have had a serious and continuing commitment to make citizen participation meaningful.

Conflict versus Cooperation

If these five cities represent unusual cases of strong, institutionalized neighborhood associations, does it follow that they also are characterized by distinctive patterns of business-neighborhood interaction? That is, has business adapted to these neighborhood competitors so that it behaves differently from business in cities without well-functioning citizen participation systems?

A critical difference between the neighborhood activism of cities without well-functioning citizen participation systems and that in the five cities is predictability. In typical American cities developers are tempted to try to make their projects *faits accomplis* by getting them as far along as possible without any kind of public input. If significant resistance does emerge, they will turn to sympathetic administrators to help them overpower it. In the five cities, there is the *assurance* of neighborhood reaction. There is no way around it; the rules and norms require neighborhood involvement. City administrators resolutely enforce the requirements of citizen participation and work with neighborhood associations to ensure that development projects are fully reviewed by affected communities.

The consequences from this difference are clear. Knowing that neighborhoods can kill all but the grandest of projects, businesspeople will

15. The conventional wisdom would hold that the fragmentation of city government through creation of a system of neighborhood associations would make it easier for business to dominate the governmental process. In the five cities at least, the decline of business worked against this. See Alan A. Altshuler, *Community Control: The Black Demand for Participation in Large American Cities* (New York: Pegasus, 1970), p. 46.

conclude that it is a good *business* decision to seek peace with the neighborhood. Even though the ideological sentiments of developers may hold that, as a matter of personal freedom, they should be able to do what they want with the property they own, living out that philosophy in these cities is not practical.

Even businesspeople not experienced in the ways of the neighborhood associations will be strongly socialized as soon as they come into contact with city hall agencies. Citizen participation is part of the organizational routines for project approval. Moreover, concern for neighborhood preferences becomes part of the agency mission in these cities. As one Portland administrator put it, "[What's] important from my perspective is the kind of ingrained training that everybody in this region has gone through: that it doesn't make sense . . . to try to do it without citizen participation." A developer who seeks the cooperation of city administrators is making a de facto request for participation by the neighborhood associations. However, administrators face demands from developers that the process move along expeditiously and that their proposals be free from unreasonable requests. At the same time, they face demands from the neighborhood associations, which want to exert influence over what is to be built in their communities. The administrators' goal, therefore, is to get both sides to believe that bargaining and compromise are the optimum arrangement.

Just how different the behavior of businesspeople in the five cities is from that elsewhere is hard to say. What can be concluded, though, is that the citizen participation systems induce businesspeople toward cooperative behavior that helps them to achieve their business goals. For their part, the neighborhood associations engender cooperation by seeing it as their responsibility to let reasonable development projects be built. Since the cities encourage businesspeople to organize into neighborhood-based groups that interact in an ongoing way with the neighborhood association in their area, the problems of local businesspeople are very much on the minds of people active in the neighborhood associations.

Co-optation?

Some strong believers in grassroots citizen advocacy feel that it is self-defeating to channel such efforts through city-sponsored programs. If citizen participation takes place through organizations dependent on the city for funding and recognition, those organizations will inevitably be compromised. The neighborhood associations will always be pressured to go along with city hall because they need its support over the long run. Thus the argument is that the true interests of the neighborhoods may not be served because their organizations are not completely free to do and say whatever they want.

When Saul Alinsky wrote in 1965 about public participation in the war on poverty, he argued that entrenched interests in city politics wielded their power and money to undermine challenges to the status quo. In his words, "Poverty funds are . . . used to suffocate militant independent leadership and action organizations which have been arising to arm the poor with their share of power. . . . Good potential . . . leadership is seduced by payoffs, rentals of premises, jobs and specialized pressure such as money grants or projects to . . . rivals."[16] In a similar vein, Piven and Cloward have suggested that governments respond to challenges by pursuing co-optation and conciliation.

> [During periods of public protest] . . . political leaders . . . will try to quiet disturbances . . . by making efforts to channel the energies and angers of the protestors into more legitimate and less disruptive forms of political behavior . . . by offering incentives to movement leaders or, in other words, by coopting them . . . . [Conciliation is usually] achieved through new programs that appear to meet the moral demands of the movement, and thus rob it of support without yielding much by way of tangible gains.[17]

These are serious charges, reflecting the views not only of intellectuals on the left but of the organizers of COPS as well. COPS has steadfastly refused participation in activities that could be construed as cooperative endeavors with the city's government. The organization's leaders regard its independence as crucial to its effectiveness as an advocate for San Antonio's Hispanic community.

Such critics of city-sponsored citizen participation might look at our data on the relations between business and the neighborhood associations and reach some rather different conclusions from those offered here. They might argue that the neighborhood associations work to business's advantage by co-opting business's potential adversaries. The citywide

16. Saul D. Alinsky, "The War on Poverty: Political Pornography," *Journal of Social Issues*, vol. 21 (January 1965), p. 42.

17. Frances Fox Piven and Richard Cloward, *Poor People's Movements: Why They Succeed, How They Fail* (Vintage, 1979), pp. 30–31.

systems direct opposition to development into forums that give the neighborhoods a voice but ultimately speed development projects along. Some evidence exists to support this charge. As will be documented in chapter 8, those who are active in the neighborhood associations are less likely to continue fighting when they disagree with a decision made by their neighborhood association than are people who are active in other types of political organizations.

Overall, however, neighborhoods gain far more protection from the citywide systems of citizen participation than they lose from the pressure to compromise with the businesspeople who come before them. The data here simply do not support the conclusion that the neighborhoods get co-opted by big business and city hall. The issue narratives indicate that the neighborhood associations have been formidable adversaries for private economic interests. There is always pressure under these systems for all parties to compromise, but the neighborhood associations have shown that they are not afraid of an open fight when they cannot accept a development proposal.

Neither does the subset of issues involving large-scale development offer convincing evidence of co-optation. The degree to which neighborhood associations opposed the large development projects differed, and the overwhelming strength of the development side meant that in some cases only the most affected homeowners were opposed. When projects have the enthusiastic backing of business and city hall, and the public wants economic development, they are difficult to stop. Although neighborhood associations may, in fact, be less likely than an ad hoc group of homeowners to file lawsuits or use other delaying tactics, it is hard to see evidence of direct co-optation. Generally, these projects did not become compromises between the neighborhood associations and big business; a number of the issues resulted in outright defeats for the neighborhood associations. In these cases, the neighborhood associations may have lost the battle, but they were certainly not co-opted.

If the neighborhood associations had relatively weak powers, the requirements that developers bring their projects before them for approval might indeed be a way the neighborhood could be co-opted. If a neighborhood association knew that a project would eventually be built anyway when the developer went over its head to city hall, the association would certainly have an incentive to take whatever crumbs the developer offered as concessions. But the neighborhood associations' strong controls over zoning give them considerable leverage over developers. How could a neighborhood group having no affiliation with the city and no formal powers be in a better position to represent its community? Even if an independent neighborhood group were effectively organized on a long-term basis—a dubious assumption in urban politics—it would have to rely on much more difficult tactics to accomplish what a neighborhood association in the four cities can do in a single evening.

The neighborhood associations in the citywide systems enjoy substantial freedom to do and say what they want. They are not expected to toe the line or follow city hall's lead. Only in some parts of Birmingham has city hall tried to mobilize support in the neighborhood associations for the administration in office. The operative culture of these neighborhood associations is that they are independent organizations that will not be punished for taking stands unpopular with city hall.

The argument here is that the neighborhood associations have not been co-opted; but this is not to deny that there is a bias in these cities—and all other cities—in favor of business and economic development. The fundamental power of business in politics rests on society's need for the jobs and wealth that it produces. No citizen participation system can alter that. Cities are particularly vulnerable to the demands of business: an enterprise that does not get what it wants often moves a short distance across a boundary to another city that will grant its wishes. "Developmental policies," writes Paul Peterson, "come at the expense of other communities."[18] What citizen participation does do is create some popular control over the city's ongoing need to increase its wealth. Left to their own devices, city governments often find it more efficient to take development decisions out of the normal, visible political process and leave the division of the spoils to a highly autonomous bureaucracy.[19] Clearly, cities must pursue development. What the citywide systems of neighborhood associations accomplish is that they allow citizens to have some say over just how much and what kind of development. That is no small achievement.

Citizen Participation and Responsiveness

Although city residents want enough economic growth for their cities to prosper, it is not clear to what extent policy responsiveness to business

18. Paul E. Peterson, *City Limits* (University of Chicago Press, 1981), p. 148.

19. Stephen L. Elkin, *City and Regime in the American Republic* (University of Chicago Press, 1987), pp. 61–82; and Robert P. Stoker, "Baltimore: The Self-Evaluating City?" in Clarence N. Stone and Heywood T. Sanders, eds., *The Politics of Urban Development* (University Press of Kansas, 1987), pp. 244–66.

is supported by the general citizenry. When local governments respond to business, even after incorporating the position of neighborhood associations, how does this response compare to citizens' preferences? Stated another way, when issues important to business get resolved, are they resolved in ways that are satisfactory to a broad array of citizens?

In the analysis of policy responsiveness based on resolution of specific issues, analysts often ascertain how the issues were resolved and what kinds of interest groups and organizations supported that resolution and then make assumptions about who "won." Yet this approach minimizes the role of public opinion and the efforts of policymakers to respond to popular preferences. The research here is designed to determine the extent to which the general population and subgroups of the population seem to have been in favor of resolving the issues as they were eventually settled.

To examine the question of outcomes and public preferences, we compiled from the elite interviews and from a variety of news sources a list of pressing issues already on the agendas in each of the five cities. The second-wave citizen surveys contained a variety of city-specific issue questions so that citizen preferences could be identified. These were nonroutine issues that seemed clearly on the public agenda and about which specific proposals or solutions had been offered. These issues, described in appendix 6-1, were not necessarily the issues the general public thought should be on the agenda and may not have been among the issues citizens would have volunteered as being most important at that time. They were, however, receiving considerable attention in the press and at city hall. There is little overlap between this current list of issues and those discussed in the previous section and in chapter 5. Most of the previously discussed economic development issues derived from the elite interviews had already been resolved when those interviews were conducted. This list of issues was compiled just before the second wave of citizen surveys, some eighteen months after the field research was completed.

Our public opinion surveys sought to present the pending issue to the general public and to elicit responses that matched as closely as possible the solutions or proposals already being put forth.[20] For example, in San

20. The fact that a solution was put forth does not necessarily mean that it had any real support in the general population. In the one extreme case, for example, there was widespread recognition of a "drug problem" in Portland, and among the solutions raised to deal with it was legalization of crack and cocaine use, an idea that, as might be expected, was never seriously considered. Rather than assuming what the public response would be to this proposal, we simply included it as a question in the survey.

Antonio, one of the proposed policy changes involved developing a new ground source of drinking water. There was fairly uniform concern in the city about the adequacy and quality of the existing aquifer. Several different solutions to this problem were offered, including the city-sponsored plan to develop a new open-air reservoir. Some suggested that this solution would not be satisfactory and argued that alternative sources of new water had to be found. Others maintained that the real problem was too much unregulated economic and population growth and not enough attention to water conservation and growth limits. These three options were presented to survey respondents.

Nearly three years after the second-wave interviews, we examined each issue to determine how it was resolved. We relied on multiple sources, such as newspapers and interviews with city agency officials, neighborhood association officials, and others.[21] Then we compared the resolution with the responses of people who reported in the surveys that they would like to have seen the issue resolved in a particular way. The issues and how they were resolved are listed in appendix 6-1.

This comparison between how these issues were resolved and how the public said it wanted the issues resolved forms the basis for this analysis of policy responsiveness. In each city, an average percentage of people whose policy options were actually pursued by city hall was calculated across all issues. The resulting average percentage is called the index of policy responsiveness (IPR). If everyone agreed on what the city should do about each issue, and the city actually did it, then this index would be 100. If everyone agreed on each issue, and the city did not pursue the preferred courses of action, the IPR would be zero.

Although the IPR may not be a perfect indicator of every aspect of local government's responsiveness to people, it does provide some concrete information on a range of specific issues addressed in each city. Perhaps the most important aspect of the index is that it clearly indicates how responsive the city is on the selected issues rather than how acquiescent citizens are to decisions already made. Because of the time dimension in this study and the fact that the decisions had not yet been made when the surveys were conducted, citizens' answers and decision preferences could not simply reflect the decisions that were actually made. Instead, the resulting index is a fairly unambiguous measure of the extent to which city officials made decisions in line with the previously expressed preferences of the public.

21. In the five cities combined, we asked questions in the second-wave public opinion surveys about a total of five issues whose resolution could not be determined.

As shown by the indexes of policy responsiveness in table 6-3, the cities with greater community participation had a strong tendency to make decisions in line with the preferences of larger portions of the general population. In San Antonio, the decisions that were made across all issues were, on average, responsive to about 40 percent of the people, while in Portland the decisions were in line with the attitudes of almost 63 percent of the people. These percentages, by themselves, may not mean that much, but the relative differences between the cities are important because they tell us something about the general tendencies of these governments to match policies to public preferences. In St. Paul and Portland during the period of this study, compared with other cities, decisions were typically made only after a significantly higher level of public approval or support was achieved.[22]

As noted earlier, policy responsiveness bias has been found to be the product of uneven political organization and influence. Such biases result from the different abilities of people to organize or become active in organized interest groups, and the unrepresentative character of those who participate, especially with respect to their socioeconomic status. Analyses by Schumaker and Getter suggest that if the neighborhood associations in the cities with greater community participation perform the same functions as well-organized interest groups in cities with no system of neighborhood participation, then these cities should also experience greater responsiveness bias than the cities with somewhat less community participation.

In chapter 4 we showed very little evidence to suggest that the systems of community participation in the five cities can be characterized as being more severely unrepresentative of the cities' broader populations than elsewhere. Additionally, the more participatory of the five cities did not tend to draw in people who might have made the neighborhood associ-

22. The index of policy responsiveness can be affected not only by the way public officials respond to their populations when making decisions, but also by the nature of cleavages within the population. Public officials making decisions in a city that is usually evenly split on specific issues would find it very difficult to be responsive to relatively large segments of the population. Officials in cities where cleavages are less severe, where the general public tends to have reached greater consensus, would find it much easier to be responsive but would also be much less responsive if they made their decisions contrary to the consensus alternative. This opens the possibility that these results are simply a reflection of how evenly split the cities' populations are on how to solve these issues. Yet the average difference between the percentage of the population favoring each solution across all issues suggests that the people of San Antonio, Dayton, and Birmingham are not more evenly split than the people of St. Paul or Portland. The average differences are San Antonio, 34.7; Dayton, 28.3; Birmingham, 21.1; St. Paul, 41.1; and Portland, 35.9.

TABLE 6-3. Public Approval of Issue Resolutions

City and issue	Percentage of the population who wanted the issue resolved the way it was finally resolved
San Antonio	
Increase taxes for more police substations	18.3
Build Alamodome	21.9
Retire city debt before building Alamodome	23.2
Increase taxes to hire more police	25.0
Increase taxes to support citizen crime prevention training	28.7
Pay for Alamodome with private funds only	30.8
Bring professional football to San Antonio	35.3
Use city funds for Alamodome	42.7
Develop Applewhite Reservoir	43.8
Increase taxes 0.5 percent for Alamodome	50.5
Increase taxes for more police patrols	53.3
Attract major events to Alamodome	64.0
Sell city-owned utility	82.8
Average index of policy responsiveness	**40.0**
Dayton	
Increase city spending for redeveloment	13.0
Implement affirmative action in police and fire hiring	29.6
Increase downtown parking and shuttle	42.9
Increase historic preservation	45.1
Implement New Futures program	46.6
Increase spending on public relations	56.1
Annex adjacent areas	56.2
Promote regional development	81.6
Average index of policy responsiveness	**46.4**

ations overrepresentative of advantaged citizens. In chapter 5 we failed to find any consistent pattern where the local public agenda was biased in favor of those who participate. Does this mean that the cities with more community participation are not more responsive to those who participate? Or could it be that these cities still find a way to respond more to frequent participants?

To analyze this question, the IPR was calculated separately for people who participated in the systems of neighborhood associations and for higher SES people. Although the higher community participation cities tend to be more responsive both to community participants and to higher SES people than the lower community participation cities, these cities are no more responsive to community participants and higher SES people than they are to their respective general populations. In other words, the

TABLE 6-3 (continued)

City and issue	Percentage of the population who wanted the issue resolved the way it was finally resolved
Birmingham	
Use eminent domain to build UAB clinic	21.0
Close or convert Turf Club	35.3
Ensure horseracing at racetrack	38.3
Start greyhound racing	41.4
Build the UAB health clinic	47.1
Encourage private operation of Turf Club	60.5
Divorce city government from Turf Club	60.8
Rezone Lake Purdy area	68.8
Average index of policy responsiveness	**46.7**
St. Paul	
Continue 1984 affirmative action plan	17.4
Expand affirmative action in city government	44.8
Develop riverfront	46.5
Change zoning of areas with pornography	56.6
Distribute low-income housing evenly	61.1
Offer incentives for alternative uses of properties where pornographic materials sold	71.2
Change pornography regulations	79.1
Eliminate affirmative action in government	85.8
Average index of policy responsiveness	**57.8**
Portland	
Provide social services for the homeless	33.6
Increase taxes for increased drug treatment	52.4
Increase taxes for neighborhood crime watch	54.8
Increase taxes to hire more police	63.6
Cut other services to increase police	82.2
Legalize use of crack and cocaine	91.0
Average index of policy responsiveness	**62.9**

higher community participation cities are more responsive to everyone, not just those who traditionally are well represented. The indexes and differences suggest that Portland and St. Paul are not more responsive to those who participate or to higher SES people than Birmingham, Dayton, or San Antonio (see table 6-4). Clearly, greater community participation does not translate into policy bias or imbalance in favor of those who participate or those who have greater personal resources.

But the functioning of citizen participation programs raises issues of other kinds of policy biases and imbalances. Citizen participation pro-

TABLE 6-4. Indexes of Policy Responsiveness for Community
Participants and Higher SES Respondents

City	General population index	Community participants		Higher SES	
		Index	Difference	Index	Difference
San Antonio	40.0	42.0	2.0	41.5	1.5
Dayton	46.4	45.2	−1.2	47.1	0.7
Birmingham	46.7	48.5	1.8	51.3	4.6
St. Paul	57.8	58.9	1.1	58.6	0.8
Portland	62.9	66.5	3.6	66.3	3.4

grams, especially those associated with the war on poverty, have been
criticized for creating serious biases or imbalances in government responsiveness. The antipoverty programs were thought to create too much
access to decisionmaking for the poor and for racial and ethnic minorities
at the expense of the white middle class. Indeed, in general, studies have
shown that when disadvantaged citizens are able to organize and present
their demands through the activities of local groups, they tend to be able
to generate favorable government responses.[23] The problem, of course,
is that disadvantaged people typically have a much more difficult time
organizing.

Do the systems of neighborhood associations help make city officials
more responsive to the disadvantaged? Or are the disadvantaged left out
when it comes to getting public officials to act? To answer these questions, IPRs were computed for lower SES and African-American respondents in each city (see table 6-5). Only in San Antonio do decisions seem
more likely to be in line with what poorer people want than the population as a whole. Issue decisions were made in line with what some 40
percent of the general population preferred but in line with what almost
50 percent of what lower SES people wanted. In all of the other cities,
there is no evidence of a bias in favor of or against poorer people.

This general lack of responsiveness bias with respect to lower SES
does not carry over to race. San Antonio, St. Paul, and Portland do show
marked tendencies to make decisions more in line with what their respective African-American citizens want. Dayton and Birmingham show
no such tendency. Indeed, in these latter two cities, there is no evidence
of bias for or against blacks. On its face this may seem to indicate that
the systems of participation sometimes provide too much access for racial

23. Schumaker and Getter, "Structural Sources of Unequal Responsiveness."

TABLE 6-5. Indexes of Policy Responsiveness for African
Americans and Lower SES Respondents

City	General population index	African Americans		Lower SES	
		Index	Difference	Index	Difference
San Antonio	40.0	55.5	15.5	49.4	9.4
Dayton	46.4	46.8	0.4	45.4	−1.0
Birmingham	46.7	45.4	−1.3	47.7	1.0
St. Paul	57.8	67.9	10.1	57.6	−0.2
Portland	62.9	72.0	9.1	61.1	−1.8

minorities. However, there is another side to this story. The three cities
showing responsiveness bias in favor of blacks are the three cities with
the smallest black populations.[24] If cities find it difficult to be responsive
to relatively small minority populations, this does not seem to be a
problem in Portland and St. Paul. Perhaps in these cities the systems of
community participation are able to overcome any biases that work
against small minorities by providing guaranteed opportunities to be
heard through the neighborhood associations. Without a baseline from
other cities with small minority populations against which to compare
these results, our tentative conclusion must be that if there is responsiveness imbalance that comes from greater community participation in cities
that are overwhelmingly nonminority, it is in favor of the black population.

Conclusion

The neighborhood associations are impressive in their ability to compete with business once matters get on the agenda. They were the most
frequent opponents to business, which, in turn, was the most infrequent
winner among all initiators. Conflict between neighborhood associations
and business, however, is mitigated by the citizen participation systems
as businesspeople learn that coming to agreement with the affected community is the shortest route to reaching their goals. For their part, the
neighborhood associations are not usually antagonistic toward business
and are not inveterate opponents of development. At the same time, the
citywide systems have been able to work with business without being

24. Black percentages of the populations from the 1980 census are St. Paul, 4.9 percent;
San Antonio, 7.3 percent; and Portland, 7.6 percent; compared with Dayton, 36.9 percent;
and Birmingham, 55.6 percent.

co-opted by it. The success of these systems in forging cooperation and negotiation between neighborhoods and businesspeople contrasts with the experience of cities like Hartford, Cleveland, and Berkeley, where progressives took control of city hall. Business-led backlashes subsequently occurred in these cities because of the conflict that came to characterize business-government relations.[25] None of the five cities included in this study has been subject to a business-led backlash against its citizen participation system.

Although business must take the neighborhood associations seriously, the need for economic growth gives business a unique advantage in city politics. City governments pursue development not because they are manipulated by elites but because their constituents want the jobs and wealth that come with economic expansion. Citizens are willing to pay some costs for this expansion; they do not inevitably feel that new businesses or factories are fine as long as they are in someone else's backyard. People want to find the right balance between the city's economic growth and the quality of life in their community. The systems of neighborhood associations provide a vehicle through which citizens come together to try to define where that balance lies.

The analyses based on the indexes of policy responsiveness provide even more evidence of the capability offered by the systems of neighborhood associations. Policy responsiveness tended to increase as structured community participation increased. Public officials in Portland and St. Paul, the cities with greater levels of community participation, made decisions that were considerably more in line with what people said they wanted the cities to do than was the case in Birmingham, Dayton, or San Antonio. Perhaps more impressive is the fact that the cities with greater community participation were able to be more responsive without much evidence of biases or imbalances.

The central question in this chapter is whether cities' policies can be made to be more responsive to what people want. In particular, can systems of neighborhood-based citizen participation improve the way city governments respond to their citizens? Our analysis presents abundant evidence that cities that have more structured community participation are better able to respond to a broad range of the demands of citizens than other cities and appear better able to balance the myriad demands of diverse groups and interests.

25. Pierre Clavel, *The Progressive City: Planning and Participation, 1969–1984* (Rutgers University Press, 1986), p. 219.

Appendix 6-1: Issues and Their Outcomes in Five Cities

Portland

The crime problem. A significant issue for Portland residents in recent years has been the dramatic rise in drug dealing, gangs, and burglaries. The perception of the city quickly changed from one of a safe haven to one of fear and "back East" style crime. In fact, for a few years in the late 1980s the city ranked among the highest in the nation in reported thefts from homes. The city has gone through several police chiefs within a few years in the attempt to deal with the problem.

City response and resolution. The city has done a great deal in response to the situation. Mayor Bud Clark came up with a "Safer City Plan" involving everything from increased police presence in target neighborhoods to training for city and utility employees to serve as crime-watch auxiliaries. The Police Bureau's budget rose by more than 25 percent from 1989 to 1991, with a corresponding increase of over 80 officers. The budget for crime prevention employees, working out of the neighborhood coalition offices, nearly doubled over this period, totaling 19 full-time people by early 1992. A major community policing initiative was coupled with a plan for hiring 200 additional sworn police personnel with blocks of time available to implement proactive community policing strategies. However, the passage of Measure 5, Portland's Proposition 13 style tax limitation, required a leveling off of police hiring in 1992, so the plan was not fully implemented. A newer program put added emphasis on drug offenders with a tenfold increase in effort in counseling and detoxification programs (including a court counseling program) between 1988 and 1992 and a special effort to reduce rates of recidivism.

The homelessness issue. In the mid-1980s, the homeless population on the streets of Portland had become a topic of major concern to residents, social service providers, visitors, and business owners alike. The mayor had proposed, and a nonprofit organization called Central City Concern had implemented, a twelve-point plan to provide shelters, transition housing, and basic services for the homeless in Portland. At the time of the interviews in Portland, implementation of the plan had already been going on for more than a year.

City response and resolution. Despite the efforts described above, in 1989 the Clark–Shields agreement between the mayor and a number of business and community leaders was reached to put a cap on the total number of shelters plus transitional housing in the "skid row" area of downtown Portland, where most of this housing had been developed at that time. Nevertheless, from 1988 through 1991, more than 400 units of single resident occupancy (SRO) housing had been developed, primarily through renovation of old hotels mainly in this same area. Only about 30 of these units were covered by the agreement that included the planned reduction of shelter beds. By 1992, some observers came to believe that the key need was no longer beds, but services and supervised situations to provide a way out of homelessness. Many of these services are the responsibility of the county, but the city has been a key catalyst in the process.

St. Paul

Low-income housing. The need for certain types of low-income housing, namely SRO housing, has been clear, as in most cities, for those coming out of prison, and from drug and alcohol treatment programs and simply as a step out of homelessness. The strength of the District Councils and their neighborhood focus enabled them to raise sharp objections if they thought they were being treated unfairly by SRO placement programs and to prevent the programs from being sited.

City response and resolution. A task force was formed from both human service providers and neighborhood representatives. After a year of meetings, the task force developed a set of recommendations for state legislation and local ordinances that would help the city meet the specific goal of distributing community residential facilities evenly across the city. By early 1992, these proposals were in the process of being implemented.

Riverfront development. In 1986 the two-year-old Riverfront Commission proposed a fifteen-year, $58 million redevelopment plan for St. Paul's share of the Mississippi riverfront. Plans included development of the Kellogg shopping mall, building of a park on Navy Island, widening and moving of a riverfront road, a major development of a marina at Harriet Island Park, construction of the Minnesota Revenue Department office building, and construction of broad pedestrian walkways along both sides of the river.

City response and resolution. The commission is no longer in existence. A few of the proposed projects, such as the shopping mall, the office building, and a flood wall along one stretch of the river were completed. Others, like the reconstruction of Shepard Road, are still in development stages. The development that did take place was evenly divided between the two sides of the river. But in general the grand plans of the commission have not been carried out. Very little citizen participation was evident in the commission's work, either in favor of or against riverfront development.

Affirmative action. A temporary affirmative action plan for St. Paul had been in effect since 1984. With its expiration in the summer of 1987, a major controversy developed about what should replace this 1984 plan. Some wanted to keep it in force without change; others, like the Human Rights Commission, wanted to strengthen it; and still others, like the firefighters' union, wanted to weaken or abolish it.

City response and resolution. The original plan called for qualification of not only the top three scorers on the civil service tests, but also a "reachdown" to the highest scoring minority, woman, or disabled person scoring within the top one-third of the applicants. New proposals called for a "100 percent reachdown" to the highest scoring protected-class person regardless of where they scored among applicants. Finally, after an eight-month battle with particular attention on the ability of women as firefighters, the personnel department and the city council reached a compromise with the union on a provision strengthening the original affirmative action provision. The final plan called for a 45 percent reach out provision for every opening at the original entry level (thus not applicable to promotions). The first two women were subsequently employed in the fire department.

Pornography. For more than a year in 1986 and 1987, a battle raged between residents of the low-income University-Dale area of St. Paul and the owners of X-rated theaters and bookstores in their neighborhood. Efforts ranged from pray-ins and picketing to proposed zoning changes, buyouts, and other measures to restrict these businesses to very limited parts of the city. One complaint about some of these proposals is that they would just push the activity into other neighborhoods.

City response and resolution. Eventually, the area got rid of the pornographic establishments through both a new zoning ordinance that declared the area a redevelopment site for the city and a buyout of some of the property by the city. A state department of public safety office building was constructed on one corner and a park on another. The pornographic establishments had not relocated to any other part of St. Paul by early 1992.

Birmingham

Development near Lake Purdy. A 1,200-acre $300 million mixed-use development was proposed by J. Brooks Emory for the area around Lake Purdy. The land is part of the watershed for the lake, which supplies 60 percent of the city's drinking water, and many citizens and environmentalists felt that development would harm water quality. Other large sectors of the community encouraged the development for its beneficial economic impact.

City response and resolution. Development around Lake Purdy was blocked. Environmentalists and other opponents won this battle, but it is unclear whether development is possible in the future. The Waterworks Board did not renew the proposed developer's option to purchase, and the area remained a watershed into 1992.

Using eminent domain for the UAB Clinic. A city block containing a dozen businesses was proposed for the development of a new University of Alabama–Birmingham (UAB) health clinic. The area is located between the UAB campus and the city's downtown, on the edge of the Five Points South neighborhood, home of one of the strongest neighborhood associations in the city.

City response and resolution. The city used its powers of eminent domain to take the land and evict the businesses that were there. The leaders of the opposition were the owners of a restaurant and a fish market that had been there for years. They took the city to court over the issues and, as of this writing, appear to have lost. There was very little neighborhood involvement: Betty Bock, leader of the Five Points South neighborhood association, informally supported the businesses at one point, but the property taking and eviction never became a major issue for the community.

Birmingham Turf Club. The Turf Club thoroughbred racetrack was supported by the city as an economic development measure. Shortly after opening, the track started losing money and eventually filed for bankruptcy. Many subsequent proposals were made to support the track; one that would establish greyhound racing was defeated by residents in a referendum vote. Another horse racing operation by Delaware North, Inc., was approved by the managers, but it also failed financially, leaving the future of the facility uncertain.

City response and resolution. The racetrack is currently owned by the bank that foreclosed. It is trying to lease the track to a group that would run greyhound racing. This proposal would need to be voted on by residents, who previously rejected greyhound racing.

Dayton

Affirmative action in municipal hiring. In late 1987, a coalition of local civic groups called for greater minority representation in public agencies, specifically the police, fire, and sheriff departments. The mayor invited a "friendly lawsuit" against the city to push the issue further. A group of black ministers brought the suit in 1988.

City response and resolution. Affirmative action in the hiring of police, fire, and sheriff officers has remained "status quo," according to the Dayton Police Department. The city's affirmative action plan is still in place but has not been revised or expanded as a result of a 1988 lawsuit. The presiding judge in the invited lawsuit decided "not to decide."

The New Futures program. The goals of Dayton's New Futures plan were to improve students' academic skills, increase school attendance, decrease youth unemployment, and reduce adolescent pregnancy. Conservative groups voiced their opposition to parts of the original plan, especially potential counseling and referrals for abortion and the dispensing of contraceptives.

City response and resolution. Dayton was awarded a $10 million, five-year Casey grant in 1988 to develop programs in all community sectors to aid at-risk youth. The city is still receiving money under the grant and has developed programs that do not give abortion counseling or dispense contraceptives. Referrals for both are actively given through an interagency program.

Historic preservation. Dayton has a long history of historic preservation both in the residential neighborhoods—through designated historic districts—and in the preservation of original facades in the downtown area. This was a major issue in the Dayton Arts Complex, the Victoria Theater restoration, and a host of other projects.

City response and resolution. There is no evidence of a significant change in preservation policy. Both development and preservation seem to be conscious policies of existing government.

Economic development strategies. Five actions were proposed to improve Dayton's struggling economy: annexing land, pursuing regional development plans, increasing redevelopment efforts in blighted areas, developing an improved national image, and increasing downtown parking.

City response and resolution. Since 1988, Dayton has annexed more than one square mile of land through voluntary efforts and continues to encourage the movement toward annexation. Parking has been increased downtown partly through underground lots in two new high-rise buildings, the Arcade and Civic Center. Other regional projects have also been encouraged through the EDGE (Economic Development Government Expenditures) program, designed to promote the development of the region through funds shared with other communities. The city has spent substantial sums on the program, which never got off the ground and will probably be replaced sometime in 1992. Two large public relations campaigns, the City of Neighbors and the 1991 All-America City promotions, were intended to make Dayton appear more visible and vital. Specific projects to reduce urban blight do not seem to be in evidence.

San Antonio

Applewhite Reservoir. The city of San Antonio developed a plan to supplement its aquifer water supply by building on Applewhite Road a broad, shallow reservoir to capture and store surface water. Opposition to the plan came from individuals concerned with the reservoir's water quality and the lack of water conservation measures to reduce demand. Property owners near the proposed site also opposed the plan, which would have destroyed land and wildlife habitats.

City response and resolution. The proposal to build the Applewhite Reservoir was approved by the city council in 1988. During the following year, opponents used numerous blocking tactics, including court action, and finally Applewhite was defeated in a referendum. The city has imposed some conservation measures but has not limited growth in any way. Additional measures were investigated to increase the flow of water into the aquifer, such as raising the level of the contributory lake, buying irrigation rights, and building additional recharge dams. To date, little has been done to ensure that the aquifer does not become polluted.

Sale of the city-owned utility. The city was approached by a private firm wanting to buy City Public Service, the municipally owned gas and electric company, for approximately $2 billion. The sale would have yielded approximately $200 million a year for the city's use on various projects. Opponents contended that the price offered was too low and that the utility was yielding a yearly profit of $100 million for the city already. They maintained that future control of utility rates would be sacrificed.

City response and resolution. The company was not sold to a private corporation. The city council passed a resolution preserving public ownership of the utility but will continue to review the benefits of a potential sale in the future.

The crime problem. In 1988 San Antonio had a severe crime problem, and several suggestions were made to correct the situation. Many people felt that the number of officers on the police force was inadequate. Mayor Cisneros proposed five substations to provide a link to communities and to encourage increased community participation in crime prevention.

City resolution and response. In mid-1988, before the second-wave interviews were conducted, money ran out for hiring additional police officers for deployment in problem areas. Two mobile substations were funded with community development block grant money. In 1990, officers started riding bikes to enhance police visibility. Bikes were bought and maintained through donations by businesses. Citizen crime prevention training continues but has not been strongly emphasized.

Building Alamodome. The Alamodome was proposed as a general-use stadium and the future home of a National Football League (NFL) team. Proponents felt that the dome was needed and that significant economic benefits would result. Controversy arose over the method of funding and the site location.

City response and resolution. The Alamodome has proceeded full speed ahead. A 0.5 percent increase in city sales tax to fund the dome was passed in a citywide vote, and the dome is expected to be completed in 1993. The city has been actively promoting events for the dome. A National Basketball Association (NBA) team has decided to move to the new facility, and an NFL franchise is being sought. Conventions, other events, and shows have been actively recruited.

CHAPTER 7

The Neighborhood Voice

AN ESSENTIAL INGREDIENT in all of the strong democratic cities of our study is the neighborhood association. Neighborhood groups have been an important factor in American political life since the turn of the century. They gained recognition first through the settlement house movement and later in civic clubs and neighborhood improvement associations, in the community organizing of Saul Alinsky, in urban renewal committees of the 1950s, and in poverty programs of the 1960s, in the organizing projects of the "new left," and finally in what has been called the "new populism" of the 1970s.[1] Many see this last wave of neighborhood activity as a direct expression of and reaction to the strident calls for participatory democracy made during the late 1960s.[2] This is when the key organizational forms that energized the strong democratic communities were initiated.

In spite of the pervasiveness of neighborhood movements throughout most urban areas in the country, little agreement has developed about their role in the political process. The importance of neighborhoods to urban life has been clearly portrayed by such influential observers as Jane Jacobs, Herbert Gans, Suzanne Keller, and Gerald Suttles.[3] In many ways they are responsible for taking the inner-city neighborhood out of its

1. Some of the best historical overviews of neighborhood movements of this century include Sidney Dillick, *Community Organization for Neighborhood Development—Past and Present* (William Morrow, 1953); Howard W. Hallman, "The Neighborhood as an Organizational Unit: A Historical Perspective," in George Frederickson, ed., *Neighborhood Control in the 1970s: Politics, Administration, and Citizen Participation* (New York: Chandler, 1973), pp. 5–16; and Robert Fisher, *Let the People Decide: Neighborhood Organizing in America* (Boston: Twayne, 1984).

2. See, for example, Fisher, *Let the People Decide*, pp. 126–52.

3. Jane Jacobs, *The Death and Life of Great American Cities* (Random House, 1961); Herbert J. Gans, *The Urban Villagers: Group and Class in the Life of Italian-Americans* (New York: Free Press of Glencoe, 1962); Suzanne Keller, *The Urban Neighborhood: A Sociological Perspective* (Random House, 1968); and Gerald Suttles, *The Social Construction of Communities* (University of Chicago Press, 1972).

"ghetto" status and infusing it with at least the potential of becoming the city's vibrant core. Later writers, including Albert Hunter, Roger Ahlbrandt, Irwin Altman, and Abraham Wandersman, have described the broader social and psychological contexts in which these communities function.[4] But others have questioned the very existence of the neighborhoods as true social organisms in modern mobile society and doubted that they could ever fulfill the definition of a political entity.[5] These critics imply that neighborhood associations can be no more than, in David Easton's terms, "parapolitical systems," along with such institutions as churches, universities, and other nonprofit organizations.[6]

At the opposite end of the spectrum are those who have argued that the neighborhoods, not the cities, are the natural political entities. Milton Kotler, one of the leading proponents of this point of view, advocates full-scale neighborhood governance to enable neighborhoods to regain the political and economic vitality that the "downtown interests" have taken away from them over the past several decades.[7] In a similar vein, David Morris and Karl Hess paint a vivid picture of a future in which Americans' quality of life could be vastly increased through social, political, and economic decentralization of activities down to a more human scale.[8] A range of other authors have made strong claims for the importance of neighborhood councils, decentralization, and community control.[9]

4. Albert Hunter, "The Urban Neighborhood: Its Analytical and Social Contexts," *Urban Affairs Quarterly*, vol. 14 (March 1979), pp. 267, 288; Roger S. Ahlbrandt, Jr., *Neighborhoods, People, and Community* (New York: Plenum, 1984); and Irwin Altman and Abraham Wandersman, eds., *Neighborhood and Community Environments* (New York: Plenum, 1987).

5. An excellent examination of the role of the neighborhood as a polity, its critics, and its supporters, is given in Matthew A. Crenson, *Neighborhood Politics* (Harvard University Press, 1983), pp. 8–20.

6. David Easton, *A Framework for Political Analysis* (Prentice-Hall, 1965), especially pp. 50–54.

7. Milton Kotler, *Neighborhood Government: The Local Foundations of Political Life* (Indianapolis: Bobbs-Merrill, 1969).

8. David Morris and Karl Hess, *Neighborhood Power: The New Localism* (Beacon Press, 1975).

9. Three very different views, for example, are provided by Alan A. Altshuler, *Community Control: The Black Demand for Participation in Large American Cities* (New York: Pegasus, 1970); Howard Hallman, *The Organization and Operation of Neighborhood Councils, A Practical Guide* (Praeger, 1977); and Burt W. Griffin, *Cities Within a City: On Changing Cleveland's Government* (Cleveland State University, College of Urban Affairs, 1981).

While this debate continues, the neighborhood clearly is more than just another "parapolitical" organization. As Matthew Crenson points out:

> Like any parapolitical system, the neighborhood can sometimes be a direct participant in the political process, and it performs internal functions that seem to imitate those of the political system itself. Unlike other groups, however, it is set up on the same terms as the political system itself. Membership comes as an adjunct to geographic location. . . . The necessary qualifications for being a neighbor are about as indiscriminate and inclusive as the requirements for citizenship. . . . This inclusive and near-compulsory character differentiates the neighborhood from virtually all other private groups in the society. In fact, the central point is that the residents of a neighborhood do not constitute a private group at all, but a miniature "public"—more like citizens than like members of a private association.[10]

These conclusions are buttressed by extensive practice and policy that give neighborhoods and their organizations special status, particularly in planning, development, and community organizing. Since at least the urban renewal days of the 1950s, neighborhood groups of various types, from blue ribbon commissions appointed by the mayor to neighborhood leaders elected block by block, have been seen as "representatives" of the neighborhood interest in the planning process. A voluminous literature has grown up that describes how effective neighborhood-based planning can be carried out.[11] Even more extensive is the literature on neighborhood development practice and theory.[12] We have noted earlier

10. Crenson, *Neighborhood Politics*, pp. 16–17.

11. See for example, Rick Cohen, "Neighborhoods, Planning, and Political Capacity," *Urban Affairs Quarterly*, vol. 14 (March 1979), pp. 337–62; Phillip L. Clay and Robert M. Hollister, eds., *Neighborhood Policy and Planning* (Lexington, Mass.: D.C. Heath, 1983); William M. Rohe and Lauren B. Gates, *Planning with Neighborhoods* (University of North Carolina Press, 1985); and an excellent overview of the field by Barry Checkoway, "Neighborhood Planning Organizations: Perspectives and Choices," *Journal of Applied Behavioral Science*, vol. 21, no. 4 (1985), pp. 471–86.

12. The wide range of this literature is indicated by such works as James V. Cunningham, *The Resurgent Neighborhood* (Notre Dame, Ind.: Fides Press, 1965); Roger S. Ahlbrandt, Jr., and P.C. Brophy, *Neighborhood Revitalization: Theory and Practice* (Lexington, Mass.: Lexington Books, 1975); Philip L. Clay, *Neighborhood Renewal: Middle Class Resettlement and Incumbent Upgrading in American Neighborhoods* (Lexington, Mass.: Lexington Books, 1979); Anthony Downs, *Neighborhoods and Urban Development* (Brookings, 1981); Ed Marciniak, *Reversing Urban Decline* (Washington: National Center

that in development issues neighborhoods often reign supreme. They do so, in part, because neighborhood associations are often seen as the legitimate bearer of neighborhood interests on questions that affect the direct physical status of the neighborhood. Finally, community organizing, at least since Saul Alinsky's initial work in the 1940s, has been seen by those involved as a means of political empowerment.[13] The entire nature of the organizing process is expressed in terms of "the interests of the community" and its ability to allow those interests to be served.

In the five cities we studied, neighborhoods are taken seriously. They embody many of the attributes that students of communities and neighborhoods seem to value most. Central to these communities is the role the neighborhood associations play in facilitating face-to-face interaction among residents. In some cases citywide participation mechanisms—including several budget committees and citywide advisory boards—are an important component of the participation system as well, but they would be isolated, rather meaningless tokens of participation without the neighborhood organizations and support networks that continuously renew the participation process.

In each city, the part of the system closest to citizens, the neighborhood associations themselves, take on any and all issues that residents bring before them. They are intrinsically multi-issue groups. This does not mean that they are not focused on one or two particular issues at any time—reducing noise from a local racetrack, siting a landfill nearby, dealing with new housing developments, launching a crime prevention task force, recycling, or whatever the group decides are its current priorities. Some of these are developed very informally at monthly meetings, and others come out of a formal survey process of residents that groups

for Urban Ethnic Affairs, 1981); Jeffrey R. Henig, *Neighborhood Mobilization: Redevelopment and Response* (Rutgers University Press, 1982); and Neil S. Mayer, *Neighborhood Organizations and Community Development: Making Revitalization Work* (Washington: Urban Institute Press, 1984).

13. A few samples of the literature that ties community organizing and governance questions includes Janice E. Perlman, "Grassrooting the System," *Social Policy*, vol. 7 (September–October 1976), pp. 4–20; Joan E. Lancourt, *Confront or Concede: The Alinsky Citizen-Action Organizations* (Lexington, Mass.: Lexington Books, 1979); Harry C. Boyte, *The Backyard Revolution: Understanding the New Citizen Movement* (Temple University Press, 1980); Rachell B. Warren and Donald I. Warren, *Neighborhood Organizers Handbook* (University of Notre Dame Press, 1977); Robert Cassidy, *Livable Cities: A Grassroots Guide to Rebuilding Urban America* (Holt, Rinehart, and Winston, 1980); and James V. Cunningham and Milton Kotler, *Building Neighborhood Organizations* (University of Notre Dame Press, 1983).

occasionally undertake. Many of the issues grow out of individual resident concerns, others are responses to city initiatives, and still others are reactions to a dramatic event such as discovery of toxic materials in the water supply or a proposal for a multiblock shopping center.

Each city also has a mechanism—or more often several mechanisms—to bring before city hall the concerns of residents that develop in these meetings. The first stage of this is different in each city: it is represented by the District Coalition Boards and staff in Portland; the Priority Boards in Dayton; the citywide COPS organization in San Antonio; and the community representatives, Citizens Advisory Board, and community resource officers in Birmingham. Only in St. Paul does no intermediate structure of this kind exist; the individual staff of the District Councils work directly with individual agencies and city councillors, with the exception of a single citizen participation coordinator who works out of an office in the Planning and Economic Development Department. St. Paul does have, however, its Capital Improvement Budget Committee (CIB), the most powerful neighborhood-based body we found in any city.

Except in St. Paul, where the District Council staff perform the function, this coalition level provides the administrative and technical support and staff to help neighborhoods formulate, communicate, and implement solutions to the neighborhood problems they have identified. At this level the interests of each neighborhood are aggregated—by formal neighborhood representatives in Portland, Birmingham, and San Antonio, and by Priority Board members elected largely by precinct in Dayton. The CIB representatives of St. Paul's District Councils, in a similar manner, explicitly weigh neighborhood needs and priorities within the context of capital expenditures.

From this intermediate point, a number of direct routes to policymakers and the policymaking process are taken. The neighborhood needs process in Portland and Dayton is one such link. The Administrative Council in Dayton is another. Meetings between coalition staff and agency administrators and city councillors are a routine part of the systems' operations. St. Paul's CIB is the initiator of all capital budget proposals in each biannual cycle, its proposals going directly to the mayor and city council for ratification. Similar committees, with somewhat less clout and somewhat more agency representation, exist on a wide range of policy issues in all the cities. Some are ongoing, like Portland's Budget Advisory Committees, while others are focused on special issues, like St. Paul's task force on residential housing facilities or Dayton's water pollution control committee.

The success of these participatory models depends on three critical features: the strength of the links between citizens and neighborhood associations; the strength of the links between those associations and city policymakers; and the balance in the strengths of the associations that represent citizens of differing ethnic, social, and economic characteristics.

In order for the participatory model to work, both links must be open and effective. Concerning the first link, we need to ask, How representative and responsive are the neighborhood groups to the people in their neighborhoods? The central question about the second link becomes, How effective are the groups in making their own case before city hall? Two questions emerge about the balance in the associations' strength. Do all neighborhoods have an equal voice at city hall? And do the neighborhoods skew policy decisions toward parochial concerns rather than matters facing the city as a whole? In the remainder of this chapter, we will take up each of these questions in turn.

Neighborhood Accountability

As we have seen in earlier chapters, the neighborhood associations in the five core cities of our study do a great deal to keep the city and its participation system honest. They form a watchdog network that stretches across the city, complete with staff and resources to put teeth into that role. But who keeps the neighborhood organizations honest? What ensures that a local group's leaders will not become an exclusive, self-interested clique? Even if these leaders remain public-spirited, what evidence do we have that they remain responsive to neighborhood residents? Given such independence and power, will not many groups go off with their own agenda that is wildly unrepresentative of the neighborhood as a whole?

The evaluation of these questions is not well developed in the literature of neighborhood organizing. Douglas Yates, in *Neighborhood Democracy*, comes closest in measuring what many other observers either assume or ignore—how such neighborhood-based efforts actually perform on specific criteria of democratic practice.[14] His use of a rating scale of "representation and internal democracy," for example, enables a direct comparison of neighborhood effectiveness on eleven participatory features from "democratic selection" and "democratic procedures" to "ac-

14. Douglas Yates, *Neighborhood Democracy: The Politics and Impacts of Decentralization* (Lexington, Mass.: Lexington Books, 1973). His rating scale for representation and internal democracy is summarized on p. 82.

countability," "representation of new interests," and "participation of leaders." While the detailed definitions of each measure are open to debate, his ability to construct a series of coherent measures that can be applied to the disparate structures and processes of his seven cases enhances our understanding of the practical development of neighborhood participation.

Nor is the importance of such issues lost on community leaders in the core cities of our study. Elected officials, administrators, and neighborhood leaders alike were acutely aware that the issues of representativeness and responsiveness apply as much to the neighborhood associations as to any other public body. In general, they recognized and accepted the roles for neighborhood associations implied by these questions, as well as the limitations and responsibilities inherent in them.

The siting of the Fred Meyer superstore complex in Portland (discussed in chapter 6) illustrates the sensitivity of community leaders to these issues. In spite of extensive door-to-door efforts by at least two neighborhood associations, reaching nearly every household in their areas, the shopping center chain repeatedly charged that the organizations were not representative of the people who lived in their neighborhoods. They backed up this charge with their own opinion poll (without releasing details of the survey methodology used), which they claim showed a majority of residents supporting the development. In part by making this claim of unrepresentativeness stick (and in part because of the previous industrial nature of the site, the economic value seen for the whole city, and a compromise on landscaping and traffic patterns with neighborhood demands), the shopping center developers won their case. The issue was a stimulus for an examination of neighborhood responsiveness throughout the city, and soon thereafter agreement was reached between the city and the neighborhood associations on a set of detailed guidelines for every association. The accord ensures that all residents have a realistic opportunity to participate and have their opinions registered within the neighborhood groups.

A similar dynamic in each of the five cities has continuously promoted responsiveness. It is a process of mutual self-interest for the city and the neighborhood groups. Because the neighborhood groups exist in every part of the city, with direct staff support for their work, they can and do keep a close eye on everything the city proposes. They force a certain degree of responsiveness from public officials. In return, the city insists that the neighborhood groups be in constant communication with all residents in their communities. The cities pay for newsletters going out to every household. They ensure regular, open elections of neighborhood leaders—either at meetings, in mail ballots, or even at the polls on a special election day. Block clubs are formed, leaflets are handed out, and organizers are sent around door to door to alert residents to issues that will affect them. This process of outreach, far more extensive and continuous than anything in traditional politics beyond the election campaign itself, is demanded as a condition for legitimacy.

If left to the city alone or independent citizen organizations alone, such an outreach effort would often fall by the wayside when funds get low or time runs short. In these cities, however, the political interests of both the city and the neighborhood groups work to ensure the continuation of an extensive effort. For the city, the outreach is evidence that the neighborhood groups are keeping in touch with the entire community and not alienating a large bloc of voters. For the associations, it is the basis for their continued legitimacy as a voice for all residents of their neighborhood.

Does all this effort produce results? Two questions from our public opinion surveys provide direct evidence of the success of the attempts to promote neighborhood openness and responsiveness. The first was part of a series of questions to each respondent about his or her reactions to a major neighborhood problem. We asked, "Let's say that your local neighborhood association was going to address this issue at its next meeting. Do you think you would be offered the opportunity to become involved in the neighborhood association process?" Of those who answered the question, 62.9 percent said yes, they would be offered the opportunity to participate. A second question directly asked if there were "any group or organization that represents your community's interests better than the neighborhood association." A total of 88.5 percent of our respondents who had an answer said no, there was no more representative organization.

These results clearly show that the neighborhood organizations are widely trusted in the community. The fact that so few people feel that some other organization represents their views more effectively demonstrates the vital niche the neighborhood associations fill within the larger political framework. Fewer respondents, but still a solid majority, are secure in their opportunity to participate in these associations. These responses are particularly impressive when compared with our respondents' perceptions of how higher-level bodies would respond to their needs. For example, only 40 percent felt that city officials, when approached about a "major neighborhood problem you were having,"

TABLE 7-1. Effect of SES on Perceptions of Neighborhood
Association Openness and Representativeness

Percent agreeing with question

Question	Respondent's socioeconomic status				N	Chi square
	All	Low	Middle	High		
Neighborhood association would offer me opportunity for involvement in major issues	62.9	53.9	66.3	74.6	6,213	176.4**
No other group represents my community's interests better than the neighborhood association	88.5	89.4	88.7	86.7	4,468	4.7

**Significant at the 0.01 level.

would "give your point of view serious attention." As will be seen in chapter 10, this pattern is repeated when comparing city officials with the still lower levels of trust citizens give to federal officials.

But does this level of trust hold up for all segments of the population? The next three tables provide some answers. First, it is clear that income and education, which we have found to be strong factors in participation of all kinds, are important here as well, although they are not dominant. As table 7-1 indicates, a clear majority of respondents, regardless of their SES category, felt that the neighborhood associations were both open and representative. While the perception of neighborhood representativeness varied less than 3 percent among SES categories, however, the variation in perception of openness was much greater. Only 53.9 percent of the low-SES respondents felt they would be offered the opportunity to participate, while 74.6 percent of high-SES respondents expressed this belief.

We have noted before, however, that low-SES people are much less inclined than high-SES people to participate in political activities of any kind. Perhaps the perception of openness of the neighborhood groups could be explained largely as a consequence of this disinclination to participate. The data in table 7-2 demonstrate that this is not the complete explanation, however. There is indeed a very strong relationship between level of activity, as expressed by the respondent's position on our index of community participation, and perception of neighborhood openness. The more active a person is, the more likely he or she will feel that the neighborhood process is open. This relationship is very significant, statistically, at all SES levels. More than 20 percentage points separate the

TABLE 7-2. Effect of Level of Community Activity
on Perceptions of Neighborhood Association Openness
and Responsiveness

Percent agreeing with question

Question and SES status	Respondent's position on ICP scale[a]						N	Chi square
	0	1	2	3	4	5		
Neighborhood association would offer me opportunity for involvement in major issue								
Low SES	46.0	54.0	60.5	69.9	72.6	70.7	2,545	75.7**
Middle SES	58.1	64.0	67.4	76.7	79.2	78.3	2,366	52.3**
High SES	65.2	73.8	70.2	80.1	81.0	86.1	1,296	30.7**
No other group represents my community's interests better than neighborhood association								
Low SES	93.6	86.6	88.0	85.7	87.0	76.2	1,729	31.1**
Middle SES	95.9	88.3	86.6	86.8	80.9	81.9	1,733	38.9**
High SES	92.4	88.9	86.7	84.7	79.8	84.8	1,001	9.7

**Significant at the 0.01 level.
a. Scale ranges from least active to most active in ascending numerical order.

highly active from the inactive in each case. Nevertheless, in spite of this exceptionally strong relationship, SES continues to be a significant factor above and beyond levels of activity. Even at the highest levels of activity, low-SES people are still much less likely to perceive the neighborhood system as open to them. From 8 to nearly 20 percentage points separate high- and low-SES respondents in every activity category.

These figures suggest both success and failure in the neighborhood-based participation system. On the one hand, as people become more aware and involved in community concerns, they increasingly see the opportunities available in the system. Involvement does not induce frustration and cynicism (a point that will become particularly clear in the analysis of chapter 8). On the other hand, the system fails to overcome the "politics as usual" bias against low-SES people—even those low-SES citizens who are very active in other ways often feel they will be excluded from the decisionmaking process.

Not all organizational involvement is the same, however. The index of community participation incorporates a wide range of citizen group activity. It does not distinguish among the many types of organizations in which an individual may be active. The results in table 7-3 demonstrate that the kind of organizational involvement in which a citizen is engaged has a very significant effect on his or her perception of neighborhood openness. Not surprisingly, those who are most active in neighborhood

TABLE 7-3. Effect of Type of Organizational Activity
on Perceptions of Neighborhood Association Openness
and Responsiveness

Percent agreeing with question

Question and SES status	Type of organization in which respondent is active					N	Chi square
	None	Service or social group	Crime watch	Issue group	Neigh- borhood group		
Neighborhood association would offer me opportunity for involvement in major issue							
Low SES	49.9	54.0	60.8	63.0	80.6	2,541	61.3**
Middle SES	61.7	63.8	71.3	72.7	84.4	2,362	53.2**
High SES	67.7	73.1	74.7	78.2	86.4	1,294	32.1**
No other group represents my community's interests better than neighborhood association							
Low SES	92.2	81.3	89.7	82.5	84.8	1,726	34.5**
Middle SES	93.1	84.1	86.4	83.5	84.0	1,731	34.3**
High SES	91.2	85.5	85.5	83.0	84.3	999	9.9*

**Significant at the 0.01 level.
*Significant at the 0.05 level.

groups are the most likely to see them as open. This confirms our observation that close association with the neighborhood groups does not breed cynicism about the process. Of still greater consequence, perhaps, is that issue-group participants are second only to neighborhood participants in perceiving the neighborhood process as open to them. That even those most likely to be competitors with the neighborhoods in seeking influence at city hall do not feel excluded from the neighborhood process is a strong endorsement of the legitimacy achieved by the neighborhood associations. While SES differences persist, the range of difference between high- and low-SES respondents is much lower for neighborhood group participants than for any other category—less than 6 percent, compared with as much as 18 percent for nonparticipants. Consequently, for low-SES people active in the neighborhood process, the yawning gap in perception of its openness is finally overcome.

Table 7-3 also shows the effect of community activity on the perception of the neighborhood associations as representative. In contrast to the perception of openness, activity has a relatively mild impact. Here, SES has virtually no effect at any level or kind of activity. Much of the variation with activity, which is statistically significant at all but high SES, occurs between those who are active in some fashion and those who do not participate at all in community activity. While most of the results remain at the 80 percent level or higher, the inactive respondents are somewhat *more likely* to express belief in the representativeness of the neighborhood associations than those who are active. Apparently an increased awareness of community concerns brings with it a recognition that the neighborhood associations are not the only game in town: other routes to representation of specific interests are also available and occasionally express community interests as well as or better than do the neighborhood groups.

We conclude, therefore, that the neighborhood associations in these cities do a remarkably good job of remaining open to all residents and stimulating a sense of responsiveness to them. In fact, they seem to do much better than the city governments themselves. The first link in our discussion of participatory democracy—between citizens and the neighborhood groups that serve them—is strong indeed. While only a small portion of the community devotes the day-to-day time and energy needed to participate actively in community politics, the opportunity is broadly available and apparently is used whenever the need arises.

Neighborhood Effectiveness

Although there are some ambiguities in the assessment of neighborhood openness, the strength of the neighborhoods in influencing policy is fairly clear-cut. We were told repeatedly by administrators and neighborhood participants alike that the neighborhoods generally got what they wanted on many issues affecting only their own local area. This was especially true on land use and local development issues but tended to be less true on broader issues such as protection of water quality or airport noise abatement and on huge development projects with major economic impact for the whole city. One city administrator describes a typical planning process carried out in Dayton.

> We have 16 planning districts in my area. We do a random sampling in each of these planning districts . . . about 15 households per planning district. The households are requested to give their "input." We also send that same survey and request input from all the neighborhood associations, block clubs, neighborhood watch groups . . . around 50 neighborhood associations . . . and 116 watch groups. . . . We have a series of meetings that are publicized . . . where residents are invited in to meet with me and the budget needs assessment com-

mittee. This series of meetings occurs every May. After the needs assessment is done, it's sent to the neighborhood associations for review. Then it goes to the Priority Board in June, and to the Superintendent by mid-July.

And a city councillor in Birmingham adds a sense of the value inherent in the strength of the neighborhoods.

They [the neighborhood associations] leave a councillor in a position of having a clearer picture of issues prior to making a decision. . . . You're much more likely to make the right kind of decision when you have this kind of involvement.

A citizens' group leader in Portland, however, cautions,

Control is the key word. [The neighborhood associations] do not have control. They do have early notification for early involvement and a major say. . . . If it is a development that is not in context with the Comprehensive Plan, [the hearing officer] will say "no." But when it's appealed at the Council, other politics come into it. The frustration comes from doing the homework, going through the hearings office process, testifying, working with the Planning Bureau staff, winning, and then having the developer and their lawyers appeal. . . . It's a long process, and we are all volunteers.

In fact, between 83 percent and 92 percent of the administrators, city councillors, and citizen group leaders we interviewed felt the neighborhood associations were effective. The lowest agreement level, 83 percent, came from the those who might be seen as the closest competitors to the neighborhoods, the citizen groups. While citizen group observers concur in the effectiveness of neighborhood groups, they do not find the city closed to themselves. Just over 80 percent of the group leaders interviewed also told us that their group had "real influence on the city." An important characteristic of a healthy participation system is that it not only develops a clearly defined mechanism—such as the neighborhood associations—to gain impact, but it also continues to provide the opportunity for input from independently organized sources. The evidence here, from the independent citizen groups themselves, is that these participation systems meet these criteria well.

TABLE 7-4. Effect of Level of Community Activity on Perceptions of Neighborhood Association Effectiveness

Percent agreeing with question

Question and SES status	Respondent's position on ICP scale[a]						N	Chi square
	0	1	2	3	4	5		
Neighborhood association does a good job of representing community								
Low SES	53.3	63.5	51.8	57.3	68.5	75.0	775	14.0*
Middle SES	63.6	56.4	58.1	63.1	64.3	60.2	895	3.4
High SES	64.7	60.9	67.5	67.6	64.0	69.3	651	2.1

*Significant at the 0.05 level.
a. Scale ranges from least active to most active in ascending numerical order.

Our broader telephone poll of citizens throughout each city confirms the results of the in-person interviews with elites. We asked all those familiar with the system of neighborhood associations in the city to rate the job they do in "letting the city government know what the needs of their neighborhoods are"— a good job, fair, or poor. Sixty-one percent of these respondents rated the neighborhoods as doing a "good" job, remarkably high for a three-category response set. The evaluation did vary with the SES of the respondent, ranging from a low of 57.7 percent for low-SES respondents to a high of 66.2 percent for high-SES respondents (significant at the 0.01 level). This 9 percent difference, however, is much less than the 21 percent difference in response to the neighborhood openness question discussed earlier.

Further analysis of this response bears out the relatively uniform character of the high evaluation of neighborhood impact. As the data in tables 7-4 and 7-5 indicate, there is relatively little variation in the high evaluation levels with either level of community activity or with type of group in which the respondent is active. For high and moderate SES, no pattern of any kind emerges. For low-SES respondents, however, a significant increase in perception of neighborhood responsiveness does emerge for those at the high end of the community activity scale—22 percentage points above the nonparticipants at the other end of the scale. We also see that the variation with SES, within each activity category, is not nearly as strong or consistent as we found for neighborhood openness. These results are encouraging for the ability of the participation system to overcome the alienation that low-SES people tend to feel about the political system. While they still feel somewhat excluded, as we saw earlier, and they still participate at lower rates than others in the community, those who do participate gain an increased recognition of neighborhood groups' ability to represent their interests.

TABLE 7-5. Effect of Type of Organizational Activity
on Perceptions of Neighborhood Association Effectiveness

Percent agreeing with question

Question and SES status	Type of organization in which respondent is active					N	Chi square
	None	Service or social group	Crime watch	Issue group	Neigh-borhood group		
Neighborhood association does a good job of representing community							
Low SES	54.6	61.1	52.6	56.0	71.1	774	10.0*
Middle SES	59.2	58.8	56.5	54.7	68.1	895	6.4
High SES	61.8	69.9	63.3	66.0	68.4	650	2.7

*Significant at the 0.05 level.

Overall, therefore, the second link in the participatory framework—between the neighborhood associations and city hall—is reasonably strong, but not as unshakable as the first link between citizens and the associations. While the neighborhoods are seen as effective in general, they have real clout only in certain areas and very limited clout in others. In addition, the analysis here suggests that if community leaders focus on ways to draw more low-SES people into the system, an increased sense of political responsiveness will follow. Contrary to the argument of political theorists that increased participation will only draw more of the discontented and intolerant into the system, thereby destabilizing it, we find the impact of increased participation to be stabilizing. We will provide substantially more evidence of this kind in chapters 8 and 9.

Rampant Parochialism or Policy Balance?

Even if the two links of our participatory framework were in perfect condition—if individual neighborhood groups were perfect mirrors of their constituents and at the same time extremely effective in influencing city hall—the ideals of strong democracy might still be far from realization. Neighborhood participation can fail in at least two other important ways. First, some neighborhoods may be substantially more effective than others in getting their views across, eclipsing the efforts of other sections of the city with fewer or poorer political connections. This possibility is seriously considered by several researchers who have analyzed questions

TABLE 7-6. Perceptions of Equal Treatment of Groups
or Neighborhoods by the City

Percent responding yes

Question	Administrators	Citizen groups	City councillors	Total
Does any group or neighborhood get treated better?	41.2	61.5	50.0	51.7
Does any group or neighborhood get treated worse?	24.2	51.6	52.4	40.7
N	163	189	43	395

of decentralization of service delivery.[15] Second, the channeling of participation through neighborhood-based organizations may itself narrow the focus of the issues considered, producing the ironic result that the stronger the participation system becomes, the more parochial are the policy outcomes. If the participation system veers off in either direction, neighborhood associations may, instead of producing results in the best interests of all members of the community, actually become obstacles that impede public officials elected by the whole community with those interests in mind.

We attempted to assess the balance between neighborhoods within the five cities in several ways. First, we talked to neighborhood leaders from all sections of the cities, in individual interviews and in focus groups. Second, we specifically asked all of those with whom we met, from city councillors to citizen group organizers, whether they felt that any people, groups, or neighborhoods "always seem to get treated better" or "always seem to get treated worse" than everyone else by the city government. Finally, we asked the identical pair of questions of all respondents in our public opinion surveys. In each case, if the respondent did feel that some group was consistently treated better or worse, we recorded which group that was.

A summary of results from our in-person interviews is shown in table 7-6. Not surprisingly, administrators were the most likely to assert that the city treated all neighborhoods and groups fairly. Yet the overall results are split, with more than half the respondents feeling that some

15. See, for example, Robert Yin and Douglas Yates, *Street Level Governments: Assessing Decentralization and Urban Services* (Lexington, Mass.: Lexington Books, 1975); and Richard Rich, "Equity and Institutional Design in Urban Service Delivery," *Urban Affairs Quarterly*, vol. 12, no. 3 (1977), pp. 383–410.

group is consistently treated better and somewhat less than half feeling that some group is consistently treated worse than the rest of the city. Most frequently characterized as treated better, especially from the administrators' viewpoint, were "well-organized neighborhoods." As a Portland administrator noted,

> Those that are better organized [win]. This has nothing to do with social, racial, ethnic, or geographical status, but with who knows how to play the game. Some people do a better job in making a case, lining up business or political support. The overall structure is pretty well balanced because the neighborhoods understand this and incorporate it into their process.

This success criterion has a self-help character as well, as described by a Dayton official.

> We've determined that our most successful projects in the neighborhoods are those the neighborhood people take on themselves. The more organized the neighborhood, the more enthusiastic [its residents] . . . [and] the more likely a project managed by that kind of group is going to succeed. . . . Projects that are city hall driven tend not to be very successful.

In San Antonio, the exceptional organizational skills of COPS were repeatedly mentioned as the reason for that group's unusual influence on issues in the city. In each city, effective community organization was seen as a major means of achieving results for one's neighborhood, and some neighborhoods were seen as more effectively organized than others. This is true even in those cities where a conscious attempt is made to ensure that a neighborhood organization at least exists in every neighborhood.

More than organization, however, the answers to the "always treated better" question most often focused on either economic clout or majority-group status—naming "wealthy areas," "yuppies," "the downtown area," "business interests," or "whites." Conversely, the "always treated worse" answers most often focused on low status and minority areas— "the poor," "elderly people," "blacks," "low-income neighborhoods," or specific areas of the city where large numbers of the poor or minorities reside. Respondents were as likely to name the population group involved

TABLE 7-7. Effect of SES on Perceptions of Equal Treatment of Groups or Neighborhoods by the City

Percent agreeing with question

Question	Socioeconomic status				N	Chi square
	All	Low	Middle	High		
No group or neighborhood gets treated better by the city	62.0	63.6	59.4	63.6	5,550	9.9**
No group or neighborhood gets treated worse by the city	62.6	64.8	60.5	62.3	5,570	8.6*

**Significant at the 0.01 level.
*Significant at the 0.05 level.

as they were to name a specific neighborhood or area of the city where that group is most concentrated.

The citizenry was somewhat less pessimistic than these community leaders. Fewer than 38 percent of the respondents in our population survey felt that some group or neighborhood was consistently treated better or worse than everybody else. As with our community leader interviews, a majority of those who did feel that some group was treated better or worse classified them on the basis of economic status or race. More often than in the leader interviews, the reference was to population groups ("wealthy people") rather than to specific high-status neighborhoods or areas of the city. In addition to high-income people, a significant number of respondents, about 12 percent, felt that "welfare recipients" or "minorities" were treated *better* than everyone else by the city. This attitude is not unexpected in light of the strong antiwelfare currents generated in the 1980s. The remainder of the responses were scattered over a wide range of groups. A common response outside the economic and racial categories was government employees and politicians; nearly 10 percent of our respondents felt that these groups consistently received special treatment from the city.

The effects of respondents' SES status and participation activity on their perception of an imbalanced treatment of the city's population are shown in tables 7-7 and 7-8. The data in table 7-7 show that a significant difference between respondents of different SES status does occur, although to a much smaller degree than the perception of neighborhood openness and effectiveness that we examined earlier. More surprisingly, it is the middle-SES respondent, not the lower SES respondent, who is most likely to feel that others are treated better. This seems to be yet another reflection of the middle-class anger that politicians have tried to

TABLE 7-8. Effect of Level of Community Activity on Perceptions of Equal Treatment of Groups or Neighborhoods by the City

Percent agreeing with question

Question and SES status	Respondent's position on ICP scale[a]						N	Chi square
	0	1	2	3	4	5		
No group or neighborhood gets treated better by the city								
Low SES	71.9	60.0	55.9	53.3	57.7	55.6	2,193	52.7**
Middle SES	68.3	58.8	55.2	53.9	55.8	55.4	2,160	27.5**
High SES	78.7	64.4	59.7	59.3	64.6	54.7	1,191	28.8**
No group or neighborhood gets treated worse by the city								
Low SES	71.3	62.1	58.8	60.5	55.4	52.8	2,214	35.1**
Middle SES	70.6	60.3	56.1	53.0	60.0	50.7	2,158	40.0**
High SES	77.4	67.4	57.5	57.6	58.8	52.6	1,193	33.4**

**Significant at the 0.01 level.
a. Scale ranges from least active to most active in ascending numerical order.

respond to in recent years. Moreover, we find that, unlike our earlier results, the perception of unequal treatment is not overcome by increased community activity (table 7-8). In fact, the opposite is the case. A highly significant relationship exists between increased community activity and decreased perception of equal treatment for all. While a majority in all activity categories feel that treatment is equal, that majority varies widely. For example, for high-SES respondents to the "always treated worse" question, the perception of equal treatment ranges from 77.4 percent for the least active to 52.6 percent for the most active.

This large, consistent difference in perception of equal treatment might lead one to conclude that increased community activity creates frustrated and embittered participants. All of our other data, however, including that presented in the two previous sections of this chapter, clearly indicate that this is not true—participants are more, not less, likely to feel personally efficacious and to see the neighborhood groups as being effective. In addition, the data in table 7-9, while confirming that nonparticipants have the highest perception of equal treatment, also suggest that neighborhood group participation is more successful in overcoming this tendency than are other issue-oriented groups. This is particularly true for low- and middle-SES respondents.

The combined results suggest that an alternative to the disenchantment model describes the situation more accurately. Apparently, with increased activity, participants not only become more convinced of the effectiveness of their work and of those around them, they also become more aware

TABLE 7-9. Effect of Type of Organizational Activity on Perception of Equal Treatment of Groups or Neighborhoods by the City

Percent agreeing with question

Question and SES status		Type of organization in which respondent is active				N	Chi square
	None	Service or social group	Crime watch	Issue group	Neigh- borhood group		
No group or neighborhood gets treated better by the city							
Low SES	67.2	55.4	62.7	52.7	57.9	2,190	27.7**
Middle SES	63.2	56.1	56.1	51.1	59.5	2,157	16.7**
High SES	69.7	61.9	60.3	58.1	59.7	1.190	12.3*
No group or neighborhood gets treated worse by the city							
Low SES	67.6	60.3	60.8	56.6	58.3	2,212	16.0**
Middle SES	64.0	57.4	63.4	48.0	62.1	2,155	26.0**
High SES	70.6	57.9	62.7	57.0	55.4	1,192	22.3**

**Significant at the 0.01 level.
*Significant at the 0.05 level.

of the specifics of political action and the consequences of biases and pressures. Increased clarity about social injustices need not be alienating; under some conditions it may be energizing. On the whole our findings are encouraging for the strong participation communities: through participation, people become more aware of community problems at the same time that they are more motivated and empowered to do something about them. In the context of these participation systems, the result does not generally seem to be frustration, but rather a heightened community spirit and increased support for others attempting to deal with perceived problems.

Our question remains about the type of problems these neighborhood groups deal with and encourage the city to deal with. Does the neighborhood structure itself—and its very effectiveness—promote an unhealthy parochialism? Our answer, based particularly on our in-person elite interviews, is yes and no. Yes, the neighborhood organizations do promote the interests of their neighborhood as their top priority. But, no, that promotion of neighborhood interests is not unhealthy. Instead, our respondents tended to agree, it provides a healthy balance to a political system that might otherwise be excessively focused on development of the central business district.

A summary of the responses to our parochialism question is presented in table 7-10. The neighborhoods do, in fact, often focus on their own

TABLE 7-10. Elites' Views on Neighborhood Parochialism
Percent unless otherwise indicated

Question	Administrators	Citizen groups	City councillors	Total
Do you feel that the neighborhood associations tend to promote what is good for the people of [your city] as a whole, or do the associations tend to focus on neighborhood issues at the sacrifice of what is good for the city as a whole?				
What's good for city	37.2	41.7	47.6	40.4
What's good for neighborhood association	50.0	58.3	52.4	54.1
Neither	11.5	0.0	0.0	4.9
Both	1.3	0.0	0.0	0.6
N	78	84	21	183

neighborhood-based issues. A majority of all respondent categories—city councillors, administrators, and citizen group leaders—felt that a somewhat parochial attitude existed. But many went on to say either that this was the way it should be or that an overall balance resulted. For example, one Birmingham administrator observed,

> I do think it has made it [the decisionmaking process] better in that there has certainly been more attention paid than was paid before to the concerns of neighborhoods. And I don't think it has been at the expense of any easily identified citywide issue. I don't think we have paid any major price in terms of things that might have happened by being more sensitive to neighborhood concerns, and I think that has given people a greater sense of stake in their neighborhoods.

A St. Paul official saw more of a love-hate relationship:

> It's probably a wash in the final analysis. You get into the small groups or neighborhoods that make a lot of noise because they want something there, whether that really serves the city as a whole. My professional judgment would sometimes say no it does not. On the other hand, I could think of instances where the opposite is true, that from the standpoint of sitting here, it makes a lot of sense to [do] something close to the community's perspective. . . . So I suspect it balances out, on volatile issues.

And a still more skeptical viewpoint was expressed by a citizen group leader.

They [St. Paul's District Councils] tend to be parochial. . . For example, closing a playground, or a facility in their district. I don't know of any examples where they have done anything for the city as a whole. . . . I don't think there's any examples where the city suffered for one district either. . . . District Councils are involved with sewers in their areas, with paving the streets, and planting trees, and parks . . . and this is typical of all the neighborhood councils . . . though different problems exist in each respective district.

But a city councillor was unreservedly enthusiastic:

The citizen participation groups reflect what's good for the city. Some care more about crime, others environment, economic development, etc. They are varied in their strengths. Citizen participation doesn't lead to parochialism, it leads to action and excitement.

In addition to examining the potential for parochialism, we also explored with councillors the obvious potential for the highly organized neighborhood associations to steal their thunder on community issues. In fact, the neighborhoods do take on some of the constituent service and "local spokesperson" role that previously had been the sole province of the councillors. This concern has been examined by other researchers in a variety of contexts.[16] But when we asked, "Would you say there is a sensible division of labor between what the city council does and what the neighborhood associations do, or is there a lot of overlap and confusion?" a majority (59 percent) of the councillors saw no problems at all. In fact many of the councillors in these cities have come to their present position through the ranks of the neighborhood groups. Those who did express concerns sometimes characterized the groups as too strident or as forming too much of a buffer between them and their constituents. On the other hand, several councillors expressed gratification that the neighborhood groups were on the front lines of hot community issues, allowing the councillors to play a more reflective and solution-searching role than they otherwise would have been able to do.

16. See, for example, David J. O'Brien, *Neighborhood Organization and Interest-Group Processes* (Princeton University Press, 1975); and John Clayton Thomas, *Between Citizen and City: Neighborhood Organizations and Urban Politics in Cincinnati* (University Press of Kansas, 1986).

In other cities without strong participation systems, we have seen a much more suspicious attitude among elected officials. A typical response came from an elected official in an East Coast city with a history of "machine" politics: "But why would any politician want to give up this kind of political power to citizens?" The five cities we examined seem to have gone beyond those mutual suspicions. Overall, officials and neighborhood leaders tended to be strongly supportive of the distinct roles that each plays in the political process. In fact, the clear articulation of roles for the neighborhood groups and the sense of trust that has developed from the fulfillment of these roles have enabled the participation systems to maintain themselves through two decades of citizen action.

We are led to conclude that on our third test of the participatory model of neighborhood associations in these core cities—the test of balance of interests in the city—the communities pass with only moderate success. One important feature of the systems is that all groups in the city big enough or concentrated enough to "have a neighborhood of their own" at least have a seat at the table when the bargaining begins. They might not have this seat in cities without a neighborhood system. The cities clearly make a significant attempt to hear all of the interests that are at the table. But there remains some concern that "others are getting treated better than we are."

Although the problem of parochialism in these five cities is not severe, it should not be entirely dismissed. When one steps back and looks at the participation process as a whole, it is clear that the neighborhood-oriented roles that citizens take on are far more prevalent than the roles available to them in addressing citywide issues. These communities know well how to develop and maintain effective neighborhood organizations in every part of the city. Through strong support, information, and policymaking networks, citizens have real impact on a wide range of issues affecting their neighborhoods. Except for St. Paul's Capital Improvement Budget Committee, Portland's Budget Advisory Committees, and Birmingham's Citizen Advisory Board, few such effective structures exist at the citywide level. Under most conditions, it is rare for even the leadership of the neighborhood groups from all parts of these cities to meet together or decide issues jointly. The development of participation processes that can give citizens the kind of input on citywide issues that they now have on neighborhood issues is an important challenge each city has yet to meet.

Conclusion

We have found that the neighborhood-based participation systems in the five core cities of our study fulfill a model of democracy substantially different from the representative democracy that exists in most other American cities. These participation efforts clearly open up broad avenues for ongoing citizen involvement in policymaking, extending far beyond that which is possible through electoral politics. The neighborhood groups at the core of the system are generally recognized as responsive to their constituents and effective in influencing policy important to those constituents. Distortions caused by wealth and social status are not eliminated, but neither are they exacerbated. And the strengthening of neighborhood-oriented structures does introduce a new emphasis on parochial concerns, but in a way that tends to help balance overall policy results.

The pattern we have observed in these communities addresses a concern that many observers have expressed about the participatory model of democracy: can such a model be truly representative, or is it just another way for a special elite to gain unwarranted power? This concern is not limited to the domain of democratic theory. It is a common justification that some elected officials give for their reluctance to support initiatives for strong participatory democracy. "After all," concludes the rationalization, "who is in a better position to make decisions for the good of the whole city than those who are elected by the entire population?"

In at least one of the five cities we looked at, this question remains a front-burner issue. The neighborhood support staff in Portland, particularly in the wake of the shopping center battle discussed earlier in this chapter, have repeatedly had to defend the legitimacy and representativeness of the neighborhood groups. As one staff member noted: "We have never claimed that the neighborhood system is representative in the sense that elections are; what we have claimed, and tried to ensure, is that the system is responsive to all who choose to participate."

Responsiveness to those who choose to participate is a crucial element of the argument for strong democracy. Its proponents acknowledge that the increased demands on time and energy required by a participatory system mean that fewer people will participate. Weekly meetings take much more time than a biannual stint in the voting booth. But the payoff comes in responsiveness to those who do choose to participate—to the people who become community problem solvers and policy initiators. These people, while fewer in number than voters, are far greater in number than the handful of elected or appointed officials who would otherwise be considering and acting on community concerns. Providing ways for these participants to affect policy may in the long run turn community apathy into community consensus and action.

In the last three chapters we have examined the question of responsiveness in many different ways. Multiple tests were used because responsiveness is a multifaceted question. Different criteria must be used at each of the different stages in the policymaking process. Even at a single stage of the policymaking process no single test can measure all dimensions of the problem.

As difficult as it may be to assess, responsiveness is at the core of success for strong democracy. Even if those active in neighborhood associations do not greatly expand the number of people who participate or build communitywide consensus—difficult tasks under any circumstances—their efforts should result in enhancing the responsiveness of government to the neighborhoods. If neighborhood associations do not work to make governments consider and act on policy issues in ways that better correspond to rank-and-file preferences, they are of limited value to the community.

The data here show that the participation systems in five core cities meet this test. Residents regard their neighborhood associations as open to them and believe that these organizations are the best representatives of their interests in city politics. Clearly, the rank and file perceive that the neighborhood associations care what they think and will transmit those concerns to city officials. Participation rates for face-to-face activities in the cities are not directly linked to policymakers' concurrence scores with rank-and-file views on city issues, though there is some relationship on neighborhood issues. Participation rates are, however, related to responsiveness on actual policy outcomes.

Yet responsiveness is more than giving the people what they want, because issues can have many sides, with segments of the community having different goals. Ideally, cities should demonstrate policy responsiveness balance, with no group of people coming out winners or losers on every issue. Balance also implies that decisions incorporate sensible trade-offs between competing interests, such as the potential conflict between business development and quality of life in the neighborhoods. In the cities studied here, the need for business development is not disregarded by the neighborhood associations; economic growth is not incompatible with strong neighborhood groups working to preserve the quality of life in their communities. As noted earlier, the parochial concerns of neighborhoods seem to be balanced with the larger concerns of the community. Furthermore, policy responsiveness is not linked to the preferences of those with higher SES levels, and responsiveness does not favor neighborhood activists over rank-and-file residents.

The neighborhood associations are impressive in the way they promote policy responsiveness and balance. They deserve the high level of trust they have gained from the residents of their communities.

Part Three
Does Participation Empower?

CHAPTER 8

Three Deadly Sins:
Conflict, Alienation, and Delay

MANY SCHOLARS AND PRACTITIONERS in the art of government have argued that although broadening participation in policymaking is noble in intent, it is counterproductive in practice. Diluting representative democracy with a heavy dose of participatory democracy is said to lead to persistent conflict, eventual alienation from the political system, and unnecessary and expensive delays. These are serious charges and they are not without historical examples to lend them credence.

A Delicate Balance

The central dilemma is both an enduring question of political theory and a practical question of day-to-day politics: how much authority should be given to citizens to rule themselves and how much authority should be retained by government officials? The United States is impressive in the degree to which it allows for direct, popular control through electoral means such as party primaries and referenda and initiative provisions in many states. Outside of elections, though, little direct authority is left to the people. In the cities with citywide systems of citizen participation that we portray here, the balance is much different. Citizens, through the neighborhood associations, are given substantial authority to make decisions on some of the issues that affect their neighborhood, especially those concerning land use, crime prevention, and recreational facilities.

The popular rationale against participatory democracy is twofold: people do not want to take the time to rule themselves, and government would not work well if people participated widely. The first line of thinking is unpersuasive. Except for New England town meetings, there are few examples of people being given the opportunity to rule themselves. Thus it has not been proven that people do not want to take the time to engage in direct democracy—they simply have not had the chance.

But the second argument against citizen participation cannot be as easily dismissed as the first. Are average citizens really capable of governing themselves in a wise and conscientious manner? Furthermore, can the political system accommodate a high degree of citizen participation? In societies larger than the city-state, how much public involvement in government can be implemented before government becomes unworkable?

For many classical, normative theorists the answer was clear. Mosca and Schumpeter, for example, pointed to the inevitability of representative democracy. Elites exist in every society, and their guidance in the affairs of state is desirable. Elites must be controlled, but this can be accomplished through representative government. For others, like Rousseau, the good society could be built only through participatory government. Participatory democracy is more than just a means of determining the general will. Participation also enhances the intellect, ennobles the spirit, and nurtures a sense of community. John Stuart Mill, who argued for participation within the context of representative democracy, noted that "a political act, to be done only once in a few years, and for which nothing in the daily habits of the citizen has prepared him, leaves his intellect and his moral dispositions very much as it found them."[1]

As empirical data became available to modern political scientists, the debate continued but was grounded in findings demonstrating a very low level of participation by average citizens. Did this mean that American democracy had failed? To rationalize what they had discovered, Bernard Berelson and his colleagues argued that democracies survive by maintaining a delicate balance. The masses need to be able to control elites, but at the same time elites need the flexibility to solve problems without having to resort to demagoguery or debilitating partisanship. Thus citizens' inattention to politics was acceptable because a healthy political system had limited but meaningful participation by its citizenry.[2]

Berelson's early effort to rationalize Americans' lack of interest in politics was intriguing but ultimately unconvincing. A more sophisticated attempt to square the political apathy of citizens with the standards of a viable democracy was made by Robert Dahl. In examining interest group politics rather than voting behavior, Dahl concluded that the

1. Quoted in Carole Pateman, *Participation and Democratic Theory* (Cambridge University Press, 1970), p. 30.
2. Bernard R. Berelson, Paul F. Lazarsfeld, and William N. McPhee, *Voting: A Study of Opinion Formation in a Presidential Campaign* (University of Chicago Press, 1954).

American city was democratic, "warts and all."[3] Although typical citizens were uninterested in politics generally, they were concerned about those issues that affected them most directly. Their voices were heard at city hall through their interaction with interest group leaders and those leaders' interaction with policymakers. Dahl concluded that the entrepreneurial, coalition-building needs of politicians made the political system responsive to interest groups.

What Dahl saw as an acceptable balance between the needs of leadership and the realities of mass political behavior was seen by critics as elite domination. A generation of political scientists was consumed by the question of whether pluralism was democracy or illusion. Yet under the weight of the empirical evidence of low involvement in politics, few critics ventured forth to call for true participatory democracy. In an era of hard data, participatory democracy was a soft argument. Ironically, at the same time, outside of academe the calls for a more participatory political process reached a high water mark. Civil rights leaders and student radicals gained widespread attention for their call for "power to the people," and government tried to rekindle participation and community among inner-city residents with the "maximum feasible participation" requirement of the war on poverty.

As noted in chapter 2, the popular perception of public involvement in the community action program is that participatory democracy can be an invitation for the ignorant and irresponsible to muck around in government. Still, the push for a more participatory political system during the 1960s and 1970s was intuitively appealing. Broadening participation by bringing in those previously excluded and deepening participation by getting people more involved in policymaking were seen as a means of making government more responsive. Initially, the burden of proof fell on those who did not believe that a more participatory government would be a more democratic government. Eventually, however, the failures of the community action program and the many programs aimed at middle-class constituencies stimulated extensive scrutiny of citizen participation. The academic literature that emerged was highly critical, offering exhaustive documentation of why programs fail.

Tinkering with citizen participation programs did little to raise their overall performance, and a new, neoconservative critique emerged, ar-

---

3. Robert A. Dahl, *Who Governs? Democracy and Power in an American City* (Yale University Press, 1961), p. 311.

guing that by their very nature these programs were harmful. The gauntlet against citizen participation was thrown down by political scientist Samuel Huntington. Huntington decried the surge in citizen advocacy during the 1960s, which he said made unreasonable demands on government. "Previously passive or unorganized groups . . . embarked on concerted efforts to establish their claims" upon government.[4] Their pressure overwhelmed governmental institutions' capacities, and when new programs failed to live up to the unrealistic expectations set for them, the newly active became the newly alienated. The consequence of increased participation was decreased authority for government. In Huntington's terms, there was too much democracy and the appropriate balance of mass participation and elite leadership and expertise had been upset. His remedy, simply, was less direct democracy.

Where is the line between the value of expanded participation and its potentially harmful side effects? A first step in trying to position that line is to determine what the effects of extensive citizen participation have been. By breaking the sweeping arguments about citizen participation into more discrete propositions, we can begin to analyze the conflicting views outlined here.

Our tests will revolve around three charges that have been made against expanded citizen participation: conflict, alienation, and delay.

Government can be called the art of managing political conflict, and any type of citizen involvement in politics can be judged guilty as a primary cause of a confrontation of interests. Our concern here is to isolate an expanded opportunity for participation and to see if it causes increasing political conflict. This was the basic charge against the community action program.

If participation overloads the system, what will be the effect on those making the demands? Huntington says that alienation follows, particularly for those newly drawn into the political system. As new groups mobilize, make demands, and achieve some initial response from government, expectations are heightened. The consequence of government's failing to meet those expectations, however, is less participation. The marginal participants who come into the system are the first to leave it, taking with them a newly acquired sense of alienation from government. We need to identify this subpopulation so that we may test the alienation hypothesis.

4. Samuel P. Huntington, "The United States," in Michel Crozier, Samuel P. Huntington, and Joji Watanuki, *The Crisis of Democracy: Report on the Governability of Democracies to the Trilateral Commission* (New York University Press, 1975), p. 61.

One of the most widely leveled charges against citizen participation is that it delays action by government. Procedures for incorporating citizen participation into the administrative process can slow policymaking to a snail's pace. Different laws require studies, hearings, advisory panels, and other lengthy steps in the march toward a decision. Citizens knowing how to use the opportunities available to them can delay decisions while they mobilize opposition to a proposed policy. And when they run out of procedural opportunities to make their case before administrators, they can then go to court and create even more delay. In the trade-off between efficiency and participation, efficiency loses. The key here is to test the attitude toward governmental bodies that incorporate high levels of citizen participation. Are the "decisions" of those bodies viewed as binding settlements, or are they invitations for further activism by those who disagree with them?

Conflict

If there is disagreement in a community, does participatory democracy makes things worse than if the conflict were handled by representatives experienced in the art of compromise? That is, do neighborhood associations throw oil onto a burning fire?

The logic of this allegation against participatory democracy is that mobilization of the population brings with it many new contradictory and unreasonable demands on government. At its base, this criticism reflects a distrust of the ability of average citizens. Schumpeter minced few words on this point: "The typical citizen would in political matters tend to yield to extra-rational or irrational prejudice and impulse." Consequently, "he will relax his usual moral standards."[5] Berelson was more temperate in his language, but equally damning: "Certain requirements commonly assumed for the successful operation of democracy are not met by the behavior of the 'average' citizen."[6] Moynihan made the same charge, but he was as inflammatory as Berelson was bland. Poor blacks were seen as the main beneficiaries of the community action program, so Moynihan's argument that the poor are too uneducated and irresponsible to govern added a racial element to the case against participatory democracy.[7]

5. Joseph A. Schumpeter, *Capitalism, Socialism, and Democracy*, 3d ed. (Harper and Brothers, 1950), p. 262.
6. Berelson and others, *Voting*, p. 307.
7. Daniel P. Moynihan, *Maximum Feasible Misunderstanding: Community Action in The War on Poverty* (Free Press, 1969), pp. 136–37.

In the following chapters we will look at the capabilities of participants in the citizen participation systems of our five cities. Focusing more narrowly on the relationship between citizen participation and the expansion of conflict, we examine the proposition that is at the heart of Huntington's provocative analysis. He claims that participation leads to conflict when additional demands are placed on the system. Huntington notes that during the 1960s and 1970s, when political participation was conspicuously linked with conflict, the rate of voting actually dropped. Thus he argues that it is the mobilization of demands rather than an overall increase in the numbers of people participating in politics that is significant.

Unquestionably, the neighborhood associations make additional political demands on city government. The resources given to the neighborhood associations—including staff, technical assistance, and direct financial support for communication with neighborhood residents— guarantee that they will have the organizational capability of bringing demands forward. While some of these demands might be forcefully brought before government in cities without citizen participation systems, most would never reach city hall without some easy means to aggregate and articulate grievances and requests. Government officials must interact with the neighborhood associations on a regular basis. The resources available to the neighborhood associations in the five cities and their high expectations of responsiveness by city hall do create the potential for substantial conflict. This added layer of neighborhood government exerts more pressure on elected officials and administrators as they make decisions about the distribution of goods and services within their city. Indeed, the central purpose of these programs is to give a voice to those not normally heard at city hall.

Each of the cities has mechanisms in place to help resolve conflict. Portland has a neighborhood mediation center with that specific mission. In St. Paul, the role of the Capital Improvement Budget Committee is specifically to bring neighborhoods together and to work out competing demands for capital funds. The intermediate structures—Portland's District Coalitions, Dayton's Priority Boards, and Birmingham's Citizens Advisory Board—are specifically designed as forums for potentially conflicting demands to be at least partially reconciled with available resources.

As already demonstrated, the neighborhood associations mix a regular cadre of activists with those more marginally interested in neighborhood or city politics. For those not regularly active, involvement does not come randomly, with a small number of the curious seeking out political opportunities throughout the year. Rather, the marginally active are brought into the system because they are stimulated by an issue that deeply concerns them.

To examine the concept of marginal participation, we created a variable consisting of five categories of participants. The most relevant distinction from the standpoint of the cities' participation programs is the extent to which people can be considered either regular or marginal participants in that program. We defined "regular system participants" as those respondents who reported having taken part in activities of the participation program at least once a month. "Marginal system participants" are those respondents who participated in the program's activities but did so less than once a month on average. (Respondents in either category may or may not be active in other types of community groups.) To provide a clear comparison with these program or system participants, we created another pair of regular and marginal participants. These are the respondents who had taken part not in the participation program but in the activities of other local citizen groups.[8] A final category consists of respondents who had not participated in either the participation program or any other local citizen groups.

To assess the notion that the mobilization of additional demands through citizen participation leads to increased conflict, we asked all respondents who had heard of the neighborhood associations a simple and straightforward question:

> Sometimes public discussion of issues leads to a great deal of bitterness and increases bad feelings between people in a neighborhood. Other times public discussion of issues settles arguments and reduces bad feelings. Do you think that the way the Neighborhood Association has worked on issues in your neighborhood has *increased* bad feelings or *decreased* bad feelings between people?

An overwhelming majority of all citizens who have heard of the citizen participation system feel that the neighborhood associations defuse hos-

---

8. Our distinction between regular and marginal participants closely parallels Inglehart's "cognitive mobilization scale" used in the analysis of cross-national data. His scale takes into account both the participatory activity itself and the frequency of participation in that activity. See Ronald Inglehart, *The Silent Revolution: Changing Values and Styles among Western Publics* (Princeton University Press, 1977); and Ronald Inglehart and Jacques-Rene Rabier, "Europe Elects a Parliament: Cognitive Mobilization and Pro-European Attitudes as Influences on Voter Turnout," *Government and Opposition*, vol. 14 (Summer 1979), pp. 479–507.

TABLE 8-1. Do Citizen Participants Think Participation
Increased Bad Feelings?[a]

Percent unless otherwise indicated

Samples and responses	System participants		Participants in other local groups		Non-partici-pants
	Regulars	Marginals	Regulars	Marginals	
First wave, five cities[b]					
Increased	13.1	12.6	24.7	16.5	18.3
Decreased	86.9	87.4	75.3	83.5	81.7
N	199	143	239	176	663
Ten matched cities[c]					
Increased	...	...	17.3	6.9	16.9
Decreased	...	...	82.7	93.1	83.1
N	...	...	139	116	189

a. The question was: Do you think the way the [citizen participation system or neighborhood association] has worked on issues in your neighborhood has increased or decreased bad feelings? This question was asked of respondents who recognized that a neighborhood system existed in their city or a neighborhood association existed in their area.

b. The chi square was 14.3; significance was less than 0.000.

c. The chi square was 7.2; significance was 0.003.

tility (see table 8-1). The lopsided response pattern speaks well of these neighborhood-based organizations. Perhaps the more important pattern is revealed in the comparisons between regular and marginal participants in the neighborhood associations. Here there is virtually no difference. Marginal participants do not seem to be driven away from more consistent activism because of conflict. Instead, they seem to regard neighborhood associations as mechanisms that resolve rather than exacerbate differences. Few people want to get involved in organizations that are highly conflictual and leave participants in an antagonized state. Neighborhood association meetings are seen by both types of participants as comfortable gatherings where residents can go and discuss the problems of their community.

An interesting contrast to this is found in Jane Mansbridge's study of town meeting government in a small Vermont village. She found in her interviews with rank-and-file citizens that over a quarter of them volunteered without prompting that they were upset by the conflictual nature of the town meeting.[9] Had she asked about conflict, this figure could have been higher. Clearly the neighborhood associations are unusually successful at making people feel comfortable as they discuss the political issues before them.

9. Jane J. Mansbridge, *Beyond Adversary Democracy* (Basic Books, 1980), p. 65.

Alienation

Huntington's attack on participatory democracy is grounded in his belief that conflict and disappointment lead to alienation from the political system. This alienation, in turn, undermines the authority of government, and "the decline in governmental authority reduces still further the ability of government to deal effectively" with the problems that led people to become active in the first place.[10] Looking back at the 1960s and early 1970s, he argues that "the surge of participatory democracy and egalitarianism gravely weakened, where it did not demolish, the likelihood that anyone in any institution could give an order to someone else and have it promptly obeyed."[11]

Huntington's model of participation is thus a vicious circle. Increased participation leads to increased alienation. Increased alienation leads to declining trust in government and sense of powerlessness. Declining trust and efficacy lead to lower participation.[12] New issues, however, will eventually bring new participants back into the system, and the cycle begins anew.

This is a serious indictment of the American political system. Huntington claims not only that the end result of participatory democracy is a weakened government that cannot deal adequately with domestic problems, but also that the United States loses the respect of governments of other countries when they see that it cannot command the respect of its own citizens. If he is right, then his conclusion—that America needs not more democracy but instead "a greater degree of moderation in democracy"—is logical and compelling.[13]

The five cities of our study, however, provide specific forums—both in person and through a wide range of newsletters, community newspapers, and position papers going from the neighborhoods to city hall—that may serve as a way to overcome this sense of alienation. Any individual with an axe to grind can do so publicly, in a constructive context that includes a timely mechanism for comment and reaction from neighbors and peers. Political and administrative leaders also can use these forums to respond publicly to specific demands from individuals and neighborhoods.

10. Huntington, "The United States," p. 103.

11. Samuel P. Huntington, *American Politics: The Promise of Disharmony* (Belknap, 1981), p. 219.

12. Huntington, "The United States," p. 84.

13. Huntington, "The United States," pp. 106, 113.

Our surveys allow us to test Huntington's thesis against the potential means to reduce alienation that exists in these five cities. Using two standard questions that probe individuals' sense of political efficacy, we again divide neighborhood association participants into regulars and marginals.[14] We use efficacy questions rather than alienation questions because of recurring criticism of the validity and reliability of the latter group of questions.[15] (Chapter 11 provides a more complete discussion of the nature of these efficacy questions.)

The goal here is not to determine whether participation is positively related to a sense of personal political efficacy—that has been well established. Instead, we want to look beneath that pattern to compare the relative levels of political efficacy of different segments of a city's activist population. Specifically, the focus is on the relationship between marginal participation and political efficacy. (A fuller investigation of the relationship between community participation and political efficacy is also found in chapter 11.)

The responses to the statements "People like me don't have any say about what government does" and "Sometimes politics and government seem so complicated that a person like me can't really understand what's going on" are revealing (see table 8-2). Among those involved in citizen participation systems, there are no consistent differences between regular and marginal participants. Whatever keeps people from staying involved on a regular basis, it is not a sense of powerlessness. In contrast to the system participants, local group participants, both regular and marginal, are less likely to feel politically efficacious.

These conclusions are bolstered even more by the patterns found in the panel data. There is remarkable stability in personal efficacy over time, and this stability persists for all five participation groups. During the period between the two sets of interviews, marginal participants in

14. Although our survey included modified National Election Study (NES) efficacy questions that refer to the respondent's city, the analysis here is based on the national questions because they tap a more generalized attitude of personal efficacy toward government. Also, our data show that the respondents in the five cities score much higher in levels of personal efficacy and trust in government when the standard NES questions refer directly to the resident's city. Thus the national questions are a more exacting test of our hypotheses.

15. Ada Finifter, "Dimensions of Political Alienation," *American Political Science Review*, vol. 64 (June 1970), pp. 389–410; Herbert Asher, "The Reliability of the Political Efficacy Items," *Political Methodology*, vol. 1 (Spring 1974), pp. 45–72; and Stephen C. Craig, "Efficacy, Trust, and Political Behavior: An Attempt to Resolve a Lingering Conceptual Dilemma," *American Politics Quarterly*, vol. 7 (April 1979), pp. 225–39.

TABLE 8-2. Do Marginal Participants Exhibit Less Political Efficacy?[a]

Percent unless otherwise indicated

Sample and responses	System participants		Participants in other local groups		Non-partici-pants
	Regulars	Marginals	Regulars	Marginals	
"Any say" question					
First wave, five cities[b]					
Agree	27.6	24.2	32.3	31.7	43.5
Disagree	72.4	75.8	67.7	68.3	56.5
N	246	194	353	268	2,821
Ten matched cities[c]					
Agree	...	...	32.1	36.5	41.3
Disagree	...	...	67.9	63.5	58.7
N	...	...	396	307	818
Second-wave panel, five cities[d]					
Say diminished over time	29.7	30.3	29.8	25.7	28.5
Say stayed high	44.3	45.1	38.7	42.6	28.6
Say increased over time	7.0	4.2	7.7	8.4	9.6
Say stayed low	18.9	20.4	23.8	23.3	33.3
N	185	142	248	202	1,715
"Complicated" question					
First-wave, five cities[e]					
Agree	42.2	39.2	49.0	46.8	63.4
Disagree	57.8	60.8	51.0	53.2	36.6
N	244	194	351	269	2,861
Ten matched cities[f]					
Agree	...	...	53.0	56.2	64.5
Disagree	...	...	47.0	43.8	35.5
N	...	...	396	308	832
Second-wave panel, five cities[g]					
Got more complicated over time	13.4	11.7	13.5	16.7	12.9
Got less complicated	9.1	12.4	12.7	12.3	13.6
Stayed too complicated over time	32.3	29.7	36.7	34.0	50.3
Stayed uncomplicated	45.2	46.2	37.1	36.9	23.3
N	186	145	245	203	1,749

a. Two questions were asked. The first asked respondents to agree or disagree with the statement "People like me don't have any say about what government does." The second asked them to agree or disagree with the statement "Sometimes politics and government seem so complicated that a person like me can't really understand what's going on." "Disagree" responses represent greater efficacy.

b. The chi square was 65.2; significance was less than 0.000.

c. The chi square was 10.0; significance was less than 0.000.

d. The chi square was 62.8; significance was less than 0.000.

e. The chi square was 110.6; significance was less than 0.000.

f. The chi square was 17.0; significance was less than 0.000.

g. The chi square was 101.4; significance was less than 0.000.

both the system and group categories were not more likely than regular participants to suffer a diminished sense of personal efficacy.[16]

A counterargument to our general findings might be that we cannot equate neighborhood politics of the mid-1980s with the turbulence of the 1960s and 1970s that so disturbed Huntington. In his eyes, the time between 1960 and 1975 was one of this country's periods of "creedal passion."[17] We are not entirely sure what creedal passion is, and we are even less sure how to go about measuring it. But while acknowledging that some periods of American political history are more emotional than others, we are less inclined to accept that this passion is a wholly compartmentalized dimension of political behavior. The instincts to participate or to be alienated during such periods cannot be completely divorced from the same instincts at other times. In short, it is not only justifiable but absolutely necessary to test Huntington's propositions by examining them against well-defined dimensions of behavior and conventional forms of participation. Since Huntington failed to prove empirically that alienated participants subsequently dropped out of the political system at a greater rate than the general population, his argument is highly speculative. It is also inconsistent with the evidence provided here.

Delay

A less global but still troubling criticism of participatory democracy is that it makes government inefficient by needlessly slowing down the policymaking process. Critics charge that agencies can be held hostage to liberal elites who know how to manipulate the system to gain advantage for their point of view. Citizen participation procedures may lead to changes in policy, but not because of reasoned discussion of alternatives between administrators and a cross-section of the public. Rather, as D. Stephen Cupps concludes,

16. The analysis was pressed further to examine the impact of SES on the results. Since participation generally is strongly correlated with SES, comparisons were made within SES levels rather than between them. In comparing marginal participants in citizen participation systems with regular citizen participation system participants, we found that the two populations were consistently similar in their feelings of personal efficacy and perceptions of conflict at each level of SES. In the comparison of system participants and group participants, statistically significant differences emerged only among those citizens who fell into the middle of the SES scale. The thrust of these findings from basic cross-tabulations was confirmed through log-linear analysis.

17. Huntington, *American Politics*, pp. 167–220.

Some citizen groups seem committed to extending administrative hearings and legal proceedings interminably in hopes that lengthy delays, the growing frustration of other groups, and the unwillingness of private parties to tolerate continuing uncertainty and expense will ultimately assure them of success.[18]

Such delays not only are costly to government, but they also can be harmful to the broader public, which is unaware that its interests are being damaged by extended citizen involvement in agency policymaking. In a study of housing developments in the San Francisco Bay Area, Bernard Frieden found that citizen groups used public participation requirements, procedural safeguards in the administrative process, and litigation as leverage to alter, if not altogether stop, real estate development proposals.[19] Typically, an ambitious housing proposal would be scaled down by developers to meet the objections of citizens; the developers simply could not tolerate the delays and continuing administrative reviews because they were costing them too much money. Frieden concluded that the big loser in all of this was the housing consumer. Fewer new homes and apartments being built meant that buyers and renters paid higher prices. The counterargument, which we heard in the five cities of our study, was that the participation systems, while taking time to let people understand the proposal and its alternatives, often overcome the substantial delay that projects face when strident objections are raised after substantial resources have already been expended. Such objections cause more delay than they would if dealt with earlier and also may lead to high costs for redesigning a project.

We approached this problem from both sides of the street, examining the attitudes of residents and policymakers in our five cities. We asked our citizens what they would do if their neighborhood association decided an issue in a way they disapproved of. This was an open-ended question, and interviewers were instructed not to prompt their subjects.[20]

18. D. Stephen Cupps, "Emerging Problems of Citizen Participation," *Public Administration Review*, vol. 37 (September–October 1977), pp. 478–87.

19. Bernard J. Frieden, *The Environmental Protection Hustle* (MIT Press, 1979).

20. This question was the last in a sequence of questions about a hypothetical issue affecting the respondent's neighborhood. The first question read, "Let's say the people who run [name of city] are considering *a proposal to change city services or to change your community in a way you and your neighbors disapprove of*. What do you think you would do if such a situation arose?" The next two questions asked respondents whether they thought they would be offered the opportunity to be involved at the next neighbor-

Responses fall into two broad categories. The responses grouped under "consent" are those where respondents indicated that they either accepted the decision (even though they didn't like it) or would do nothing more than passively oppose it. If our subjects said that they would contact officials to try to change their minds, organize or join an existing group to fight the decision, engage in protest, or otherwise try to disrupt the government's plans, we concluded that their activities could cause delay. These responses were coded as "active opposition."

The data suggest that citizen participation in the five cities does not lead to delay (see table 8-3). On the contrary, those involved in the neighborhood associations are the most likely to consent to decisions that went against their preferences. This is true of both regular and marginal participants. The people most likely to engage in actions that will delay implementation of a decision are those who are active in other types of local groups.

These findings are even more impressive in light of the above results in which participants in the neighborhood associations scored the highest in their feelings of political efficacy. Consequently, the people in our analysis who are most likely to believe they are capable of getting government to listen to them are generally the least likely to pursue policy changes after they have been defeated at the neighborhood level. The neighborhood associations are apparently successful in getting activists to buy into a decision by letting them participate in its formulation. Even when they lose, most activists appear to regard the decision as legitimate.

Although citizens may feel that the decisions of the neighborhood associations are legitimate and conclusive, administrators and city councillors might see the citizen participation process in a different light. Procedures that citizens perceive to be fair and prudent could be seen as slow and cumbersome by policymakers. Considering the professional expertise that they possess and the time they spend analyzing issues, policymakers may find that citizen participation does little more than slow everything down.

As noted in chapter 5, each administrator and city councillor was asked for a detailed chronology of an issue that he or she had worked on. Although this question did not specify that respondents discuss only an issue in which citizen participation played a role, public involvement

---

hood association meeting, and if they would take advantage of such an opportunity. They were then asked what they would do if the neighborhood association decided against their preferences.

TABLE 8-3. How Would Citizens React to an Unfavorable
Decision?[a]

Percent unless otherwise indicated

	System participants		Participants in other local groups		Non-participants
Response	Regulars	Marginals	Regulars	Marginals	
Consent	58.1	54.6	45.4	43.4	46.2
Accept decision	29.8	29.1	26.4	29.8	25.9
Passively oppose	28.3	25.5	19.0	13.6	20.3
Active opposition	36.1	39.0	51.4	54.6	35.6
Contact officials	11.5	16.3	13.0	17.7	7.8
Organize, join group	20.4	17.0	29.9	27.8	16.7
Protest, disrupt	0.5	0.0	1.1	2.0	1.1
Other action	3.7	5.7	7.4	7.1	10.0
Don't know	5.8	6.4	3.2	2.0	18.2
N	191	141	284	198	2,402

a. The question was: If the neighborhood association decided this issue in a way you disapprove of, how do you think you would respond? The chi square was 178.9; significance was less than 0.000.

was often part of the story we heard. All the evaluative comments about the neighborhood associations or the citizen participation system were subsequently coded as being supportive or critical of the public involvement process.

Of 105 administrators and 28 city councillors, a total of 69 offered at least one evaluative comment on citizen participation in their city. The positive comments outnumbered the negative by about two to one, as table 8-4 shows. Yet 42 percent of the policymakers who made an evaluation did mention delay as one of the consequences of citizen participation. To broaden our analysis of these responses, we read through the original interview transcripts and looked at the context of the entire answers. The predominant response was that citizen participation produced delay *and* brought about resolution of issue differences at the same time. This is not as contradictory as it may sound. Policymakers thoughtfully and dispassionately described the citizen participation process as one that did slow things down by requiring thorough review at the neighborhood level. They recognized this as an added and time-consuming step. Yet such delays were typically thought to be a more than equitable trade-off for what the city got in return. Most respondents believed that citizen participation was worth the price in the end because

TABLE 8-4. Policymakers' Evaluation of Citizen Participation
Programs in Five Cities

Comments or evaluations	Number agreeing	Percent of policymakers making an evaluation
Negative		
Delays the process	29	42
Creates conflict	10	14
Creates frustration among participants	11	16
Polarizes sides in a dispute	3	4
Yields fragile solutions	1	1
Creates more opposition	2	3
Positive		
Expedites the decision process	15	22
Resolves conflict	19	28
Creates participant satisfaction	30	43
Builds consensus/better communication	17	25
Produces more durable solutions	25	36
Creates more support for final decision	12	17

it builds consensus, gets people to buy into decisions when they participate in their formulation, or makes subsequent appeals by dissatisfied
parties illegitimate after the neighborhood association has its say.

A St. Paul administrator summarized her feelings about the city's
citizen participation process in this way:

> The quality [of decisions] is better because of citizen participation.
> Sometimes it makes things longer and more painful. Because the people
> have ownership of the decisions, they are more durable; there is more
> consensus.

For many respondents, like this Portland administrator, adapting to
the city's participatory environment was simply a matter of pragmatism:

> If you want to get a significant policy through [the City] Council,
> boy, you really need to have done your homework with the neighbor-
> hoods, meeting with them and talking with them and making sure
> they've reviewed the proposal well in advance and had input into
> it. . . . Otherwise, you're asking for trouble.

Another Portland administrator recalled that "if we had an in-house
relief process for this contract discussion, we could have wrapped it up

in thirty days. It took us four months and the reason was that we went and involved people. So time is an inefficiency." But he also noted that this process "improved the political salability of the final decision. By involving citizens to that degree you diminish the ability of people to come in at the last minute and attack the process and attack the product of the process."

An interesting contrast to Frieden's charges was the point emphasized by an economic development administrator—that even private developers support the citizen participation program because it makes local policymaking predictable.

> A developer came up to me and said, "I'd much rather work with the city of St. Paul because . . . [it has] a citizen participation process that addresses any issues at an early stage in the project. You don't put a lot of money into it and then go down to city hall and then all of a sudden all the people who show up are negative and kill it."

Developers could, of course, like the St. Paul system because it channels potential opponents into a single organization that can be more easily co-opted. As noted in chapter 6, the underlying question is whether neighborhood residents would be better off with a completely independent neighborhood organization or with an organization linked to city government. A city-sponsored group could certainly be influenced by norms that encourage compromise and accommodation with business. An independent group, especially one that is ad hoc and not a repeat player in city politics, would be less restrained by the expectations of city officials and businesspeople themselves.

The routinization of policymaking that comes with city-sponsored programs should not be equated with co-optation. As argued earlier, what is most significant about the relationship of business and neighborhoods in these citywide systems is that the neighborhoods have considerable power—they bring a good deal of leverage to the bargaining table. Although an independent neighborhood group has no formal power, businesspeople must contemplate the possibility that the delays it could cause would raise the real costs of a project and conceivably even kill a project. But city-sponsored neighborhood associations can also kill projects that do not have large economic consequences for the city—the vast majority of cases that come before them—and they can force costly and unanticipated changes in developers' plans. What developers gain from working with officially sanctioned neighborhood associations—namely speedier and more binding decisions—they pay for by conceding a share of control over project design to the associations.

Conclusion

When cities create real participatory structures to involve citizens in local policymaking, those in government pay a high cost. City councillors and top administrators give up some of their power and in turn empower a large number of people who can use their new resources to challenge city hall. Yet government officials rarely have to confront the dilemma of whether they should give up their own power in the name of good government. Instead, they can rationalize that there is no reason to build a substantive citizen participation structure because public involvement programs do not work. Why should they try something that has been shown to be a failure? Building a substantive citizen participation system has not been actively considered in most cities because such a system seems to be counterproductive.

This conventional wisdom about citizen participation is built not merely on convenient myth but on social science research as well. Beyond the inflammatory attacks by Moynihan, Huntington, and others, a body of empirical literature demonstrates that most programs are failures. Moreover, the literature lacks a convincing reform message: no coherent set of steps guides those who might push for more participatory forms of government. And changing the procedures and structures of government is not enough; city administrators can undermine citizen participation programs if they are not committed to them.[21]

Unfortunately, social scientists have largely given up on participatory democracy. Without a convincing message of how citizen participation can be made to work, they have played a major role in ensuring that it is a nonissue in city politics. As demonstrated here, though, citizen participation is not destined to fail. The literature that paints a bleak picture of citizen participation in city politics has unfairly stigmatized public involvement as the cause of unavoidable and damaging problems. The data here show that when administrators make a good-faith effort to make citizen participation work rather than trying to undermine it, the performance of public involvement programs is dramatically different from that described in the literature.

21. Jeffrey M. Berry, Kent E. Portney, Mary Beth Bablitch, and Richard Mahoney, "Public Involvement in Administration: The Structural Determinants of Effective Citizen Participation," *Journal of Voluntary Action Research*, vol. 13 (April 1984), pp. 7–23.

The findings from our surveys could not be more clear. Participants in the neighborhood associations (as well as nonparticipants who know about them) believe that the citizen participation process in their city is nonconflictual. The neighborhood associations defuse hostility rather than create it. The mobilization of marginal participants through the neighborhood associations does not cause feelings of personal political inefficacy. Both regular and marginal participants in neighborhood associations actually had higher feelings of efficacy than did comparable populations of activists in conventional community groups. Marginal participants did not demonstrate a distinctive tendency toward declining efficacy over time. Participants in these cities' programs were less likely to volunteer that they would take action that could lead to administrative delays if a decision went against them than were community group participants. A large proportion of administrators did indicate that delay was a consequence of citizen participation, but they overwhelmingly felt that the benefits outweighed the costs.

CHAPTER 9

Tolerance and Intolerance

Is DEMOCRACY AT RISK when too many people participate? In chapter 8 we found that, contrary to some theoretical arguments, strong democratic methods do not unduly promote conflict, alienation, or long-run delay in the policymaking process. But should American democracy leave well enough alone? Even if carefully designed participation systems work well for those who now choose to participate, can the expansion of democracy to include more and more people actually weaken democracy itself?

Several political analysts, drawing upon the frameworks of elitist theories of democracy, have argued that the answer is emphatically yes. They claim that the large majority of the population, which does not actively participate, holds attitudes that are authoritarian, racist, and intolerant of any deviation from the cultural norm—or at least that these attitudes are much more prevalent among "the masses" than among those few who now dominate political decisionmaking. Therefore, the argument goes, if more of these people are drawn into active political life, these attitudes will play a much larger role in the political process, thereby undercutting the very values necessary for democracy to survive.

In the wake of the worldwide movement toward democracy, when a curious collection of political analysts and practicing politicians are becoming born-again democrats, this question is gaining new relevance. This chapter looks at how the essential ingredients of the elitist theory of democracy hold up to the facts of strong participation observed in our study. The main tool of this analysis will be a series of survey questions concerning freedom of speech, education, and the press for groups that many people ardently oppose.

Elitism and Intolerance

The belief that increased participation may undermine democracies was catalyzed by two very different events: the collapse of the Weimar

Republic into fascism and the invention of the public opinion survey. The former suggested that high levels of mass participation could lead to the conversion of a democracy into a totalitarian regime. The latter made it clear that support for some of the bedrock principles of democracy were dangerously low among the general public in the United States and other Western democracies, particularly among people of low socioeconomic status.

Joseph Schumpeter was one of the first to recognize that what he termed the "classical" theory of democracy had to be drastically revised.[1] He argued that this theory required every citizen to be aware, rational, and thoroughly involved in political decisionmaking. Yet his observations of the common man, as we noted earlier, precluded the existence on a broad scale of such characteristics and attitudes. Therefore, a democracy must be held together by other means. In Schumpeter's mind an influential elite was critical because such guardians better approximate the ideal citizens of classical democracy.

During the next twenty years, scholars developed this point of view,[2] arguing strongly that in all known democracies one or more groups of elites rule and asserting with varying degrees of emphasis that this may be good thing—that limited popular participation may be desirable. The latter argument rests on several considerations: the need to obtain at least a temporary consensus for a particular political course, the desirability of social and economic stability rather than too-rapid change, and the need for active participants in a democratic process to support its underlying tenets.

This third consideration, the role of the nonauthoritarian attitudes of an elite in shaping and maintaining a democracy, has been particularly important in legitimating a distinct distrust of participatory democracy by many political scientists. The argument in some form has been important in the work of most contemporary democratic theorists. Its moderate form has been advanced by advocates for pluralist politics. Lester Milbrath, for example, explains,

1. Joseph A. Schumpeter, *Capitalism, Socialism, and Democracy*, 3d ed. (Harper, 1950).

2. See, for example, Bernard R. Berelson, Paul F. Lazarsfeld, and William N. McPhee, *Voting: A Study of Opinion Formation in a Presidential Campaign* (University of Chicago Press, 1954); William Kornhauser, *The Politics of Mass Society* (Free Press, 1959); Seymour Martin Lipset, *Political Man: The Social Bases of Politics* (Doubleday, 1960); Giovanni Sartori, *Democratic Theory* (Greenwood Press, 1976); and Harry Eckstein, *Division and Cohesion in Democracy: A Study of Norway* (Princeton University Press, 1966).

Although it can be argued that participation in politics develops character, there is doubt that the society as a whole would benefit if intense interest and active involvement in politics became widespread throughout the population. . . . If this analysis is correct, present levels and patterns of participation in politics do not constitute a threat to democracy. . . . The political processes of that democracy may not be close to the ideal of the classical theorists, but they may well be the best possible approximation to popular control of government that can be achieved in modern, industrialized, mobile, mass society.[3]

Even Dahl, the consummate pluralist, notes the importance of the elitist argument. He explains the basic fear that increased political activity among certain classes of people could threaten his version of a working democracy, the polyarchy:

Current evidence suggests that in the United States the lower one's socioeconomic class, the more authoritarian one's predispositions and the less active politically one is likely to be. Thus if an increase in political activity brings the authoritarian-minded into the political arena, consensus on the basic norms among the politically active certainly must be declining. To the extent that consensus declines, we would expect . . . that, after some lag, polyarchy would also decline.[4]

While Dahl provides an example of the complexity of the relationship between increased participation and a stronger polyarchy, other authors are not so cautious. Thomas Dye and Harmon Ziegler assert the proposition of democratic values versus participation in perhaps its strongest form:

It is the irony of democracy that democratic ideals survive because authoritarian masses are also generally apathetic and inactive. Thus, the capacity for intolerance, authoritarianism, scapegoatism, racism, and violence of the American lower classes is seldom translated into organized, sustained political movements.

3. Lester W. Milbrath, *Political Participation: How and Why Do People Get Involved in Politics?* (Chicago: Rand McNally, 1965), pp. 147, 154.
4. Robert A. Dahl, *A Preface to Democratic Theory* (University of Chicago Press, 1956), p. 89.

The survival of democracy is not based upon mass support for democratic ideals. It is apparently not necessary that most people commit themselves to a democracy; all that is necessary is that they fail to commit themselves actively to an antidemocratic system.[5]

To evaluate the empirical evidence for the impact of expanded participation on the democratic political system, we need to examine the main points of reasoning that lie behind the elitist argument concerning authoritarianism and tolerance. This reasoning proceeds through four essential arguments:

1. People of high socioeconomic status are much less likely to have intolerant attitudes than people of low socioeconomic status.

2. People of high socioeconomic status are much more likely to participate politically than those of low socioeconomic status.

3. Therefore, people who do participate in politics are much less likely to have intolerant attitudes than those who do not participate. The rejection of authoritarian attitudes among those participating elites enables the institutions of democracy to be maintained in spite of the intolerance and antidemocratic attitudes of the nonparticipating majority.

4. Therefore, expansion of the democratic process beyond the existing equilibrium point would bring more people into the process who have increasingly intolerant attitudes. Since the views of the new participants are antithetical to the process of democracy, the expanded participation base would yield policies that would tend to undercut the process of democracy and would destabilize the government.

The Stratification of Tolerance and Participation

Since the first major compilation of public opinion polls dealing with tolerance issues by Herbert Hyman and Paul Sheatsley in 1953 and particularly with the landmark work of Samuel Stouffer in 1955, it has been clear that the levels of tolerance among the general public fall far short of the "classical democracy" ideal.[6] Stouffer's study found, for

5. Thomas Dye and L. Harmon Zeigler, *The Irony of Democracy: An Uncommon Introduction to American Politics*, 4th ed. (North Scituate, Mass.: Duxbury Press, 1978), p. 135.

6. Herbert H. Hyman and Paul B. Sheatsley, "Trends in Public Opinion on Civil Liberties," *Journal of Social Issues*, vol. 9, no. 3 (1953), pp. 6–16.; and Samuel Stouffer, *Communism, Conformity, and Civil Liberties: A Cross-Section of the Nation Speaks Its Mind* (Doubleday, 1955).

example, that as few as 37 percent of his national sample would choose to allow individuals to speak "against churches and religion" in their communities, and as few as 27 percent would support freedom of speech for an "admitted communist."[7] Substantial research has tracked these tolerance attitudes over the last three decades; using the same scale that Stouffer used, these studies have found a sharp increase in tolerance over this period.[8]

There is substantial disagreement, however, about the explanation for these changes. One fairly convincing argument is that the increase in tolerance is due to the increasing levels of education in the population.[9] The original data led Stouffer to argue that "great social, economic, and technological forces are operating slowly and imperceptibly on the side of spreading tolerance."[10] In support of this perception, McClosky and Brill look back to see a tolerance and civil rights "explosion," and note that "there is a large body of intuitive and anecdotal evidence which strongly suggests that the rise in tolerance reported by Nunn et al. and Davis with respect to communism, atheism, and socialism has in fact been paralleled by dramatic expansions in other domains of civil liberties as well."[11]

These findings are not universally accepted, however, either on their own grounds or as an explanation for the rising tolerance levels measured among the U.S. population. Several studies have questioned the relationship of increased education to increased tolerance, arguing that response-set biases and superficial conditioning lead the more highly educated to respond well to abstract questions and value-laden phrases but to respond

7. Stouffer, *Communism, Conformity, and Civil Liberties*, p. 40.
8. See James W. Prothro and Charles M. Grigg, "Fundamental Principles of Democracy: Bases of Agreement and Disagreement," *Journal of Politics*, vol. 22 (May 1960), pp. 276–94; Herbert McClosky, "Consensus and Ideology in American Politics," *American Political Science Review*, vol. 58 (June 1964), pp. 361–82; James A. Davis, "Communism, Conformity, Cohorts and Categories: American Tolerance in 1954 and 1972–73," *American Journal of Sociology*, vol. 81 (November 1975), pp. 491–513; Clyde Z. Nunn, Harry J. Crockett, Jr., and J. Allen Williams, Jr., *Tolerance for Nonconformity: A National Survey of Americans' Changing Commitment to Civil Liberties* (San Francisco: Jossey-Bass, 1978); and Herbert McClosky and Alida Brill, *Dimensions of Tolerance: What Americans Believe about Civil Liberties* (New York: Russell Sage Foundation, 1983).
9. See, for example, Stouffer, *Communism, Conformity, and Civil Liberties*; Davis, "Communism, Conformity, Cohorts and Categories"; Nunn and others, *Tolerance for Nonconformity*; and McClosky, "Consensus and Ideology in American Politics."
10. Stouffer, *Communism, Conformity, and Civil Liberties*, p. 236.
11. McCloskey and Brill, *Dimensions of Tolerance*, p. 435.

with the same intolerant attitudes as poorly educated people when faced with specific challenges to their status.[12]

Another argument is that the nature of the specific groups that were the subject of the questions in Stouffer's tolerance scale—communists, socialists, and atheists—are simply not as deeply feared as they were in the early 1950s and are therefore more tolerated. Specifically, this argument asserts that the intolerance once directed toward communists and socialists has merely been shifted toward other groups. To demonstrate this, John Sullivan and his colleagues have developed "content controlled" survey questions in which they first ask a person to select from a list of groups the one he or she most strongly opposes, after which they proceed to ask the tolerance-related questions about those groups in the Stouffer tradition.[13] In doing so, they find levels of intolerance comparable to Stouffer's original study. They also conclude that education and social status have little direct influence upon tolerance, but that social status is "one of the major factors influencing personality and political ideology," which are key influences on tolerance in their model.

These concerns have led to two major paths of research stemming from Stouffer's original approach: in one path Stouffer's questions are coupled with other questions identifying "right wing" targets designed to balance the "left wing" targets of Stouffer's original work; the second research path, using the Sullivan methodology, allows the respondents to identify the target groups. We applied both approaches here. For the

12. See Dean Peabody, "Attitude Content and Agreement Set in Scales of Authoritarianism, Dogmatism, Anti-Semitism, and Economic Conservatism," *Journal of Abnormal and Social Psychology*, vol. 63, no. 1 (1961), pp. 1–11; John G. Condran, "Changes in White Attitudes Toward Blacks: 1963–1977," *Public Opinion Quarterly*, vol. 43 (Winter 1979), pp. 463–76; Richard M. Merelman, "Democratic Politics and the Culture of American Education," *American Political Science Review*, vol. 74 (June 1980), pp. 319-32; Mary R. Jackman, "Education and Prejudice or Education and Response-Set?" *American Sociological Review*, vol. 38 (June 1973), pp. 327–39; Mary R. Jackman, "General and Applied Tolerance: Does Education Increase Commitment to Racial Integration?" *American Journal of Political Science*, vol. 22 (May 1978), pp. 302–24; and Mary R. Jackman and Michael J. Muha, "Education and Intergroup Attitudes: Moral Enlightenment, Superficial Democratic Commitment, or Ideological Refinement?" *American Sociological Review*, vol. 49 (December 1984), pp. 751–69.

13. Leading proponents of this skepticism are John L. Sullivan, James Piereson, and George E. Marcus, "An Alternative Conceptualization of Political Tolerance: Illusory Increases 1950s-1970s," *American Political Science Review*, vol. 73 (September 1979), pp. 781–94; and John L. Sullivan and others, "The Sources of Political Tolerance: A Multivariate Analysis," *American Political Science Review*, vol. 75 (March 1981), pp. 92–105.

TABLE 9-1. Tolerance and Socioeconomic Status

Percent giving more tolerant response

Question	Socioeconomic status			N	Chi square
	Low	Middle	High		
Should a person who is against all churches and religion be allowed to make a speech in your city?	67.6	84.2	92.5	6,267	385.16**
. . . be allowed to teach in a college or university?	46.7	62.8	76.5	6,260	341.15**
. . . be allowed to keep a book he wrote in your public library?	63.7	79.5	89.0	6,267	336.67**
Should a person who believes that blacks are genetically inferior be allowed to make a speech in your city?	57.2	68.8	82.5	6,267	256.95**
. . . be allowed to keep a book he wrote in your public library?	60.0	73.6	83.2	6,265	245.79**
Should a member of such a group [identified by respondent as a group in the city whose ideas are bad, dangerous, or with which he/she disagrees most often] be allowed to speak?	74.8	85.3	93.6	2,495	99.40**
. . . be allowed to teach in a college or university?	54.4	69.8	80.4	2,485	116.82**
. . . be allowed to keep a book he wrote in your public library?	62.1	78.6	89.5	2,485	156.67**

**Significant at the 0.01 level.

"left" tolerance target, the original Stouffer questions regarding a person who is against all churches and religion were used. For the "right" tolerance target, respondents were asked about an advocate who claims that blacks are genetically inferior. Sullivan's approach was modified slightly by allowing the antagonist to be identified in an open-ended response rather than being chosen from a predefined list.

Overall, these data confirm the very strong relationship between socioeconomic status (SES) and tolerance (see table 9-1). The percentage difference between high and low SES ranges as high as 30 percent and is at least 15 percent on every one of the eight tolerance questions used here. Since the differences are strong for the predefined opponents, on both the left and the right, as well as for the opponents identified by the respondents themselves, the Sullivan objection cannot be supported. The strength and consistency of relationship found is impressive. The work of previous researchers on the role of education and socioeconomic status in tolerant attitudes is confirmed, as is the first basis of the elitist theory.

Chapter 4 described the pervasive tendency for people of high SES to be disproportionately involved in voting, election campaigns, and other forms of political campaign activity. The relationship between SES and participation is as strong as that for tolerance, reaching more than a 30 percent difference in participation rates between high- and low-SES groups in some cases. The second hypothesis of the elitist theory is therefore strongly confirmed as well.

Participation and Tolerance

Considering the strength of the SES effect on both tolerance and participation, a significant relationship between participation and tolerance would not be surprising. To analyze this relationship, we used the index of community participation (ICP), controlling for the SES level of the participant.

The relationship between participation and tolerance is not generally as strong as the SES effect but nevertheless is highly significant (see table 9-2). For each of the eight tolerance questions, very active participants tend to be substantially more tolerant than nonparticipants. The tolerance differences between respondents at the high and low end of the participation scale ranges from 5 percent to 20 percent.

The relationship shown in table 9-2 involving people who advocate that "blacks are genetically inferior" deserves more detailed analysis, however. Obviously, the question is likely to have a much more personal impact on blacks than on whites. The results of the same pair of questions treating black and white respondents separately are shown in table 9-3. Whites show a much greater tolerance than blacks on this question. The difference between whites and blacks of the same SES and participation levels is as much as 45 percent and does not diminish with increasing SES. The comparisons of participants and nonparticipants, within each racial and SES category, on the other hand, show a much less consistent pattern.

It is also clear from table 9-2 that participation makes the most difference in tolerance for low-income people. For five of the eight questions the difference is statistically significant at the 0.01 level, and for a sixth it is significant at the 0.05 level. For high-SES people, while more active

TABLE 9-2. Tolerance, by Level of Community Participation

Percent giving more tolerant response

Question and socioeconomic status	Respondent's position on ICP scale[a]						N	Chi square
	0	1	2	3	4	5		
Should a person who is against all churches and religion be allowed to make a speech in your city?								
Low SES	62.7	68.9	72.4	79.5	75.6	68.0	2,569	31.88**
Middle SES	80.6	84.7	84.4	88.8	86.3	89.0	2,385	13.44*
High SES	91.8	90.0	91.1	93.2	96.2	96.8	1,303	10.03
. . . be allowed to teach in a college or university?								
Low SES	44.9	47.5	45.3	51.2	51.2	65.3	2,568	14.47**
Middle SES	62.0	62.5	58.8	68.1	67.9	70.8	2,380	12.93*
High SES	72.4	75.7	75.8	77.5	78.3	82.8	1,302	6.13
. . . be allowed to keep a book he wrote in your public library?								
Low SES	58.4	67.0	67.6	72.3	72.1	66.7	2,570	28.65**
Middle SES	76.4	81.9	78.4	81.9	84.7	80.5	2,383	9.40
High SES	87.9	86.5	88.9	91.0	87.9	92.5	1,304	4.90
Should a person who believes that blacks are genetically inferior be allowed to make a speech in your city?								
Low SES	53.0	58.3	61.7	65.1	61.6	58.7	2,568	18.10**
Middle SES	66.5	67.7	68.2	75.0	78.6	68.2	2,384	12.15*
High SES	78.9	79.9	83.1	84.7	81.3	88.1	1,305	7.60
. . . be allowed to keep a book he wrote in your public library?								
Low SES	54.8	64.6	63.4	69.3	59.3	60.0	2,567	26.16**
Middle SES	69.7	75.2	73.5	78.9	83.2	69.5	2,384	16.92**
High SES	80.6	80.3	82.2	85.6	84.9	89.3	1,304	8.27
Should a member of such a group [identified by respondent as a group in the city whose ideas are bad, dangerous, or with which he/she disagrees most often] be allowed to speak?								
Low SES	70.5	73.5	76.8	83.3	86.4	69.0	831	10.18
Middle SES	82.0	87.1	83.8	91.4	84.0	85.7	1,002	6.70
High SES	91.1	95.3	91.0	94.1	98.0	94.8	659	5.33
. . . be allowed to teach in a college or university?								
Low SES	54.6	50.3	54.2	59.8	65.9	48.3	824	5.09
Middle SES	67.6	73.8	65.5	79.1	64.0	68.8	1,001	11.32*
High SES	77.2	78.3	79.0	78.5	88.2	86.5	657	5.58
. . . be allowed to keep a book he wrote in your public library?								
Low SES	56.8	59.2	69.0	74.4	56.8	58.6	827	14.00*
Middle SES	71.7	83.1	75.1	89.9	78.7	75.3	998	20.57**
High SES	84.8	87.7	89.2	90.4	90.2	94.8	657	5.32

**Significant at the 0.01 level.
*Significant at the 0.05 level.
a. Scale ranges from least active to most active in ascending numerical order.

TABLE 9-3. Tolerance, by Race and Level of Community Participation

Percent giving more tolerant response

Question, race, and socioeconomic status	Respondent's position on ICP scale[a]						N	Chi square[b]
	0	1	2	3	4	5		
Should a person who believes that blacks are genetically inferior be allowed to make a speech in your city?								
Blacks								
Low SES	47.2	48.4	55.1	54.5	54.5	63.6	485	3.85
Middle SES	68.8	53.1	67.4	66.7	78.9	56.7	288	6.36
High SES	57.9	53.8	72.7	50.0	84.6	71.4	82	4.86
Whites								
Low SES	59.0	60.7	63.4	70.2	68.3	58.6	1,467	6.76
Middle SES	67.3	69.9	69.4	76.0	79.2	71.8	1,804	9.07
High SES	80.7	82.7	84.4	86.4	80.0	89.9	1,081	6.97
. . . be allowed to keep a book he wrote in your public library?								
Blacks								
Low SES	51.8	53.8	49.5	57.6	45.5	45.5	485	1.66
Middle SES	55.8	63.3	70.7	52.4	68.4	50.0	288	7.17
High SES	73.7	38.5	54.5	62.5	84.6	57.1	82	7.58
Whites								
Low SES	58.1	66.8	68.0	72.8	70.7	69.0	1,466	17.38**
Middle SES	73.1	77.9	75.4	80.7	86.5	74.5	1,804	11.31*
High SES	83.3	84.1	84.4	86.9	84.8	91.5	1,081	5.36

**Significant at the 0.01 level.
*Significant at the 0.05 level.
a. Scale ranges from least active to most active in ascending numerical order.
b. All significance tests shown in this table apply to the differences between participants and nonparticipants within each racial category. The difference between white and black respondents on this question, not shown in this table, is significant at better than the 0.01 level for both questions and all SES levels.

individuals do express more tolerant attitudes, the differences are not statistically significant in any of the eight tests.

For questions involving the person or group in the community who the respondent felt had "bad or dangerous ideas" or with whom the respondent "disagreed with the most often," the pattern is less clear-cut but still generally in the same direction. However, active participants were very different from nonparticipants in another way. Although many respondents could not identify any group in their community with "bad or dangerous" ideas, participants were able to do so more often than nonparticipants. Some 30.6 percent of the participants identified a "bad or dangerous" group, while only 20.3 percent of the nonparticipants did so. The implication here seems to be that participation is associated with

TABLE 9-4. Opposition Groups Identified by Respondents

Group	Frequency of mention	Percent of responses	Tolerance toward category[a]
Government officials and agencies	389	18.6	73.7
Racists, white supremacists	311	14.9	
Criminals, drug pushers	204	9.8	36.9
Sex peddlers	88	4.2	
Neighborhood citizen groups	65	3.1	69.8
Issue advocacy groups	265	12.7	
Church groups	206	9.9	
Political organizations	168	8.0	
Professional/business	131	6.3	
Racial groups	123	5.9	65.8
Other demographic groupings	70	3.4	
Economic groups	53	2.5	
Service/social/recreation	14	0.7	
Citizen crime prevention	1	0.0	
Total number mentioned	2,088	100.0	

a. Percentage of respondents indicating a high level of tolerance on an index combining the three questions involving opposition groups identified by respondent.

a greater awareness of specific groups or willingness to reveal that one disagrees with them.

The groups mentioned by respondents in order of frequency of mention are listed in table 9-4. Perhaps the most striking fact is that the category most frequently mentioned by this study's respondents (389 times, representing 18.6 percent of all groups or individuals indicated) was government officials. The identification question used in this study involved two parts: the first part asked for "any group of people in [respondent's city] whose ideas you feel are particularly bad or dangerous," and the second part, used only if no group was mentioned in response to the first question, sought "a group of people in the city you like the least or find yourself disagreeing with most often." Most of the government officials were mentioned in response to the second, milder form.

A second important point is that the neighborhood organizations or other participation organizations in the cities were mentioned rarely in this context, in spite of their frequent reference by respondents throughout the remainder of the survey. In fact, of the sixty-five times a neighborhood-based organization was mentioned, fifty-eight of them involved a single group, COPS, in San Antonio. As noted earlier, COPS is a highly confrontational and controversial (and powerful) citizen organization. The fact that in the other cities these highly visible participation organizations, which in some cases have quasi-governmental responsibilities, are mentioned so seldom while government officials are mentioned so frequently, speaks volumes about the credibility of these neighborhood associations with the general public. The participation organizations somehow escape the wrath of the public toward bumbling or self-interested public figures. This finding is confirmed by several other survey questions that directly sought to measure the perception of the participation groups.

When all the organizations mentioned by respondents are grouped into four major categories—government officials and agencies; criminals, racists, and sex peddlers; neighborhood organizations (including COPS); and all other groups—some clear patterns emerge, as shown in the right-hand column of table 9-4. As would be expected, tolerance toward criminals is the lowest, averaging only 37 percent, and tolerance toward government officials is the highest, averaging nearly 74 percent, with the other organizations falling in the middle. It is clear that tolerance depends on much more than education and participation alone. It also depends on levels of threat perceived from a particular opposition group and how direct and personal that threat is—such as an advocate of "black inferiority" for blacks or "criminals and drug pushers" for most population groups.

On balance, however, the third elitist argument can be confirmed—or at least the initial part of that argument dealing with the facts of the participation/tolerance relationship. Clearly those who choose to participate are disproportionately of upper and middle SES and possess greater tolerance than those who do not participate. This is true even in communities like our five core cities, which devote substantial resources toward reaching the entire residential population and make special efforts to involve low-income people.

Expanding Democracy versus Expanding Intolerance

The fourth elitist argument—involving the consequences of increased numbers of participants—is the critical one on which rides the theory that expanded democracy may be self-defeating. It is also the one for which the least evidence has been brought to bear in political science literature. In fact, most elite theorists tend to assume that the fourth argument immediately follows if the first three hypotheses are satisfied. Yet there is not a necessary logical connection between the third and fourth propositions. A number of alternative propositions could be offered that are just as consistent with the facts that have been considered so far. Two such alternatives—one concerning the participation process as a screening mechanism and the second treating it as a learning mechanism—will be considered at the end of this discussion.

We have seen that tolerance tends to increase with participation throughout the population, with the strongest effects occurring among low-SES people and at the lower end of the index of community participation. This suggests that whether participation leads to more tolerance or whether more tolerant people tend to participate more, the impact extends to the entire community. It is not just the elites who are more tolerant. A second piece of evidence strengthens this conclusion. In all the data examined here, the average levels of tolerance are similar to or greater than tolerance levels reported by other researchers in national surveys of the general population (see table 9-5). In fact, many of the levels are as great as those found among the elite interviews these researchers conducted.

Yet citizens at all SES levels in the core cities of this study exhibit higher levels of participation than citizens nationwide. The cities were specifically chosen because of their extensive and pervasive systems designed to encourage citizen participation and make it effective in influencing policy. As observed in chapter 4, people in these cities tend to participate in neighborhood, political, and issue groups more often, as a proportion of their community activity, than do their counterparts in other cities. If the elitists' fourth proposition—that wider participation undermines democracy—had any validity, these strong participation cities should show substantially lower levels of tolerance than average because they are substantially more inclusive. Exactly the opposite is true. The respondents in the most participatory cities are more likely, not less likely, to exhibit high levels of tolerance. The results for each of the eight tolerance questions and five categories of this citywide participation scale are shown in table 9-6. Consistent differences are found in most of the questions at most SES levels. These findings are particularly striking because they represent an impact on the tolerance of a cross-section of the community, not just of those who participate. Communities that generate higher levels of community participation stimulate higher levels of tolerance throughout the population.

TABLE 9-5. Surveys of Levels of Tolerance

Percent giving more tolerant response

Survey and question[a]	Tolerance level
General population	
Stouffer[b]	
Speak against churches and religion	37
Teach if against churches and religion	12
Nunn[c]	
Speak against churches and religion	62
Teach if against churches and religion	39
General Social Survey[d]	
Speak against churches and religion	65.2
Speak in support of black inferiority	60.9
Teach if against churches and religion	47.2
Elites	
Stouffer[b]	
Speak against churches and religion	64
Teach if against churches and religion	25
Nunn[c]	
Speak against churches and religion	87
Teach if against churches and religion	59

a. The form of these questions is exactly the same as used in this study, for example, "There are always some people whose ideas are considered bad or dangerous by other people. For instance, somebody who is against all churches and religion. If such a person wanted to make a speech in your community against churches and religion, should he be allowed to speak, or not?"

b. Samuel Stouffer, *Communism, Conformity, and Civil Liberties: A Cross-Section of the Nation Speaks Its Mind* (Doubleday, 1955), pp. 32–33. The survey was conducted in 1954.

c. Clyde Z. Nunn, Harry J. Crockett, Jr., and J. Allen Williams, Jr., *Tolerance for Nonconformity: A National Survey of Americans' Changing Commitment to Civil Liberties* (San Francisco: Jossey-Bass, 1978), pp. 40–41. The survey was conducted in 1973.

d. James A. Davis and Tom W. Smith, *General Social Survey Cumulative File, 1972–1982* (Ann Arbor, Mich.: Interuniversity Consortium for Political and Social Research, 1983), Frequency Addendum, pp. V142, V143, V148. The survey was conducted in 1982.

All the evidence, therefore, indicates that increasing levels of strong participation—involving more people in the policymaking process than would otherwise be involved—does not lead to participants with lower levels of tolerance. Instead, nearly every case of expanded participation has a corresponding result of expanding tolerance levels.

Conclusion

Of the four arguments that constitute the elitist analysis of tolerance and democracy, the initial three propositions, correlating socioeconomic status with tolerance, political participation with socioeconomic status, and participation with tolerance, are solidly confirmed by these data.

TABLE 9-6. Tolerance and Citywide Participation Level

Percent giving more tolerant response

Question and socio-economic status	Low community partici-pation city[a]	Moderate community participation cities		High community participation cities		N	Chi square
		Unstruc-tured[b]	Struc-tured[c]	Unstruc-tured[d]	Struc-tured[e]		
Should a person who is against all churches and religion be allowed to make a speech in your city?							
Low SES	59.2	74.2	64.1	69.1	73.6	2,576	41.07**
Middle SES	75.4	85.8	82.0	87.0	87.8	2,387	33.70**
High SES	87.9	95.7	90.0	93.1	93.9	1,304	12.88**
. . . be allowed to teach in a college or university?							
Low SES	45.5	44.5	42.0	51.6	51.1	2,575	15.49**
Middle SES	58.0	60.5	58.7	64.5	67.9	2,382	17.92**
High SES	70.4	71.3	71.9	78.3	82.4	1,303	20.55**
. . . be allowed to keep a book he wrote in your public library?							
Low SES	56.4	71.6	59.1	65.4	69.2	2,577	38.05**
Middle SES	68.6	81.1	75.0	78.9	86.1	2,385	55.88**
High SES	82.1	87.1	87.7	87.6	93.3	1,305	21.37**
Should a person who believes that blacks are genetically inferior be allowed to make a speech in your city?							
Low SES	52.4	59.4	56.6	59.9	59.4	2,575	8.03
Middle SES	63.0	72.2	67.4	70.3	70.2	2,386	9.15
High SES	79.2	87.0	74.7	85.5	84.4	1,306	16.06**
. . . be allowed to keep a book he wrote in your public library?							
Low SES	54.9	60.3	58.4	59.4	65.1	2,574	15.29**
Middle SES	64.7	75.3	70.5	76.4	77.7	2,386	26.23**
High SES	79.7	80.4	78.6	84.8	87.2	1,305	12.59**
Should a member of such a group [identified by respondent as a group in the city whose ideas are bad, dangerous, or with which he/she disagrees most often] be allowed to speak?							
Low SES	67.0	74.3	69.4	78.6	80.7	833	13.60**
Middle SES	80.2	83.7	81.8	84.3	89.4	1,003	10.73*
High SES	90.0	93.7	88.8	90.8	97.5	659	14.53**
. . . be allowed to teach in a college or university?							
Low SES	56.2	43.8	55.4	52.7	56.7	826	5.72
Middle SES	74.4	62.6	65.6	67.4	73.4	1,002	9.59*
High SES	78.0	75.8	78.7	74.3	85.0	657	7.33*
. . . be allowed to keep a book he wrote in your public library?							
Low SES	53.3	65.4	59.5	56.1	66.8	829	8.51
Middle SES	69.4	77.6	75.7	77.5	83.1	999	12.45**
High SES	81.8	87.4	88.8	92.1	92.5	657	9.96*

**Significant at the 0.01 level.
*Significant at the 0.05 level.
a. San Antonio.
b. Birmingham–Dayton comparison cities (Tucson, Omaha, Colorado Springs, El Paso, Savannah, and Wichita).
c. Birmingham and Dayton.
d. Portland–St. Paul comparison cities (Norfolk, Minneapolis, Louisville, and Buffalo).
e. Portland and St. Paul.

The fourth proposition, that expanded participation will lead to lowered levels of tolerance among participants, is not confirmed. The rejection of the elitist conclusion is based on evidence involving individual level of participation, evidence comparing overall tolerance in highly participatory cities with the national norm, and—most strongly—evidence comparing the tolerance of citizens in highly participatory communities with those in less participatory communities.

We must conclude, therefore, that the elitists have made an unwarranted leap of faith. As the discussion at the beginning of this chapter indicated, most of these theorists correctly observed or deduced the relationship between SES, tolerance, and participation embodied in the first three propositions. They note that being a participant and being tolerant are characteristics of political and economic elites. With virtually no additional evidence, however, many presume that SES is the only causal factor—that only high-SES people, only the elite, will participate in great numbers and will be tolerant toward the ideas of others. Some go even further out on a very shaky limb to conclude that even if you could get more low-SES people to participate, their tolerance and other attitudes would remain at the same level as when they were nonparticipants. In reaching this conclusion, they ignore the possibility of a direct relationship between participation and democratic values, a relationship clearly demonstrated by the evidence presented here.

Two mechanisms may serve to explain why tolerance increases with participation even while it incorporates more and more segments of society that are normally intolerant. One of these is the screening character of the participation process itself. Expanded democracy is not the same as mob rule.

The cities examined here make an extensive effort to bring people into the political process and ensure an opportunity for each person to make her or his opinions known, whatever those opinions may be. Guidelines for the neighborhood associations clearly indicate that they must be open to all opinions. Because they are designed to be the voice of the entire community that they represent, the legitimacy of the group depends upon its willingness to let all viewpoints in the neighborhood be expressed in the neighborhood forums. In Portland, for example, a written guideline calls for dissenting opinions expressed in neighborhood meetings to be fully covered in meeting reports and neighborhood newsletter articles.

A thoroughly intolerant person simply would not be able to put up with the conditions of such a process. The more intolerant of others' opinions a person is, the less attracted he or she would be to the neighborhood participation process. Most people who become involved and stay involved in a participation process are likely to be relatively tolerant toward others in that process. To the extent that the process itself is open to people of all opinions, high levels of tolerance are likely to be demonstrated, whatever other characteristics and socioeconomic backgrounds the participants may have.

The second factor is that participation itself is a learning process. People are not the same at the beginning of the process as they are at the end. Tolerance appears to be one of the lessons learned. The neighborhood associations in the five core cities depend, in many ways, upon this learning process for their continued vitality. The same neighborhood elites cannot keep running the show; regular turnover due to the contingencies in individuals' personal lives is inevitable. New people must be brought in on a regular basis, or the organization will die. The door-to-door outreach that occurs in many of these neighborhoods represents a constant search for potential new activists. Initially these new recruits tend to be hesitant to join the give-and-take of debate in the meetings. Many have a fear of disagreement. But by watching others disagree and remain in the same room—eventually reaching a consensus, or at least a group decision—and by gradually being drawn into that process themselves, they become more comfortable with opposing opinions. And most important, they learn that a decision that succeeds in accommodating many varying points of view is possible. This learning process is not expected to be universal or rapid. Many may drop out of the process rather than learn tolerance. But many, in fact, increase their willingness to let others express their point of view without undue restrictions or hostility.

The complexity of this learning process may be reflected in the finding that a stronger relationship exists for participation and tolerance between communities than within communities. Participation in a single participation process may not in itself create significant changes in individual tolerance levels. Such changes may only be produced through repeated opportunities for political participation in a range of contexts. Thus communities in which such a range of opportunities exists and in which citizens more frequently engage in such participation may, in time, exhibit higher tolerance levels than communities in which these opportunities are more limited.

It is difficult to avoid the conclusion that, within the context of the U.S. political experience at least, an expansion of opportunities for political participation will not tend to undercut the democratic process itself. On the contrary, the evidence developed here indicates that an expanded participation process will increase the attitudes necessary to maintain a strong democracy. The highly participatory structures in each of the five core cities in this study have now been maintained and have grown significantly over a fifteen-year period, in spite of financial commitments demanded by the participation processes and the heavy fiscal pressures each of these cities has faced. The exuberance of the participation activities in each city and the commitment to them that is demonstrated by administrators and citizens alike further strengthen the argument that prodemocracy attitudes and relationships—and not intolerant or authoritarian beliefs—have been fostered and advanced through structures for strong democracy.

CHAPTER 10

Building Community Confidence

WHETHER DEMOCRATIC, AUTHORITARIAN, or otherwise, all governments search for support among their constituents. Those in power want to do what they can to ensure that people perceive the institutions of government as legitimate. In democracies, failure to satisfy voter preferences can easily result in defeat for the party in office. Yet decline in support for a democratic government may indicate a much more serious problem than a misreading of the popular will by incumbents. As popular dissatisfaction endures over time, attitudes may turn from disappointment with incumbents to alienation from the system.

At the national level, unchecked dissatisfaction can lead to the dissolution of the state itself. As Arthur Miller notes, "A democratic political system cannot survive for long without the support of a majority of its citizens."[1] At the local level, rising dissatisfaction can have equally disturbing consequences. Even when strong support remains for the political system—that is, for support of the processes of democracy and political structures in general—dissatisfaction with local government can mean substantial withdrawal of support for any governmental efforts to address critical problems. Tax cuts, spending limits, and a general "Proposition 13 mentality" have left many states and towns with far fewer resources and far less flexibility to meet pressing social needs than they have had for decades. While budget-limiting ballot questions are a form of grassroots democracy, they fail to include most of the features of strong democratic talk and detailed consideration of alternatives that are the hallmarks of the participation systems we have examined. In the early 1990s more and more communities are near programmatic paralysis and several teeter on the brink of financial receivership. Dissatisfaction that reaches these proportions is a problem of the highest order.

1. Arthur H. Miller, "Political Issues and Trust in Government: 1964–70," *American Political Science Review*, vol. 68 (September 1974), p. 951.

At first glance, authoritarian forms of government may seem to possess more effective ways of restraining conflict and mobilizing support than do democracies. Yet as has been seen in Eastern Europe and in the former Soviet Union in the 1990s, the rapid disintegration of authoritarian governments often exposes a deep-rooted distrust of the governmental process running just below a surface acquiescence. In fact, democracies seem to be much better suited to retaining the support of their constituents than other forms of government.[2] People have the opportunity to organize and to make their voices heard in the political process. Conflicts are made public, debated, and usually resolved with a certain degree of acceptance by all parties to the dispute. The pressure-relief mechanism of throwing the rascals out always remains within reach of the citizenry, encouraging government leaders to find an acceptable accommodation with all major constituent interests.

Does More Democracy Mean More Support?

If the basic elements of democracy—such as contested elections, broad citizen enfranchisement, open public debate, and freedom of association—lead to increased support for the political system, it seems reasonable to ask if greater opportunities for democratic participation will strengthen this support further. If it does, increased participation may lead to a greater ability of government to face difficult social challenges and concentrate energy and resources where they are needed most. If, on the other hand, strong participation merely leads to rising expectations that cannot be met, as many argue happened during the war on poverty, then it would widen the gap between citizens and their government and make effective governmental action that much more difficult.

Developing the concept of citizen support for and trust in government and measuring corresponding citizen attitudes have been major tasks of political scientists since the 1950s. Research in this area was spurred by the turmoil of the 1960s, when many people took to the streets and criticism of government became particularly strident. During this time confidence levels eroded sharply, influenced by broad, fundamental issues facing government, especially the Vietnam War and civil rights. The decline in confidence continued into the next decade and the country's

2. Robert A. Dahl, *Polyarchy: Participation and Opposition* (Yale University Press, 1971), pp. 150–52.

collective angst seemed to reach a high water mark when President Jimmy Carter addressed the nation in the summer of 1979 and declared that the nation's "crisis of confidence" constituted "a fundamental threat to American democracy."[3]

Carter's heartfelt analysis of the American condition came across as a schoolmarmish scolding and seemed to undermine confidence in Carter himself. When Ronald Reagan took over, there was an upturn in confidence in government.[4] The improvement in trust scores quickly hit a plateau, however, and confidence levels reported in the 1988 National Election Survey were roughly similar to those around the time of Watergate. But even though the Reagan presidency had only a modest impact on confidence indices, much of the public discussion of the "crisis in confidence" evaporated. Reagan claimed that it was again "morning in America," and his sunny optimism prompted editorialists and magazine writers to look for other topics to wring their hands about. This optimism faded in the early 1990s, however, as the weak economy, the financial problems of many state and local governments, and anger at Congress led to a popular perception that the system had broken down. Yet whatever the public mood about whether or not a crisis of confidence exists, the underlying issues of citizen trust and support remain critically important to the nation's vitality.

In attempting to understand citizen attitudes toward government, scholars have recognized that the concepts of "trust," "responsiveness," and "efficacy" have multiple and overlapping implications. The first attempt to define the concept of political efficacy, for example, was made in 1954 by Campbell, Gurin, and Miller, who referred to it as "the feeling that individual political action does have, or can have, an impact upon the political process, i.e., that it is worthwhile to perform one's civic duties. It is the feeling that the individual citizen can play a part in bringing about change."[5]

As measurement efforts increased, this unidimensional description was seen to have at least three relatively independent components: beliefs about one's individual powers (internal efficacy), beliefs about one's

---

3. "Transcript of President's Address to Country on Energy Problems," *New York Times*, July 16, 1979, p. A10.

4. Arthur Miller, "Is Confidence Rebounding?" *Public Opinion*, vol. 6 (June–July 1983), p. 17; and Seymour Martin Lipset and William Schneider, "The Confidence Gap during the Reagan Years," *Political Science Quarterly*, vol. 102 (Spring 1987), pp. 1–23.

5. Angus Campbell, Gerald Gurin, and Warren E. Miller, *The Voter Decides* (Evanston, Ill.: Row, Peterson, 1954), p. 187.

ability to influence the political system (external efficacy), and beliefs about the responsiveness of the governmental system and the incumbents in office. The importance of the latter distinction, between citizen judgments of government per se and their judgments about the people holding the offices of government, was emphasized by David Easton:

> Some types of evaluations are closely related to what the political authorities do and how they do it. Others are more fundamental in character because they are directed to basic aspects of the system. They represent more enduring bonds and thereby make it possible for members to oppose the incumbents of offices and yet retain respect for the offices themselves, for the way in which they are ordered, and for the community of which they are a part.[6]

Ideally, these concepts should distinguish between sentiments about government policies, ongoing events, incumbent approval, and alienation from the political system itself.[7] Recently, Craig and Niemi have revisited these distinctions using a factor analysis involving thirty-five attitudinal questions.[8] They conclude that at least four separate measures are necessary: internal efficacy, external regime-based efficacy (a sense of "the expectation that conventional rules and procedures for policy formation and implementation facilitate, rather than impede, citizen inputs"), incumbent-based trust, and regime-based trust.[9] Our examination of internal efficacy and external regime-based efficacy is deferred to the next chapter. Here we examine the relationship of participation to the two forms of trust and the related concepts of responsiveness—and to the "respect for community" to which Easton alluded.

We will focus on the hypothesis that three key attitudes are important in reflecting a positive relationship between citizens and their government. The first is the sense of community that enables people to feel that they can have a productive role in working with other people to solve

6. David Easton, "A Re-Assessment of the Concept of Political Support," *British Journal of Political Science*, vol. 5 (October 1975), p. 437.

7. Jack Citrin, "Comment: The Political Relevance of Trust in Government," *American Political Science Review*, vol. 68 (September 1974), p. 987.

8. Stephen C. Craig and Richard G. Niemi, "Political Efficacy and Trust: Results from the 1987 NES Pilot Study," paper prepared for the 1988 annual meeting of the Midwest Political Science Association.

9. Using the definition of Richard D. Shingles, "Sense of Political Efficacy, Political Trust, and the Dimensions of Political Support," cited in Craig and Niemi, "Political Efficacy and Trust."

community problems. Second is the perception that government responds to what they feel, so that citizens will be inspired to take action to affect government policymaking. The third attitude is a sense of trust that government will take the kinds of action that can lead to effective resolution of community problems.

Of Nation and Community

People think differently about their local government than they do about the national government. And they are able to act differently toward it. People recognize that the national government sets the broad framework in which the economic, political, and social activities of people's daily lives are carried out. Yet the local government is expected to carry out many of the functions, from education to police protection to road repair, that directly affect their quality of life.

Participation in national politics, noble as it may be, is tied to events that are distant and influenced by forces beyond any individual's control. Individual participation in a political campaign for state or federal office is only one small cog in a very large machine. Strong democracy activities in one's neighborhood are something else entirely. Working with one's neighbors, being exposed directly to contrary arguments, and devising policies and strategies aimed at consensus influence one's perceptions of the capabilities and limitations of government. The neighborhood associations in the cities studied here also bring participants into direct contact with government leaders, providing ample opportunity to try to influence city officials and to hear their side of the story.

We begin this examination of the trusting relationship or lack thereof between citizens and their government with a look at the relationship between citizens and their community. The logic of Tocqueville leads us to expect that concern for community may be inextricably tied to participation. Tocqueville's small town had no government separate from the people themselves. To trust government was to trust one's neighbors. In contemporary America, the nature of government is much more complex, but the starting point is the same—the ties between citizens and their neighbors in the quest of a better community.

Yet there are as many scholarly approaches to "community" as there are approaches to governmental trust and responsiveness. Robert Booth Fowler, in his recent book, *The Dance with Community*, describes six widely varying "images of community" in current social and political thought, ranging from the relatively private search for community in the traditions and roots of family life to the emphasis on the global village and the encompassing community of the world. Particularly relevant for us is Fowler's description of the "participatory community." This is the idea of community built upon the ideals of Athens and Rousseau and reflected in the passion of the populists of the 1890s, the stridency and idealism of the new left of the 1960s, and the critical analysis of today's participatory pragmatists such as Jane Mansbridge, Benjamin Barber, and Michael Walzer. As Fowler notes, this image of community involves, in addition to the core concept of face-to-face self-governance, "the ideal of community as a public group, a group of citizens, each respected and heard, united by common purpose, encouraged by shared human sympathies."[10]

This sense of community is seen as an essential mechanism of conflict resolution. Harry Eckstein, in his study of the preconditions for stable and effective democracies, notes three ways a balance can be obtained, in practice, between "cohesion and division." One comes into play when a high degree of homogeneity exists in the population, a second involves a high degree of cross-cutting associations and cleavages, and the third depends upon an overarching attitude of solidarity or feeling of community.[11]

A sense of community, then, is viewed as a central building block of a connected, productive, and stable polity. How do the levels of participation in this study relate to the development of this perspective? Is it, as are so many other political refinements, available only with the luxury of time and resources possessed by the relatively well off and well educated? Is community enhanced by political structures or specific forms of participation? In particular, do the regular, face-to-face meetings that occur in most of the neighborhoods of our core cities affect the sense of community in a positive way? And perhaps most crucially, is community developed by participation at all, or are only those with a strong sense of community inclined to participate in the first place?

We found some striking answers to these questions. Contrary to the picture of America as an alienated society, a substantial proportion of the respondents express a high degree of solidarity with their neighbors. The question was posed as follows:

10. Robert Booth Fowler, *The Dance with Community: The Contemporary Debate in American Political Thought* (University Press of Kansas, 1991), p. 43.

11. Harry Eckstein, *Division and Cohesion in Democracy* (Princeton University Press, 1966), p. 197.

TABLE 10-1. Effect of Level of Community Activity on Sense of Community

Percent indicating strong sense of community

Socioeconomic status	Respondent's position on ICP scale[a]						N	Chi square
	0	1	2	3	4	5		
Low	25.6	30.5	40.6	40.1	60.5	52.7	2,493	89.29**
Middle	27.9	30.5	40.1	37.4	44.2	44.1	2,352	37.54**
High	23.7	23.6	42.9	36.8	46.2	53.2	1,284	63.12**

**Significant at the 0.01 level.
a. Scale ranges from least active to most active in ascending numerical order.

Some people say they feel like they have a sense of community with the people in their neighborhood. Others don't feel that way. How about you? Would you say that you feel a strong sense of community with others in your neighborhood, very little sense of community, or something in between?

In response, 34.2 percent of the entire fifteen-city sample expressed a "strong sense of community," while only 22.7 percent noted "very little" sense of community. The remainder were in the middle. These findings are particularly important in light of the fact that these are all residents of central cities, which by many analyses include the most alienated of the populace.

Also relevant is our finding that sense of community is not dependent on socioeconomic status. Among all 6,132 respondents, 32.7 percent of low-SES people expressed a strong sense of community, while 36.2 percent of high-SES people felt the same way (with a chi-square value of only 4.99, this difference is not statistically significant). Very few political attitudes seem as independent of SES. Apparently the opportunities for developing a sense of community exist nearly as often among those who just scrape by in making a living as among those who have plenty of time and resources for leisure pursuits.

In sharp contrast to this egalitarian response, a comparison of individual participation and sense of community showed one of the strongest relationships of the entire study (see table 10-1). Up to thirty percentage points separated the most active from the least active. Over 50 percent of respondents at the highest end of the community participation scale expressed a strong sense of community. And the results were virtually independent of SES, with a good share of the highest levels of community emerging from the lowest SES respondents. These results make clear that participation and sense of community are closely intertwined. People who

TABLE 10-2. Effect of Citywide Participation Level on Sense of Community

Percent indicating strong sense of community

Socio-economic status	Low community partici-pation city[a]	Moderate community participation cities		High community participation cities		N	Chi square
		Unstruc-tured[b]	Struc-tured[c]	Unstruc-tured[d]	Struc-tured[e]		
Low	30.2	36.7	36.7	34.9	28.8	2,495	14.76**
Middle	37.3	31.7	38.9	33.5	32.5	2,353	8.55
High	40.3	33.0	40.6	34.5	34.5	1,284	5.06

**Significant at the 0.01 level.
a. San Antonio.
b. Birmingham–Dayton comparison cities (Tucson, Omaha, Colorado Springs, El Paso, Savannah, and Wichita).
c. Birmingham and Dayton.
d. Portland–St. Paul comparison cities (Norfolk, Minneapolis, Louisville, and Buffalo).
e. Portland and St. Paul.

participate in the life of the community share a strong appreciation of its riches. There is no evidence that a sense of community is in any way adversely affected by higher levels of participation.

A further review of the role of participation structures in sense of community, however, reveals a much less clear picture (table 10-2). The lowest city on the strong participation scale has some of the highest scores for sense of community, and the most participatory cities have some of the lowest scores. Yet this forms no pattern of a reverse effect either. Only at low SES values are the differences between city groups significant, and in this case, the cities at the middle of the participation scale are highest in sense of community. The structures of participation neither enhance nor degrade the sense of community that is associated with individual levels of participation.

In spite of the lack of effect at the citywide level, another aspect of citizen participation structure, the type of community organization in which a respondent is involved, shows a substantial impact (table 10-3). Participation in neighborhood associations is the most likely to be related to high levels of community, followed at some distance by participation in crime prevention groups. The effect is most pronounced for low-SES people, with more than 57 percent of such neighborhood participants expressing a high sense of community, compared with only 27 percent of the low-SES nonparticipants.

Our look at cities around the nation leaves no doubt, then, that participation is an important partner of community building. If a sense

TABLE 10-3. Effects of Type of Organizational Activity on Sense
of Community

Percent indicating strong sense of community

Socioeconomic status	Type of organization in which respondent is active					N	Chi square
	None	Service or social group	Crime watch	Issue group	Neigh-borhood group		
Low	27.1	37.8	49.3	41.3	57.3	2,490	92.41**
Middle	30.5	34.2	45.9	31.4	53.8	2,347	56.35**
High	26.1	38.8	41.9	37.4	51.3	1,282	46.88**

**Significant at the 0.01 level.

of community is an integral part of the health of a democracy, high levels
of participation must also be achieved. And we have seen that neighborhood-based organizations are one of the most fruitful ways to increase
both participation and community.

Yet this information alone is not enough to tell us which comes first.
Does participation cause increased sense of community, or does a strong
sense of community lead to increased participation? If the latter were
true, "artificially" increased levels of participation, through extensive
outreach efforts and heavily promoted involvement programs, might actually bring in more people with a low sense of community and other
"antidemocratic" attitudes. This possibility is particularly disturbing in
light of the lack of discernible influence of highly structured participation
on sense of community; perhaps the structure does offset the value of
participation by drawing in more people who weaken the commitment
to the democratic process.

We addressed the "chicken-or-egg" question through the second
round of interviews with the same people in each community, nearly two
years after the first round was completed. To examine the relationship
of participation to community over time, the responses to the question
about sense of community in the first and second interviews were compared with the change in participation status of the individual. The
following four basic categories of respondents were compared: (1) those
who were not participating in the neighborhood system at the time of
either interview, (2) those who were participating at the first interview
but had stopped participating by the second interview, (3) those who
began participating between interviews, and (4) those who were partic-

TABLE 10-4. Effect of Changes in Participation on Sense of Community[a]

Percent unless otherwise indicated

Participation status	Sense of community			N	Mean value of sense of community[b]
	Lost	Same	Gained		
Continued nonparticipation	25.8	53.9	20.2	2,012	2.07
Stopped participation	25.7	58.4	16.0	257	2.30
Began participation	20.5	54.2	25.3	249	2.37
Continued participation	17.6	65.1	17.3	272	2.55

a. Chi square was 20.98, significant at the 0.01 level.
b. The scale runs from 1, indicating "very little sense of community," to 3, indicating a "strong sense of community."

ipating in the neighborhood system all along. Each person's sense of community was characterized according to whether it had increased, decreased, or stayed the same (see table 10-4).

Not surprisingly, for those who continued in a steady state—either as participants or as nonparticipants—the loss of community generally balanced out the gains. For participants, about 17 percent gained a greater sense of community and about 17 percent lost it. For nonparticipants, the losses outran the gains 26 percent to 20 percent. The greatest net loss of community (26 percent loss versus 16 percent gain) occurs among those who stopped participating in the interim, and the greatest net gain (25 percent gain versus 20 percent loss) occurs among those who began participating in the interim.

So far, these results suggest an impressive cause and effect relationship between participation and sense of community. But are the effects significant? And under what conditions do they operate? The next two tables provide a clear answer. Table 10-5 shows the effects of participation on respondents who started out with weak, moderate, or strong senses of community. In all three cases, participants increased or maintained their sense of community more often than nonparticipants. For example, 72 percent of the participants who started out with a strong sense of community maintained it, compared with only 54 percent of nonparticipants who started out with the same strong sense of community. The higher gains and reduced losses of participants who started out with a moderate sense of community are equally impressive. Only those who started out with a low sense of community seem little affected by their participation; about half in either case failed to improve and about half increased a notch above their low community feeling.

TABLE 10-5. Effect of Participation on Changes in Sense
of Community

Percent

Original sense of community and participation status	Change in sense of community		
	Lost	Same	Gained
Weak sense of community[a]			
Participants	. . .	46.6	53.4
Nonparticipants	. . .	47.2	52.8
Moderate sense of community[b]			
Participants	17.5	49.7	32.8
Nonparticipants	21.1	57.1	21.8
Strong sense of community[c]			
Participants	27.9	72.1	. . .
Nonparticipants	46.1	53.9	. . .

a. The number of respondents was 545; chi square was 0.0095.
b. The number of respondents was 1,206; chi square was 10.24 (significant at the 0.01 level).
c. The number of respondents was 1,079; chi square was 29.661 (significant at the 0.01 level).

TABLE 10-6. Effect of Sense of Community on Changes
in Participation

Percent

Original participation status and sense of community	Change in participation		
	Stopped	Continued	Began
Participants[a]			
Weak sense of community	67.8	32.2	. . .
Moderate sense of community	50.8	49.2	. . .
Strong sense of community	43.4	56.6	. . .
Nonparticipants[b]			
Weak sense of community	. . .	94.1	5.9
Moderate sense of community	. . .	90.2	9.8
Strong sense of community	. . .	84.9	15.1

a. The number of respondents was 531; chi square was significant at the 0.01 level.
b. The number of respondents was 2,314; chi square was significant at the 0.01 level.

Table 10-6 shows the reciprocal effect of community on participation.
It too is significant. Participants with a strong sense of community were
much more likely to keep participating than those with a weak or moderate sense of community. Likewise, nonparticipants with a strong sense
of community were more than twice as likely (15 percent versus 6 percent) to begin participating compared with those with a weak sense of
community.

Both sides in the chicken-or-egg controversy, in this case, are winners. Some degree of mutual or reciprocal causation and support prevails. Participation leads to a greater sense of community, which in turn leads to more participation. The extremists of both sides are wrong: strong participation does not undo itself by simply bringing in more people with anticommunity, antiparticipatory attitudes. It does bring them in, but it also develops their sense of community. Conversely, sense of community does not merely follow in the wake of participation, it also leads.

This happy relationship is not common among measures of political attitudes and participation. In fact, the same analysis applied to the next questions, concerning responsiveness and trust, yields no clear pattern of causation in either direction. Participation and sense of community are more closely associated and more able to engender one another than nearly any other pair of characteristics of the citizenry we have examined.

The Perception of Government Responsiveness

Many of the earlier attempts to explore concepts related to support for government revolved around a sense that political action can have an impact on policymakers. In many ways, this is the essence of legitimacy for a democratic government. As Steven Finkel notes, democratic theorists—and particularly those Dennis Thompson called "citizenship theorists"—believe:

> Participation in politics is thought to make the citizen more likely to consider the institutions, norms, and values of a given regime morally proper, to promote an increase in satisfaction with the system as a whole. Through taking part in the decision-making processes of government, the participant begins to see the system as more legitimate, and to accept more readily collective decision and policy outcomes.[12]

We consider here measures of citizen perceptions of government responsiveness, as distinct from the issue-based measures used in earlier chapters to establish actual levels of government responsiveness. These perception-based measures are somewhat broader, capturing not only

12. Dennis F. Thompson, *The Democratic Citizen: Social Science and Democratic Theory in the Twentieth Century* (Cambridge University Press, 1970); and Steven E. Finkel, "The Effects of Participation on Political Efficacy and Political Support: Evidence from a West German Panel," *Journal of Politics*, vol. 49 (May 1987), p. 443.

how well policymakers respond on specific issues, but also the whole range of relationships between citizens and policymakers—relationships that lead citizens to conclude that their public officials are or are not acting in a responsive manner. These perceptions have been measured by several standard questions in the regular national surveys of the Center for Political Studies of the Institute for Social Research at the University of Michigan. One of the questions is "Over the years, how much attention do you feel the government pays to what people think when it decides what to do—a good deal, some, or not much?" Other questions in this responsiveness set deal more specifically with political parties, elections, and Congress.

Craig and Niemi found that the "attention" question relates most strongly to "regime-based efficacy" measures but also is linked to incumbent-based efficacy and incumbent-based trust.[13] In our study the question seemed to exhibit a substantially different pattern of results than the external efficacy question. For the local level, it seems almost equivalent to the broader "regime-based trust" questions of Craig and Niemi. Within the context of a "democratic system" determined by national politics, the local responsiveness question captures the essence of how local government is expected to act. It is key in addressing the sense of legitimacy as it applies to the local level. As such, we adapted this question for use as a prime measure of responsiveness, substituting "government in Dayton" or "government in St. Paul," and so on, for the word "government" in the questions with national referents.

To focus on the issue of local government responsiveness in the context of community participation, respondents were also asked,

> How do you think the people who run your city or town would react if you let them know about a major neighborhood problem you are having? If you explained your point of view to the officials, what effect do you think it would have? Would they give your point of view serious consideration, would they pay only a little attention, or would they ignore what you had to say?

The responses to these two questions work together to reveal the impact of participation. The focus is on the percentage of those who responded

13. When running their factor analysis without constraining the number of primary factors, however, Craig and Niemi found that the "attention" question along with the "elections" question in this responsiveness series came out together as an additional primary factor.

TABLE 10-7. Effect of Level of Community Activity on Perception of Government Responsiveness

Percent perceiving most responsiveness

Question and socioeconomic status	Respondent's position on ICP scale[a]						N	Chi square
	0	1	2	3	4	5		
The government pays a good deal of attention to what people think								
Low SES	28.7	29.8	31.3	35.2	34.9	36.0	2,535	5.53
Middle SES	32.1	33.3	38.3	41.1	34.1	43.6	2,353	14.17*
High SES	45.8	41.0	47.2	47.7	45.3	49.0	1,290	3.64
The government would give serious attention to my views about a major neighborhood problem								
Low SES	25.7	36.5	32.2	38.2	48.2	42.9	2,346	40.30**
Middle SES	35.4	41.4	38.7	44.2	43.7	59.3	2,274	30.83**
High SES	47.6	49.6	53.7	56.3	59.8	59.2	1,236	8.70

**Significant at the 0.01 level.
*Significant at the 0.05 level.
a. Scale ranges from least active to most active in ascending numerical order.

"a good deal of attention" to the first question or "serious consideration" to the second question.

In contrast to the "sense of community" questions, answers to these responsiveness questions exhibit the more typical strong dependency on socioeconomic status. Among low-SES respondents, 30.2 percent thought their local government paid "a good deal" of attention to what citizens think and 31.6 percent thought city officials would give serious attention to their views on a neighborhood problem. The corresponding figures for high-SES respondents were 45.7 percent and 53.4 percent. The percentage spread between high and low SES here is more than five times that found for sense of community. The relationship between participation and perception of responsiveness, on the other hand, is not as strong as the relationship between participation and sense of community (see table 10-7). For low- and middle-SES respondents, three of the four statistical tests yield significant results. In all but one of these cases, the highest participation level yields the highest perception of government responsiveness, and the lowest participation level yields the lowest responsiveness results. The progression from low to high is not always uniform, however, and neither of the tests for high-SES respondents yields significant results. It seems safe to conclude that participation is related to an increased perception of responsiveness for low- and moderate-SES citizens. Apparently higher income people have nearly as much reason to believe that government is responsive whether or not they participate in community activities.

TABLE 10-8. Effect of Citywide Participation Level on Perception of Government Responsiveness

Percent perceiving most responsiveness

Question and socio-economic status	Low community partici-pation city[a]	Moderate community participation cities		High community participation cities		N	Chi square
		Unstruc-tured[b]	Struc-tured[c]	Unstruc-tured[d]	Struc-tured[e]		
The government pays a good deal of attention to what people think							
Low SES	27.9	32.0	26.8	28.6	34.8	2,573	14.05**
Middle SES	34.0	31.0	28.2	40.7	41.5	2,368	32.63**
High SES	30.8	42.2	39.7	50.0	54.2	1,296	38.46**
The government would give serious attention to my views about a major neighborhood problem							
Low SES	27.5	32.5	29.8	32.7	34.9	2,350	8.63
Middle SES	35.5	41.8	38.4	45.1	42.2	2,275	7.61
High SES	44.8	56.8	43.8	58.3	58.1	1,237	20.23**

**Significant at the 0.01 level.
a. San Antonio.
b. Birmingham–Dayton comparison cities (Tucson, Omaha, Colorado Springs, El Paso, Savannah, and Wichita).
c. Birmingham and Dayton.
d. Portland–St. Paul comparison cities (Norfolk, Minneapolis, Louisville, and Buffalo).
e. Portland and St. Paul.

In spite of their comparatively moderate relation to individual participation activities, increased citywide participation levels lead to clear results in levels of perceived responsiveness (table 10-8). Unlike the inconclusive relationship of sense of community with participation, most of the statistical tests here are definitive. In general, the cities at the high end of the participation scale have higher perceived responsiveness scores, and those at the low end have lower scores. The differences between Portland–St.Paul and their comparison group and between Birmingham–Dayton and their comparison group are not consistent, however. Clearly, participation at the citywide level does make a significant difference in attitudes of citizens toward government responsiveness, but participation structure alone is not the dominant factor.

The type of group in which a respondent participates continues to be a major factor in perception of responsiveness (table 10-9). Neighborhood groups again lead the pack, but interest groups, rather than crime watch organizations, are generally in second place. Surprisingly, the social and service organizations make a strong showing as well. Apparently any activity that tends to stimulate politicians to respond—perhaps by getting them to come out to speak to the group or to bless it with special

TABLE 10-9. Effect of Type of Organizational Activity on
Perception of Government Responsiveness

Percent perceiving most responsiveness

Question and socioeconomic status	None	Type of organization in which respondent is active				N	Chi square
		Service or social group	Crime watch	Issue group	Neigh-borhood group		
The government pays a good deal of attention to what people think							
Low SES	28.6	34.8	29.1	33.3	37.6	2,523	10.18*
Middle SES	33.0	38.6	35.1	39.6	40.5	2,348	9.86*
High SES	45.2	45.9	37.8	46.8	48.5	1,288	2.77
The government would give serious attention to my views about a major neighborhood problem							
Low SES	27.9	38.3	32.0	35.8	49.6	2,343	38.61**
Middle SES	36.0	44.4	40.0	46.9	50.7	2,270	26.38**
High SES	48.0	59.0	43.2	59.6	56.3	1,234	15.90**

**Significant at the 0.01 level.
*Significant at the 0.05 level.

recognition or favors from time to time—leads to an increased sense of governmental responsiveness. But for members of crime watches who tend to be recipients of similar political gestures, this potentially favorable activity may be countered by disappointment in government attempts to deal with crime and a self-help attitude made necessary by a failure of government to do its job.

Overall, participation—and particularly participation within neighborhood organizations—does relate to an increased sense of government responsiveness. The effect is present at the individual level, the organizational level, and the citywide level. The effects during the two-year period between the two rounds of interviews did not yield consistent implications for causal relationships between these two variables, however. Apparently, the relationship between participation and perceived responsiveness is not nearly as direct and unencumbered as that between participation and sense of community. Once again, however, the negative argument—that high levels of participation lead to increased frustration and disenchantment with government—is disproved. The fears based on experiences with the community action program in the 1960s and other federally mandated involvement are unfounded in the fifteen cities explored. Participation does not ensure that governments will be responsive or will be seen to be so, but it does make it easier for confidence to be built between citizens and their government.

In Government We Trust?

Perhaps the most common survey question used in assessing confidence in government is one involving a basic measure of trust:

> How much of the time do you think you can trust the government in Washington to do what is right—just about always, most of the time, or only some of the time?

While sense of community questions tap the first stage of connection between citizens and the larger society and the responsiveness questions address the legitimacy of democratic structures, trust questions deal with the end product of governance—the bottom line of the confidence ledger. If government cannot be trusted to do the job, of what value are any positive attitudes about the intermediate stages of the process? If trust is permanently missing, how long can a democratic government survive and thrive?

As important as trust is, however, assessing an individual's trust in "government" is not nearly as straightforward as, for example, assessing that person's trust in a close friend or business partner. In the first place, evaluations of incumbent office holders, of the institution of the presidency or of Congress, and of the political system tend to be thoroughly mixed together. For example, answers to the standard question given above, which does not mention incumbents, are found to be highly correlated with opinions about the incumbents.[14] In fact, Craig and Niemi concluded that this question was most related to their "incumbent-based trust" category, with a lesser but still substantial connection to the broad evaluation of the democratic system as a whole and to the perceived responsiveness of incumbents.

In addition, the relation of a lack of trust, as measured by such questions, to support for the political system are not as direct as one might expect. One might assume, for example, that those who demonstrate a great deal of cynicism are more likely to withdraw from the political system than those who have more confidence in government. Yet a number of studies have shown that the cynical and confident do not differ significantly in their propensity to vote, participate in campaigns, or

14. Paul R. Abramson and Ada W. Finifter, "On the Meaning of Political Trust: New Evidence from Items Introduced in 1978," *American Journal of Political Science*, vol. 25 (May 1981), pp. 297–307. See also Stanley Feldman, "The Measurement and Meaning of Trust in Government," *Political Methodology*, vol. 9, no. 3 (1983), pp. 341–54.

follow politics. As Jack Citrin put it, "The politically cynical [are] as likely as those expressing trust in government to be eligible for good citizenship awards."[15]

Alternatively, perhaps confidence in government does not in and of itself change participation patterns but can affect participation under the right circumstances. An intriguing hypothesis was generated by William Gamson, who suggested that low confidence in government combined with a high sense of personal political efficacy was the optimum mixture of traits that would stimulate participation.[16] This appears reasonable. People who feel angry about how things are going and who also feel they are personally capable of influencing events would be the most likely to try to do something about changing the system. Despite this apparent logic, the relationship is not evident when survey data are analyzed. The efficacious and mistrustful are not more likely, in general, to get involved in the political process than those who are efficacious and trustful.[17]

Finally, examining the effect of local participation on local government is a step removed from the goals of more common measurements of trust involving national population samples. We have no illusions that working to solve local problems will substantially affect a person's basic cynicism (or lack thereof) about the larger political system. There is no reason to expect that increased trust in one's local government will automatically translate into the same degree of trust in the national government. In fact, a certain level of cynicism is expected to remain due to more basic personality traits as well as to long-standing perceptions of politics as a whole, no matter how trustworthy a local government proves itself to be.

The design of this study helped us to sharpen the definition of trust and focus it on the local community. To establish a common base with previous work in the field, two of the most frequently used questions for

15. Citrin, "Comment: The Political Relevance of Trust in Government," p. 984. See also Seymour Martin Lipset and William Schneider, *The Confidence Gap: Business, Labor, and Government in the Public Mind* (Free Press, 1983), p. 341.

16. William A. Gamson, *Power and Discontent* (Homewood, Ill.: Dorsey, 1968), p. 48.

17. John Fraser, "The Mistrustful-Efficacious Hypothesis and Political Participation," *Journal of Politics*, vol. 32 (May 1970), pp. 444–49; Brett W. Hawkins, Vincent L. Marando, and George A. Taylor, "Efficacy, Mistrust, and Political Participation: Findings from Additional Data and Indicators," *Journal of Politics*, vol. 33 (November 1971), pp. 1130–36; and Meredith W. Watts, "Efficacy, Trust, and Commitment to the Political Process," *Social Science Quarterly*, vol. 54 (December 1973), p. 623–31. For a different conceptualization of this problem with findings in line with the Gamson prediction, see Jeffrey M. Paige, "Political Orientation and Riot Participation," *American Sociological Review*, vol. 36 (October 1971), pp. 810–20.

measuring trust in government were asked—the question presented above and a companion question: "Would you say the government is pretty much run by a few big interests looking out for themselves or that it is run for the benefit of all the people?" (For the latter, answers were recorded not only in the categories of "big interests" and "all the people," but also in a separate response category of "both the big interests and the public at large.") Both questions have been a long-standing part of the Center for Political Studies' measure of trust and were shown by Craig and Niemi to combine trust and efficacy components in nearly identical ways.

In addition, a series of matched questions replaced the references to "the government in Washington" and "the government" with a specific reference to the government of the respondent's city. Thus Birmingham residents were asked, "How much of the time do you think you can trust the government in Birmingham to do what is right—just about always, most of the time, or only some of the time?" The same technique was used for both questions, in each of the fifteen cities in these surveys.

We then took as the measure of trust the difference in response between the local version and the Washington version of each question. This allowed us to factor out the constant component of trust or cynicism inherent in a person's outlook on politics in general. What remains in this measurement is the difference in trust between the local government and the national government, which could be expected to be more directly related to the performance of local government itself.

Our overall results indicate a high level of local trust. More than 37 percent of all respondents felt that local government was more likely than the national government to "do what is right," compared with only 13 percent who were more trusting of national government. The remainder, about 50 percent of the sample, gave equivalent trust ratings to local and national governments. The "for the benefit of all" question yielded similar results, with nearly 31 percent being more favorably disposed toward local governments, while only 8 percent were more favorably disposed toward the national government. This confirms long-standing observations that people are able to trust governments close to home more readily than those they see only at a distance and through the eyes of the television camera.

Trust does vary significantly with socioeconomic status. Higher income people are more likely to feel that the local government will do "what is right" (40.1 percent) and will look out for the good of all the

TABLE 10-10. Effect of Level of Community Activity on Trust in Local Government

Percent indicating more trust in local government

Question and socioeconomic status	Respondent's position on ICP scale[a]						N	Chi square
	0	1	2	3	4	5		
Local government can be trusted more often than national government to do what is right								
Low SES	32.7	34.4	35.7	34.1	43.8	45.3	2,468	14.84
Middle SES	32.1	40.7	37.0	41.3	37.9	39.9	2,340	22.15**
High SES	33.0	30.4	46.9	46.2	40.0	44.2	1,287	33.68**
Local government is more likely than national government to look out for the good of all the people								
Low SES	25.1	26.0	31.1	39.2	31.0	33.8	2,098	26.48**
Middle SES	27.4	34.9	31.8	32.1	36.7	44.2	1,960	24.72**
High SES	32.6	33.5	33.1	45.4	34.5	30.4	1,031	13.79

**Significant at the 0.01 level.
a. Scale ranges from least active to most active in ascending numerical order.

people (34.7 percent). The corresponding figures for low-SES people were 34.5 percent and 27.7 percent. The difference between high- and low-SES attitudes of trust is statistically significant at the 0.01 level and is greater than the difference for a sense of community, but it is substantially less than for the perception of responsiveness.

Participation also makes a major difference (see table 10-10). In general, those who participate least have the least local trust; this is true for all income levels. Those who participate most, however, do not always exhibit the most local trust; sometimes they are eclipsed by higher levels for the moderate participants. Other anomalies are also exhibited. Low-SES people appear to remain more skeptical of government's ability to do what is right except at the very highest levels of participation, while high-SES people, regardless of their level of participation, have a fairly constant sense that local government works for the good of all the people. The raw trust scores, which do not factor out variation in broader trust measures, show no significant relation at all to participation levels. Apparently the relationships uncovered here are often masked by enduring differences in personal cynicism or inclination to trust that do not relate to an inclination to participate.

On the other hand, the relationship between citywide participation structure and trust is the strongest of any confidence measure found here (table 10-11). All six statistical tests—including one for each question

TABLE 10-11. Effect of Citywide Participation Level on Trust in Local Government

Percent indicating more trust in local government

Question and socio-economic status	Low community partici-pation city[a]	Moderate community participation cities		High community participation cities		N	Chi square
		Unstruc-tured[b]	Struc-tured[c]	Unstruc-tured[d]	Struc-tured[e]		
Local government can be trusted more often than national government to do what is right							
Low SES	31.7	33.4	31.7	34.0	39.6	2,505	32.66**
Middle SES	36.3	31.6	32.0	34.7	43.9	2,355	52.58**
High SES	32.3	32.7	31.0	35.9	51.1	1,293	59.73**
Local government is more likely than national government to look out for the good of all the people							
Low SES	21.4	25.0	26.7	21.7	35.2	2,128	50.02**
Middle SES	26.6	25.8	27.9	25.4	41.9	1,973	70.76**
High SES	21.2	32.2	34.3	35.6	40.6	1,037	38.16**

**Significant at the 0.01 level.
a. San Antonio.
b. Birmingham–Dayton comparison cities (Tucson, Omaha, Colorado Springs, El Paso, Savannah, and Wichita).
c. Birmingham and Dayton.
d. Portland–St. Paul comparison cities (Norfolk, Minneapolis, Louisville, and Buffalo).
e. Portland and St. Paul.

and for each SES level—show a very significant pattern in the same direction. The cities at the high end of the citywide participation scale receive the highest trust ratings, in some cases with nearly twice as high a percentage of respondents expressing trust in the local government as in the cities at the lowest end of the citywide participation scale. In most cases, the more structured participation cities also exhibit greater trust levels than their matched groups of cities. Thus, while citywide partici-pation levels seem to have little influence on sense of community and only a little more on perception of responsiveness, the bottom line of trust in government's ability to do its job is substantially enhanced by strong participation.

This impact is seen in graphic terms in several of the core cities we examined. In Dayton, for example, the passage of several bond measures in recent years was directly attributable to the existence of the partici-pation system. Each time, the city made a careful effort to present its best case for passage of the measure to each Priority Board and asked the board members to work in their communities for the measures. In the case of one school bond measure, the Priority Boards had enough

clout to bargain their support for the measure in return for a new structure of citizen councils in each school. The measure passed, and the
councils were established and continue to operate today. In Portland, a
progressive city councillor who had originally won office by appealing
to neighborhood support gradually came to be perceived as taking that
support for granted and was voted out of office. She was replaced by a
much more conservative candidate who nevertheless rekindled that neighborhood confidence.

Why confidence in government tends to be fostered by the participation systems in these core cities becomes quite clear upon examination
of their operational style. In each city—through neighborhood coalition
offices, a citywide advisory group, a budget initiatives board, or citizen-
administrator bodies, neighborhood representatives sit down on a regular
basis with government officials. They have the opportunity to express
their concerns, thank the officials for responding to a previous request,
and discuss areas where government action has been inadequate. This
happens not just in reaction to a community crisis, but week by week
and month by month as the small and large issues arise. Neighborhood
residents are encouraged—in some cases badgered—to become part of
this process. Most of the population feel they have the opportunity to
become involved. Some groups, the American Indians and the Hmong
immigrants in St. Paul, for example, do occasionally feel left out of the
process, but for most, including the larger minority groups, the chance
to have their voice consistently heard at city hall generates a sense that
government officials care about their views and act on their concerns.

Finally, in contrast to other measures of community confidence used
here, trust in local government seems to be relatively unaffected by the
type of organization in which citizens are individually involved (table
10-12). Participants in neighborhood groups are most often high on the
trust scale, but those in issue groups and social or service groups also do
well. A mix of organizational incentives seems to affect trust in government. Involvement in work on political and community issues is one
route for citizens to come to a recognition that local officials are worthy
of some degree of trust. On the other hand, for many participants in
service and social organizations, increased contact with political and
governmental leaders may be as powerful at encouraging trust. As with
the other measures of community confidence, however, there is no evidence that involvement in any type of organization is likely to lead to
increased frustration with or alienation from the governmental process.

TABLE 10-12. Effect of Type of Organizational Activity on Trust in Local Government

Percent indicating more trust in local government

Question and socioeconomic status	None	Type of organization in which respondent is active				N	Chi square
		Service or social group	Crime watch	Issue group	Neigh-borhood group		
Local government can be trusted more often than national government to do what is right							
Low SES	32.9	38.1	33.3	40.4	38.0	2,458	8.99
Middle SES	35.0	40.7	35.7	39.1	41.2	2,335	8.43
High SES	32.5	47.7	40.5	43.7	44.7	1,285	28.08**
Local government is more likely than national government to look out for the good of all the people							
Low SES	26.6	28.8	22.6	38.4	32.3	2,088	25.46**
Middle SES	29.6	35.1	32.4	35.0	39.5	1,956	11.88
High SES	31.0	36.9	34.4	37.8	38.0	1,030	6.85

**Significant at the 0.01 level.

Conclusion

The relationship between strong participation and high levels of community confidence in local government is not simple. In general, increased participation does lead to greater sense of community, increased governmental legitimacy, and enhanced status of governmental institutions. In general, the fears that expanded participation efforts will engender rising and unmet expectations or promotion of antidemocratic or antisystem attitudes are unfounded. But many factors work toward both positive and negative relationships between citizens and their government.

On an individual level, the relationship of participation to a sense of community is the clearest and most mutually supportive. Participation builds community, and procommunity attitudes generate participation. Neighborhood organizations are among the strongest promoters of this sense of community. But community-oriented attitudes do not automatically extend to the citywide level. Developing a strong neighborhood system and conducting extensive outreach to encourage participation throughout the city does not ensure that the broad cross-section of the city will capture the spirit.

For low- and middle-SES residents, participation also generates a sense that city hall is more responsive. Even though participants do not get everything they seek, they feel that government is listening to what they have to say. This feeling is strengthened as participation becomes more frequent and consistent. Neighborhood, political, and issue advocacy groups help to further their members' sense that they can have an impact. And at a citywide level, high levels of participation, but not necessarily extensive participation structures, tend to reinforce the confidence of citizens that the government is paying attention.

The final outcome of efforts to build community confidence—the trust of citizens that their government is taking appropriate actions and conducting programs for the benefit of all citizens in the community—is clearly supported by participation activities. When measured against similar attitudes toward the national government, local institutions come out far ahead. Participation is one of the reasons for this local advantage, with the strong participation structures having the most impact. Cities with such structures and cities with high levels of community participation in general generate substantial citizen confidence. Apparently citizens develop a sense of their government not only through their own direct experiences, but also by recognizing the institutional arrangements for public decisionmaking that government has helped to establish. These structures tend to create a climate in which all the people—whether or not they are active participants—are more likely to feel that government is looking out for their interests.

Strong participation is no panacea. Deep-rooted social and community problems cannot be overcome with a tip of the hat and a friendly smile exchanged between the governors and the governed. Government programs will always be the subject of intense scrutiny and frequent criticism from many community sectors. In a functioning democracy, such scrutiny is essential. But participation can lead to greater mutual understanding among citizens and between citizens and their leaders. It can lead to greater appreciation of the limitations and potential of government. Above all, it can encourage and nurture cooperative efforts to address community concerns—cooperation that is critical in a time of rapid social change and increasingly intense economic pressures.

CHAPTER 11

Enhancing Citizen Capacity

Aɴ ɪᴍᴘᴏʀᴛᴀɴᴛ ᴠɪʀᴛᴜᴇ of participatory democracy is that it is a means of nurturing citizens. In the collective vision of various theorists, participation works to educate people about the operations of government, affords them the opportunity to understand the potential and limits of their own personal influence, sharpens their cognitive skills, and gives them the experience necessary to develop self-confidence in their abilities. The logic is simple and compelling: one learns to be a citizen through experience.

Political Efficacy, Self-Actualization, and Knowledge

The surveys for this study were designed with many of these claims about participation and citizenship in mind. Political scientists who have worked in this area have largely focused on the notion of "political efficacy." Unfortunately, the study of the relationship between participation and political efficacy has been hampered by methodological problems related to the questions used in survey research to tap efficacy. Beyond the difficulties of question wording and reciprocal causation is another issue: the perceived sense of efficacy is only part of what theorists have in mind when they trumpet the virtues of participation.

According to theorists, the development of feelings of effectiveness and empowerment through participation involves two other sources of personal growth: increases in knowledge and self-actualization. For this reason we expand our focus to the notion of "capacity," beyond the more conventional analysis and measurement of efficacy. By *capacity* we mean the overall ability of an individual to take part in the political process. This incorporates a practical dimension (the knowledge necessary to know how to participate), a psychological dimension (the belief that one can influence the system), and an experiential dimension (the drawing of lessons from activity in politics that makes one believe it is worth participating again).

The clearest and most direct benefit of participation is that one *learns*. John Stuart Mill emphasized this, noting for example that "We do not learn to read or write, to ride or swim, by being merely told how to do it, but by doing it, so it is only by practicing popular government on a limited scale, that the people will ever learn how to exercise it on a larger."[1] Since Mill was an exponent of representative democracy, just how far the knowledge gained by participating "on a limited scale" could be used on the national level is not apparent. Mill is a bit contradictory on this point. He saw local government as something of a minor league of politics for the ordinary citizen, but noted that the "higher ranks" would not be attracted to local politics. Thus, while activity on this level was truly open to the "lower grade" in society and gave them the chance to participate and learn, the higher ranks did not need this kind of seasoning or gained it elsewhere.[2]

Tocqueville was more egalitarian than Mill, considering participation in local politics an end in itself. He marveled at how the residents of small-town New England "imbibe" the spirit of liberty through participation.[3] Moreover, Tocqueville regarded rank-and-file citizens as fully capable of learning whatever is valuable in the science of governing. But while Tocqueville's optimistic assessment of the capabilities of ordinary citizens is part of our heritage, so too are harsh judgments of the cognitive abilities of Americans. Walter Lippmann, for example, held that few citizens were disciplined enough to spend the time and apply the rigor necessary to make learned judgments about politics. As small-town America disappeared, citizens lost their point of reference for interpreting politics and were faced with a much more difficult task in understanding what was going on about them. Few had the wherewithal to learn about the larger and more complex political world.[4]

1. Quoted in Carole Pateman, *Participation and Democratic Theory* (Cambridge University Press, 1970), p. 31.

2. John Stuart Mill, *Considerations on Representative Government* (Harper and Brothers, 1862), pp. 288–89.

3. Alexis de Tocqueville, *Democracy in America*, ed. Richard D. Heffner (Mentor Books, 1956), p. 61.

4. Walter Lippmann, *Public Opinion* (Free Press, 1965). See also Dennis F. Thompson, *The Democratic Citizen: Social Science and Democratic Theory in the Twentieth Century* (Cambridge University Press, 1970), pp. 22–24.

Ideally, participation allows people to gain knowledge not only about the political system but also about themselves. Their actions in the political world are part of their personal growth and psychological development. What may be termed "self-actualization" is the process by which one tries to reach his or her fullest human potential.[5] This is an essential difference between representative and participatory democracy. In a representative democracy politics is not seen as a primary vehicle for the development of one's capacity for thought and feeling.[6]

In a participatory democracy, individual action in the affairs of the community is a critical part of the way that people mature. For modern communitarians, participation is a key to transforming individuals so that they develop bonds with their neighbors, come to understand shared values, and take on new identities. However, empirical analysis suggests that such maturation is a long-term process. Competence in political participation is something people learn through practice and experience.[7]

The concept of self-actualization is modern, but the fundamental idea of personal growth through political action is a traditional concern of participatory theorists. For Mill and Rousseau, participation not only allowed people to learn more about government and political issues, but it was a means for raising people above their basest instincts. They believed that there is moral instruction in politics. For Tocqueville, too, experience in politics leads people to look beyond their self-interest to acquire feelings of responsibility toward others. As he noted,

> The native of New England is attached to his township because it is independent and free: this co-operation in its affairs insures his attachment to its interest; the well-being it affords him secures his affection; and its welfare is the aim of his ambition and of his future exertions.[8]

Thus, the developmentalists see participation as a means for people to get beyond their self-interest in their relations with government.

5. See Abraham Maslow, *Eupsychian Management* (Homewood, Ill.: Irwin, 1965).
6. Arnold Kaufman, "Human Nature and Participatory Democracy," in Carl J. Friedrich, ed., *NOMOS III: Responsibility* (New York: Liberal Arts Press, 1960), p. 272.
7. C. H. Kiefer, "Citizen Empowerment: A Developmental Perspective," *Prevention in Human Services*, vol. 3 (1984), pp. 9–36; and Paul Florin and Abraham Wandersman, "Cognitive Social Learning and Participation in Community Development," *American Journal of Community Psychology*, vol. 12 (1984), pp. 689–708.
8. Tocqueville, *Democracy in America*, p. 61.

Workplace Democracy

Social scientists who have examined the link between participation and capacity have focused on workplace settings as well as on politics. There are a number of reasons why the workplace has received considerable attention from participation researchers. To begin with, work is much more central to most people's lives than is politics. The workplace also approximates a community, and research can thus examine the relationship between changes in the immediate environment and participation. From a methodological standpoint, workplace studies offer the possibility of controlled experiments; such research is difficult in the political world. Finally, in the context of political science, workplace studies are important because political activism may be linked to certain work roles.

The most common approach used in workplace research is to introduce participatory decisionmaking into a unit of a factory where autocratic decisionmaking had been the norm. Comparisons in productivity can then be made with workers in a control group who perform the same tasks as those carried out in the participatory group. Measures are also taken of various attitudes to see how giving people more control over their work affects their feelings about themselves. Generally the studies are quite positive in their assessments of the impact of participation on various measures of self-actualization.[9]

Of central importance here is whether there is a spillover effect from workplace democracy and attitudes to behavior outside the workplace.[10] A number of scholars have held that democratizing the workplace is the key to expanding participation in politics. G. D. H. Cole, the noted British socialist and political theorist, regarded the autocratic nature of industry as the bane of democracy. The individual had no role to play in a large, complex society like Britain because he had no "chance of learning the rudiments of self-government within a smaller unit." The worker is taught to take orders rather than to think for himself while on the job, and this cannot help but depoliticize individuals who come to

9. See Paul Blumberg, *Industrial Democracy: The Sociology of Participation* (New York: Schocken Books, 1969), pp. 70–138.

10. The logic of such a spillover effect is detailed in Ronald M. Mason, *Participatory and Workplace Democracy: A Theoretical Development in Critique of Liberalism* (Southern Illinois University Press, 1982), pp. 76–101. See also Melvin Seeman, "Alienation, Membership, and Political Knowledge: A Comparative Study," *Public Opinion Quarterly*, vol. 30 (Fall 1966), pp. 353–67; and Pateman, *Participation and Democratic Theory*, pp. 45–102.

expect to play the same subordinate role in their relations with government. It is the workshop, however, that is the "natural unit" for democracy to take hold. Here it is easiest for people to engage in the experiences that will lead them to believe that participation is worthwhile.[11]

The hypothesized spillover effect of workplace democracy on political activity is difficult to test in a rigorous fashion. In the United States only a small number of studies using appropriate controls have been completed. In one of the most ambitious and sophisticated investigations, Edward Greenberg surveyed workers in plywood cooperatives that are owned by their employee shareholders and operate democratically. Employees in conventional plywood mills, where the workers neither own the companies nor participate in the governing of the enterprises, were surveyed to provide a control group. As in our own study, a panel design was used to track change over time. Greenberg did find that the worker-shareholders were more politically active than the conventional workers, and the gap between the two groups grew over time.

In terms of attitudes, however, the results were disappointing. The workers in the participatory work environments were no more likely to feel politically efficacious than the workers in the control group. In addition, the worker-owners demonstrated more selfish and less public-spirited attitudes than workers in the conventional plywood mills.[12] Other studies, mostly conducted in other countries, have been more optimistic in their conclusions.[13] Nevertheless, in the United States, the argument that workplace democracy helps improve personal capacity or is an important link to participatory democracy has yet to be proven.

Political Efficacy

Since workplace democracy is relatively limited in the United States and conducting research on such workplaces is both difficult and expensive, most political scientists wishing to study the relationship between participation and capacity have relied on the Michigan Survey Research

11. G. D. H. Cole, *Self-Government in Industry* (London: G. Bell and Sons, 1918), pp. 234, 139.

12. Edward S. Greenberg, *Workplace Democracy: The Political Effects of Participation* (Cornell University Press, 1986), pp. 115–32.

13. See the literature summarized in J. Maxwell Elden, "Political Efficacy at Work: The Connection between More Autonomous Forms of Workplace Organization and a More Participatory Politics," *American Political Science Review*, vol. 75 (March 1981), pp. 43–58.

Center's periodic polls of the national electorate. More precisely, they have relied on a series of questions in these polls (and repeated in the same form in others) that tap respondents' sense of personal political efficacy.

The initial analyses of these questions revealed a positive relationship between efficacy and participation, and the questions became a standard measuring tool for political scientists.[14] Unfortunately, the original formulation of the questions was flawed; subsequent analysis revealed the battery of agree-disagree statements did not tap a unified dimension of political efficacy. It later became apparent that within a single index, there are two different attitudinal dimensions, internal efficacy and external efficacy. *Internal efficacy* is an individual's sense that he or she is capable of understanding politics and influencing the political process. The question, "Sometimes politics and government seem so complicated that a person like me can't really understand what's going on," tends to gauge this type of efficacy. *External efficacy*, or what is sometimes called "regime efficacy," is an individual's sense that the government will be responsive to his or her attempts to influence government. The question, "People like me don't have any say about what the government does," tends to measure this type of efficacy.[15]

These are subtle but telling differences. Internal efficacy gets at one's inner confidence and comes closer to measuring what we call capacity. External efficacy incorporates a belief in governmental responsiveness and might actually be a better measure of confidence in government than capacity. But even a restricted focus on internal efficacy is not satisfactory for our purposes. As noted earlier, capacity encompasses more than this sense of confidence, and the data analysis that follows will go beyond internal and external efficacy. The two questions listed above are used, however, because they can help answer some of our questions and they will provide a basis of comparison with other studies.

14. Angus Campbell, Gerald Gurin, and Warren E. Miller, *The Voter Decides* (Evanston, Ill.: Row, Peterson, 1954), p. 220.

15. George I. Balch, "Multiple Indicators in Survey Research: The Concept of 'Sense of Political Efficacy,' " *Political Methodology*, vol. 1 (Spring 1974), pp. 1–43; and Stephen C. Craig and Michael A. Maggiotto, "Measuring Political Efficacy," *Political Methodology*, vol. 8, no. 3 (1982), pp. 85–110. In the period since this current research was designed and conducted, the results of the 1987 National Election Survey Pilot Studies apparently reveal that these two efficacy questions may be less powerful indicators of internal and external efficacy, respectively, than others. The decision to use the latter question as a measure of external efficacy follows Stephen C. Craig and Richard Niemi, "Political Efficacy and Trust: Results from the 1987 Pilot Study," paper prepared for the 1988 annual meeting of the Midwest Political Science Association, pp. 6–7.

Those who have the greatest feelings of efficacy are, as we would expect, more likely to participate in politics.[16] When feelings of efficacy drop, as they have in the United States, the implications are ominous. One study, suggesting an explicit causal connection, estimates that the decline in efficacy is responsible for a little more than half of the decline in voting.[17] In addition, feelings of efficacy have been shown to vary according to the type of political participation in which people engage.[18] For example, people who engage only in personal contacting types of political behavior and those who engage in a broad array of political acts, including but not limited to personal contacting—people Verba and Nie refer to as "communalists"—exhibit significantly higher levels of political efficacy than other kinds of participants.[19]

Until fairly recently, the two strands of thought—one holding that participation causes efficacy, the other suggesting that efficacy causes participation—have coexisted without much recognition that these conclusions might be contradictory. So the question becomes, What causes what? Are the behavioralists correct that efficacy causes participation? Or are the developmental theorists correct when they argue that participation produces political efficacy? Or could there be some form of reciprocal causation at work here, where the question becomes which direction of causation is stronger?

Untangling this chicken-or-egg question is no simple task. Panel data are best suited for analyzing reciprocal causation between participation and efficacy, and efficacy and participation, because the impact of the variables can be traced over time. Looking at these two variables at only one point in time restricts analysis to measuring the degree of a relationship between the two. To see if one variable is causing the other variable, analysts must be able to determine what happens *after* each of those factors is introduced where it was not previously present.[20] For example,

16. Gabriel A. Almond and Sidney Verba, *The Civic Culture: Political Attitudes and Democracy in Five Nations* (Little, Brown, 1965), pp. 186–207.

17. Paul R. Abramson and John H. Aldrich, "The Decline of Electoral Participation in America," *American Political Science Review*, vol. 76 (September 1982), pp. 502–21. But see Carol A. Cassel and Robert C. Luskin, "Simple Explanations of Turnout Decline," *American Political Science Review*, vol. 82 (December 1988), pp. 1321–30.

18. Abraham Wandersman and Paul Florin, "Citizen Participation," in J. Rappaport and E. Seidman, eds., *Handbook of Community Psychology* (New York: Plenum, 1991).

19. Sidney Verba and Norman H. Nie, *Participation in America: Political Democracy and Social Equality* (Harper & Row, 1972), p. 88. Verba and Nie do not distinguish between internal and external political efficacy.

20. For a discussion of the problems of disentangling these variables, see Richard Shingles, "Organizational Membership and Attitude Change," in James Caporaso and

panel data could be used to locate people who did not feel politically efficacious and who did not participate in politics at one point in time and to find out what happened later to the political efficacy of those who started to participate.

One study that has used panel data is Steven Finkel's investigation of efficacy and participation in the United States during the mid-1970s. The results of Finkel's reciprocal causation model argue that feelings of internal efficacy cause voting and participation in political campaigns. The results concerning the opposite direction of causation, however, reveal that neither voting nor campaigning shows a statistically significant link to feelings of internal efficacy.[21]

Finkel's study suggests that theorists like Mill and Cole may have had it wrong, at least with respect to internal political efficacy. Participation is more likely to be the effect rather than the cause of feelings of self-confidence about one's ability to influence government. Yet voting is not a form of strong participation, and it is not clear whether campaigning can really be considered a form of strong participation.[22] The theorists discussed here clearly conceived of the types of participation we associate with strong democracy as participation in face-to-face settings. Our task then is twofold: first, to examine the relationship between strong democratic activity and political efficacy and, second, to expand the analysis to other measures of capacity.

Leslie Roos, eds., *Quasi-Experimental Approaches: Testing Theories and Evaluating Policy* (Northwestern University Press, 1973), pp. 230–31.

21. Participation does have a positive effect on feelings of external efficacy, and feelings of external efficacy are linked in the same magnitude to voting participation. Steven E. Finkel, "Reciprocal Effects of Participation and Political Efficacy: A Panel Analysis," *American Journal of Political Science*, vol. 29 (November 1985), pp. 891–913. It should be noted that Finkel used factor analysis to derive composite indexes of internal and external efficacy, each based on three survey research questions. Both of the efficacy questions used in our analysis were included in Finkel's internal efficacy factor.

22. Measures of participation other than voting have been used, but they generally do not include face-to-face activity. See Finkel, "Reciprocal Effects of Participation and Political Efficacy," pp. 903–07; Steven E. Finkel, "The Effects of Participation on Political Efficacy and Support: Evidence from a West German Panel," *Journal of Politics*, vol. 49 (May 1987), pp. 441–64; and Jan Leighley, "Participation as a Stimulus of Political Conceptualization," *Journal of Politics*, vol. 53 (February 1991), pp. 198–211. One study that does try to get at the relationship between face-to-face activities and capacity is W. Lance Bennett's study of 275 college students. He finds a positive correlation between "grassroots activism" and cognitive complexity. In contrast, there is no relationship between an omnibus measure of all types of participation and cognitive complexity. *The Political Mind and the Political Environment: An Investigation of Public Opinion and Political Consciousness* (Lexington, Mass.: Lexington Books, 1975), pp. 129–55.

Capacity and Face-to-Face Democracy

The starting point for the empirical analysis of political capacity is the hypothesis that when people engage in direct, face-to-face forms of political participation, they will experience increased senses of political efficacy, especially internal efficacy and self-actualization, political knowledge, and an ability to look beyond immediate self-interest. All of these elements of the political capacity should constructively contribute to democratic governance. If face-to-face participation is characterized by the same patterns of relationships as electoral forms of political participation, especially as demonstrated by Finkel's studies, then there should be little support for this hypothesis. Although earlier studies, including one from St. Paul, tended to find no effects of face-to-face participation on efficacy and related variables, [23] it seems plausible that face-to-face participation produces the same efficacy relationships as do other high-level acts of participation. This would be in line with Verba and Nie's work.

Additional hypotheses, however, flow from this study of direct democracy. First, face-to-face political participation may be expected to produce different efficacy and capacity consequences in some places compared with others. Whether face-to-face participation produces increased capacity might depend, in part, on the local context in which participation occurs. For example, people who live in the cities with greater community participation and who themselves engage in face-to-face participation should reap greater efficacy and knowledge benefits than people in other cities. And political participants who live in the cities with more structured face-to-face participation (Portland, St. Paul, Dayton, Birmingham, and San Antonio) might be expected to reap greater capacity benefits than participants with less structured participation.

A second set of hypotheses flows specifically from the literature on the reciprocal nature of the participation-efficacy relationship. The relationship between face-to-face participation and capacity should be stronger than the relationship between capacity and participation. In other words, participation should exert a stronger effect on capacity than capacity exerts on participation. Again, if face-to-face participation exhibits the same patterns of relationships as other forms of participation, there should be little support for this hypothesis; in particular, capacity

23. Shingles, "Organizational Membership."

TABLE 11-1. Effect of Level of Community Participation on Sense of Political Efficacy

Percent disagreeing with question

Question and socioeconomic status	Respondent's position on ICP scale[a]						Pearson's r
	0	1	2	3	4	5	
Politics and government are too complicated[b]							
Low SES	24.0	25.7	30.0	44.2	41.2	38.4	0.118**
Middle SES	36.4	42.2	45.4	52.7	53.1	67.1	0.155**
High SES	47.1	58.0	62.3	67.3	63.1	78.7	0.174**
I don't have any say[c]							
Low SES	45.6	49.7	55.5	58.1	58.8	64.4	0.104**
Middle SES	58.2	64.3	63.2	67.8	67.1	71.7	0.073**
High SES	71.4	77.0	78.8	78.5	81.9	80.8	0.660**

**Significant at the 0.01 level.
a. Scale ranges from least active to most active in ascending numerical order.
b. Responses reflect internal efficacy. Partial correlation controlling for SES was 0.147 (significant at the 0.01 level).
c. Responses reflect external efficacy. Partial correlation controlling for SES was 0.084 (significant at the 0.01 level).

should affect participation but not vice versa. However, face-to-face participation may produce capacity even where other forms of participation do not.

Does Participation Lead to Efficacy?

Although, as noted earlier, there are many ways of assessing people's political efficacy, the analysis here focuses on the two frequently used survey research questions described above, to measure internal and external political efficacy. To what extent is strong participation related to an increased sense of political efficacy? Table 11-1 shows the percentage of people who exhibit greater political efficacy at different levels of the index of community participation, separated by three levels of socioeconomic status. At any given level of SES, engaging in community participation activities is clearly and significantly related to political efficacy. People who engage in the most community participation exhibit the most political efficacy for each level of SES. Thus, even controlling for SES, face-to-face participation is strongly related to efficacy. Perhaps contrary to the findings in previous research, face-to-face participation is more closely related to internal than external efficacy, but both sets of relationships, as well as the partial correlations where SES is controlled, are statistically significant well beyond the 0.01 level. These results make it abundantly clear that people who engage in face-to-face participation have a considerably greater sense of political efficacy.

The next question involves the local context in which community participation takes place. Is face-to-face participation correlated with efficacy regardless of the overall levels or the structure of such participation in a given city? Or does strong participation seem to produce greater efficacy benefits for people who live in high community participation cities or cities with more highly structured participation? The correlations between face-to-face participation and political efficacy for people according to the city group they live in and their SES level are shown in table 11-2.

The patterns of correlation are perhaps most telling for people of low SES. Here it is clear that the correlation between face-to-face participation and efficacy, either internal or external, is somewhat higher in high community participation cities than in low community participation cities.[24] This suggests that for low-SES people, the local context does matter; low-SES people who engage in face-to-face participation in cities where there is broad-based access to such participation seem to reap substantially greater efficacy benefits than low-SES people who engage in community participation in cities where such participation is less common. If, as noted in chapter 4, the prospect of face-to-face participation intimidates people who typically do not engage in such activities, especially people of lower SES, then the participation systems offer some hope. Earlier results showed that lower SES people are not more likely to participate when there is a citywide participation system. Whether it is because of the tangible results the citywide systems of neighborhood associations are able to obtain or the type of interpersonal interactions that take place within the associations themselves, the results here suggest that when lower SES people participate within the context of a citywide system, they are more likely to experience an improved sense of political efficacy.

This pattern is less clear or nonexistent for middle- and high-SES people. For middle-SES people, face-to-face participation seems to be associated with greater external efficacy only for people in the highest and most structured community participation cities. For middle-SES people, the relationship between face-to-face participation and internal effi-

24. Although not shown here, we found precisely this same pattern for African-American respondents, regardless of SES. For blacks, community participation is more closely associated with political efficacy in the structured than in the less structured cities.

\

TABLE 11-2. Effect of Citywide Participation Level on Sense of Political Efficacy, by Local Participation Context

Respondent's SES and city participation level	Political efficacy			
	External		Internal	
	Coefficient[a]	N	Coefficient[a]	N
Low SES				
Low community participation[b]	0.032	502	0.039	532
Moderate community participation				
Unstructured[c]	0.068	294	0.049	302
Structured[d]	0.116**	684	0.162**	683
High community participation				
Unstructured[e]	0.118	210	0.082	213
Structured[f]	0.124**	758	0.180**	766
Middle SES				
Low community participation[b]	0.061	354	0.161**	354
Moderate community participation				
Unstructured[c]	0.051	384	0.143**	389
Structured[d]	0.060**	801	0.144**	801
High community participation				
Unstructured[e]	0.013	246	0.118*	246
Structured[f]	0.110**	904	0.167**	902
High SES				
Low community participation[b]	0.127*	202	0.113	203
Moderate community participation				
Unstructured[c]	−0.054	204	0.207**	204
Structured[d]	−0.036	220	0.134*	218
High community participation				
Unstructured[e]	0.027	143	0.059	142
Structured[f]	0.133**	516	0.233**	516
Partial correlations controlling for SES and local context	0.081**	6,325	0.144**	6,324

*Significant at the 0.05 level.
**Significant at the 0.01 level.
a. Pearson's correlation coefficient.
b. San Antonio.
c. Birmingham-Dayton comparison cities (Tucson, Omaha, Colorado Springs, El Paso, Savannah, and Wichita).
d. Birmingham and Dayton.
e. Portland-St. Paul comparison cities (Minneapolis, Norfolk, Louisville, and Buffalo).
f. Portland and St. Paul.

cacy does not seem to depend at all on the local context; the more these people participate, the better they feel about themselves and their abilities to get things done through the local political system. For high-SES people, direct participation is associated with greater external political efficacy only in the highly structured high community participation cities and in the very lowest community participation city (San Antonio).

Does the local context of face-to-face participation matter in terms of political efficacy? The answer seems to be yes and no, depending on SES and the type of efficacy. Face-to-face participation seems to pay efficacy dividends for everybody in the cities where access to such participation is more commonplace—where there is a citywide participation system. Except in such cities, the effect of direct participation on efficacy does not seem to depend greatly on local context for middle or upper SES citizens. Even so, controlling for SES and the city grouping, there is still a significant correlation between face-to-face participation and political efficacy.

Although these patterns suggest a particular direction of causation, they do not offer clear evidence as to what is causing what. Could it be that the direction of causation is actually the opposite of that inferred here? Could it be, for example, that when low-SES people feel greater senses of internal political efficacy (for reasons unrelated to their political participation) they are stimulated to engage in face-to-face types of political participation? This is perfectly plausible, and indeed, given the previous research investigating reciprocal causation, one might argue that these results do in fact partly reflect the effects of efficacy on participation. The results of the panel-based surveys should shed some light on the direction of causation issue.

The analysis of reciprocal causation begins with the relation between participation and efficacy at two points in time. The relation between face-to-face participation at time 1 and efficacy at time 2 is compared with the relation between efficacy at time 1 and participation at time 2. Simply stated, if participation causes efficacy, there should be a relationship between participation at time 1 and efficacy at time 2 but not between efficacy at time 1 and participation at time 2. If efficacy causes participation, the opposite set of relationships should be found. The extent of reciprocal causation depends on the relative strengths of these two relationships.

The face-to-face participation variable used in the analyses using the panel data is not exactly the same as that used in the earlier analysis

TABLE 11-3. Reciprocal Relationships between Community Participation and Political Efficacy[a]

Model segment	All cities	High participation cities	Moderate participation cities	Low participation city
External political efficacy[b]				
Efficacy$_{t1}$ → participation$_{t2}$	0.048	0.068	0.023	0.043
	(0.017)	(0.025)	(0.028)	(0.039)
Participation$_{t1}$ → efficacy$_{t2}$	0.057	0.075	0.059	0.025
	(0.018)	(0.026)	(0.032)	(0.040)
Model diagnostics				
Chi-square p	0.081	0.023	0.844	0.795
Adjusted goodness of fit index	0.993	0.979	0.998	0.995
Total coefficient of determination	0.288	0.317	0.294	0.228
Sample size	2,999	1,364	1,018	617
Internal political efficacy				
Efficacy$_{t1}$ → participation$_{t2}$	0.083	0.103	0.091	0.028
	(0.017)	(0.025)	(0.029)	(0.039)
Participation$_{t1}$ → efficacy$_{t2}$	0.042	0.057	0.034	−0.010
	(0.017)	(0.024)	(0.029)	(0.037)
Model diagnostics				
Chi-square p	0.000	0.000	0.008	0.556
Adjusted goodness of fit index	0.971	0.957	0.965	0.990
Total coefficient of determination	0.399	0.423	0.423	0.313
Sample size	3,023	1,367	1,015	641

a. The coefficients are maximum likelihood estimates produced with LISREL version 7.0 in SPSS. A representation of the full underlying path model may be found in the Methodological Appendix. Numbers in parentheses are standard errors.

b. The subscripts *t1* and *t2* mean time 1 and time 2.

because two of the questions used to construct the index of community participation were not asked in the second-wave interviews. This modified measure of face-to-face participation is different in that it cannot distinguish how frequently in the previous two-year period people engaged in face-to-face participation. It still captures the full range of face-to-face participation activities found in the earlier measure.

Initial analysis of these relationships from the panel data may be found in table 11-3. Analyses are provided for the measure of external political efficacy in the top half of the table and for the measure of internal efficacy in the lower portion. Results are presented for respondents from all five cities in the first column and then for the three subgroups of cities according to their overall level of community participation. The table presents the maximum likelihood estimated coefficients and their associated standard errors in parentheses for the paths of interest here, although these results were derived from a larger underlying path model that can be found in the Methodological Appendix. This table also provides three measures of the strength of the overall model.

The results indeed suggest that community participation plays a somewhat more important role in influencing external political efficacy than efficacy plays in determining participation. Equally important is the fact that the strength of the link between participation and efficacy diminishes as community participation goes down. Participation seems to have its greatest effect on external political efficacy in the high participation cities, less effect in middle participation cities, and virtually no effect in the low participation city. Efficacy's effect on participation can only be said to be present in the high participation cities.

The same cannot be said of internal political efficacy. In this case, where the overall "model fit" is much weaker, participation's effect on internal efficacy appears rather modest, significant only in high participation cities. Internal efficacy, however, appears to exert a fairly strong influence on community participation. This effect seems strongest in high participation cities, less strong in middle participation cities, and nonexistent in the low participation city.

What do these results suggest about reciprocal causation? They suggest that community participation works to help increase people's sense of external political efficacy but not their internal political efficacy. Although the data at hand are not sufficient to investigate this more explicitly, these results also suggest that once people develop a sense of empowerment and confidence in their own personal abilities, they become more likely to participate in face-to-face political activities. Once they start to do so, people begin to perceive that they can influence the political system and that the political system can be responsive to them.

Does Participation Contribute to Political Knowledge?

A second element of capacity relates to how much knowledge people have of the political system, politics, and public policymaking. This might include possessing rather rudimentary factual information, such as who is the president of the United States, who is the respondent's U.S. representative, or which political party controls Congress.[25] It might include knowledge about how to participate in specific types of activities—for example, how and where to vote in an election. Pertinent knowledge would also include information about how an individual might most fruitfully spend his or her time to obtain some desired result from policymakers or political officials. Finally, information about the range of problems and their possible solutions is relevant to an individual's political capacity. Unfortunately, there is no clearly recognized measure of how much political knowledge people possess.

The analysis here focuses on two indicators of political knowledge. The first measure taps people's knowledge of appropriate and potentially effective access points to local decisionmaking. It is based on survey research responses from an open-ended question asking, "Let's say that the people who run [the respondent's city] are considering a proposal to change city services or to change your community in a way you and your neighbors disapprove of. What do you think you would do if such a situation arose?" The responses were analyzed for content and for three specific answers—whether the respondent would contact the mayor's office, a city councillor, or the respondent's neighborhood association. Care was taken to clearly indicate when someone responded that he or she really would not know what to do—that is, when there was no evidence that the respondent had any knowledge about how best to gain access to city decisionmakers.

Contacting the mayor was taken as an indication of a very modest amount of knowledge about possible effective access points to city politics; contacting city councillors was taken as an indication of perhaps slightly greater knowledge; and contacting a neighborhood association was seen as reflecting a fairly substantial knowledge of the local political system. Knowing about any one of these three modes of access was contrasted with a total lack of knowledge. The expectation is that as face-to-face participation increases, people will become more knowledgeable about the contact points in city government; however, it would not be surprising if people who engage in the most face-to-face participation see less value in contacting the mayor, since higher levels of knowledge about local politics may lead to the realization that the mayor in any given city is likely to be unable to respond to all citizen demands. The

25. Craig and Niemi, "Political Efficacy and Trust," p. 25. Also see Verba and Nie, *Participation in America*, especially pp. 82–94, 369.

focus on these three channels is not meant to suggest that these are the only effective or legitimate ways that citizens can gain access to decisionmakers. There are surely others or perhaps better ones. The analysis here does provide some insight into the propensity of people who engage in different levels of direct political participation to know of these channels rather than having no idea how to influence decisionmakers. The second indicator is simply based on whether respondents were aware of the existence of their local neighborhood associations and whether those who were aware knew in which neighborhood association area they lived.[26]

In general, people who engage in direct participation are expected to exhibit more knowledge than people who do not.[27] If there is any empirical support for the developmental theorists' notions about the benefits of direct democracy, then as people increasingly engage in face-to-face political activities, they should become increasingly knowledgeable about politics and government. The earlier results show clearly that people who engage in direct participation activities are more likely to believe they understand politics and government (that government and politics are not too complicated), but does this mean that they actually know more about politics and government?

Unfortunately, the answers to the survey research question probably also contain information about how effective the respondent thinks using any particular access point would be. A respondent who fails to say she would contact a neighborhood association may not lack the knowledge that such a neighborhood association exists; she may simply believe that such associations are not effective channels through which to direct one's energies. However, implicit in this analysis is the assumption that, in the five cities, neighborhood associations are indeed effective channels for public input into local decisionmaking. More important is the distinction

26. Because of differences in the actual presence of neighborhood associations from city to city, there are differences in question wording that could certainly affect interpretation of the results. In the five core cities, each and every neighborhood is covered by a neighborhood association. Survey questions thus asked respondents whether they "have ever heard of the system of neighborhood associations in" their respective cities and, if so, whether they "happen to know which neighborhood association area" they live in. In the other ten cities, no citywide system of neighborhood associations exists, although there are many neighborhood associations. Thus, respondents were asked, "Have you ever heard of any neighborhood association, group, or community association that covers where you live?" If so, they were asked, "Do you happen to know which neighborhood association or community organization covers where you live?"

27. Seeman, "Alienation, Membership, and Political Knowledge."

TABLE 11-4. Effect of Level of Community Participation on Knowledge of Local Politics and Government

Percent unless otherwise indicated

Respondent's political knowledge	Respondent's position on ICP scale[a]					
	0	1	2	3	4	5
What would you do to try to influence local decisionmakers?[b]						
Has no idea, does not know	55.2	37.2	28.8	24.4	18.7	22.9
Would contact mayor	11.6	12.6	12.4	11.1	11.0	9.4
Would contact councillor	19.9	32.3	37.0	40.8	39.0	35.9
Would contact neighborhood association	13.2	18.0	21.8	23.7	31.3	31.8
N	1,065	713	781	316	182	223
Do you know of existing neighborhood associations?[c]						
Does not know	64.0	51.3	43.3	29.3	29.4	31.1
Knows of associations	36.0	48.7	56.7	70.7	70.6	68.9
N	2,159	1,420	1,531	649	340	399
Do you know in which neighborhood association area you live?[d]						
Does not know	62.3	44.3	39.8	30.3	16.4	19.2
Knows of association area	37.7	55.7	60.2	69.7	83.6	80.8
N	725	630	784	413	232	260

a. Scale ranges from least active to most active in ascending numerical order.
b. Chi square was 274.9 (significant at the 0.01 level); degrees of freedom = 15.
c. Chi square was 422.0 (significant at the 0.01 level); degrees of freedom = 5; Pearson correlation coefficient was 0.242 (significant at the 0.01 level).
d. Chi square was 268.0 (significant at the 0.01 level); degrees of freedom = 5; Pearson correlation coefficient was 0.286 (significant at the 0.01 level).

between people who say they would contact any one of the three access points and people who seem to have no idea whom to contact. Overall in the fifteen cities some 37.7 percent of the respondents reported that they had no idea what they would do to try to influence public decisionmakers.

The relationship between face-to-face participation and knowledge about whom to contact is fairly strong and in the expected direction. As shown in table 11-4, knowledge about accessing local government through the city council and through neighborhood associations increases as face-to-face participation increases. Perhaps most striking is the pattern for people who had no knowledge; except at the highest end of the ICP scale, as community participation increases, lack of knowledge of access points diminishes rather substantially. Additional analysis reveals that this pattern does not vary by the respondent's SES; lower SES people experience the same kind of increased knowledge with increased participation as do middle and higher SES people. Thus it seems clear that face-to-face participation is strongly associated with improved knowledge of local government.

The relationship between participation and knowledge of the community is even stronger for the second indicator, also found in table 11-4. Here it is absolutely clear that, except for the most frequent participants, people who participate more are more knowledgeable about the existence of neighborhood-based participation opportunities and about which neighborhood association covers the geographic area where they live. This relationship may seem obvious—one would expect people who participate in neighborhood associations to become more knowledgeable about those neighborhood associations—but perhaps there is more to it. First, this relationship suggests that community participation contributes to knowledge beyond one's own neighborhood to include the whole system of neighborhood associations and, thus, that participation actually helps overcome any parochial tendency for concern with only one's own neighborhood. Second, community participants consist of people who participate in not only their respective system-based neighborhood associations but also other kinds of neighborhood organizations. So even when participation in independent neighborhood organizations takes place within a city that has a system of neighborhood associations, people exhibit more knowledge about the systems of neighborhood associations.[28] Again, additional analysis reveals that this pattern is the same for people of all three SES categories. Taken together, the patterns of association provide direct evidence that participation in face-to-face activities is highly associated with increased knowledge of local governance.

These data do not establish a clear sense of the direction of causation. Could it be that community participants become active after they develop knowledge? The panel data help to address this. Table 11-5 presents information about gains in knowledge over time for those people who were not knowledgeable at the time of the first interview. In this table, "community participants" are those from the top three categories of the index of community participation combined.[29] Here it is absolutely clear that, except in San Antonio (where the small sample size precludes inferences), among respondents who lacked knowledge of the systems of

---

28. Additional analysis shows that participants in neighborhood associations are not more likely to gain knowledge than participants in issue-based organizations but are much more likely to do so than people who participate in neighborhood crime watch and similar organizations.

29. These three categories were combined because of the relatively small sample sizes and correspondingly small cell frequencies.

TABLE 11-5. Effect of Participation on Knowledge of
Neighborhood Associations[a]

Percent who gained knowledge

City participation context	Level of community participation at time 1			Chi-square (degrees of freedom)	Pearson's r[b]
	Non-participants	Non-community participants	Community participants		
Overall	40.9	48.5	57.1	8.6**	0.11**
N	357	274	84	(2)	
Low community participation	46.5	34.8	0.0	2.9	−0.21
N	43	23	3	(2)	
Moderate community participation	47.7	56.0	73.2	9.3**	0.16**
N	197	116	41	(2)	
High community participation	27.4	44.4	45.0	8.9**	0.13**
N	117	135	40	(2)	

**Significant at the 0.01 level.

a. Panel results from respondents who did not know about neighborhood association in first-wave interview but did have such knowledge in second-wave interview.

b. Pearson's correlation coefficient. Partial correlation between knowledge and participation controlling for rspondents' SES is 0.08; controlling for cities' participation level is 0.10; controlling for both SES and participation level is 0.09 (all significant at the 0.01 level).

neighborhood associations, those who were community participants were much more likely to gain knowledge of the neighborhood associations than those who did not participate. Since the community participants in this analysis did not have prior knowledge of the system, that knowledge could not have caused them to participate. The knowledge gain experienced by these respondents occurred after their participation. Thus participation appears to contribute considerably to this gain. Moreover, when the respondents' socioeconomic status and the overall level of participation in the city are controlled, the relationship persists.

But what about the structure of local participation? Do frequent participants who live in more structured participation cities gain more knowledge than frequent participants who do not have the benefit of such structure? The information shown in table 11-6 appears to suggest that structure does matter. This is revealed in two ways. First, the correlations between knowledge and level of community participation are consistently larger in the more structured than in the less structured participation cities. Community participation is more closely associated with higher levels of political knowledge in the cities with citywide par-

TABLE 11-6. Relationship between Community Participation and Political Knowledge, by Local Participation Context

| City participation context | Respondents' political knowledge | | | |
| | Knows of associations | | Knows which area | |
	r^a	N	r^a	N
Low community participation	0.187**	1,111	0.459**	233
Middle community participation				
Unstructured	0.149**	911	0.146**	308
Structured	0.239**	1,647	0.308**	1,024
High community participation				
Unstructured	0.086*	618	0.111	246
Structured	0.292**	2,211	0.327**	1,233
Overall bivariate correlation	0.242**	6,498	0.286**	3,044
Partial correlations controlling for				
SES of respondents	0.035*	3,015	0.254**	3,015
Cities' participation structure	0.036*	3,015	0.298**	3,015
SES and participation structure	0.030*	3,015	0.266**	3,015

*Significant at the 0.05 level.
**Significant at the 0.01 level.
a. Pearson's correlation coefficient.

ticipation systems than in the cities without such systems. Second, the partial correlations reveal that when the structure of participation is statistically controlled, the relationship between the level of community participation and knowledge of neighborhood associations diminishes considerably. Clearly, community participation seems to pay its greatest dividends in cities where there is a citywide participation structure.

Does Participation Increase Concern for the Community Interest?

Many developmental theories of democratic participation suggest that not only does increased self-actualization result from community participation, but that this should be accompanied by an ability and desire for people to look beyond their own immediate self-interest and to consider the interests of some larger community as well. When such theorists speak of people learning to rise above their basest instincts and becoming self-actualized, one might infer that this means transcending immediate self-interest or selfishness. Perhaps partly because there is little agreement about when someone is acting out of selfishness or out of a sense of social altruism, self-interest versus community interest is a concept that does not have a single or even a clear-cut measure.

However, to investigate the relation between community participation and community versus self-interest, our surveys included six questions developed and used by Prestby and others to reveal what it would take to get people to participate more in voluntary organizations.[30] This series of questions was asked of each respondent who reported having heard of the system of neighborhood associations in the five cities studied in depth. For those who reported not taking part in the activities of neighborhood associations, the series of questions asked why not and what it might take to get this person to start participating. For those who reported already taking part in neighborhood associations, questions focused on why the respondent participated and what it would take to get this person to participate more.

These six questions were divided into two groups of three, the first group referring to reasons reflecting what would seem to be an immediate self-interest in the benefits of participation,[31] and the second group referring to reasons reflecting self-actualization, or a more abstract and less immediate self-interest.[32] For example, when a respondent said she would participate more to achieve a "solution to a specific problem of direct concern" to her, this was categorized as being of immediate self-interest to that respondent. When a respondent said that she would participate more to "provide a useful service to the community," this was categorized as reflecting less immediate self-interest and more

30. John E. Prestby and others, "Benefits, Costs, Incentive Management, and Participation in Voluntary Organizations: A Means to Understanding and Promoting Empowerment," *American Journal of Community Psychology*, vol. 18 (February 1990), pp. 117–50. In order to make sense, these six questions were worded slightly differently when administered to people who already participated than when administered to people who had not participated in neighborhood associations.

31. The three reasons considered to reflect immediate self-interest are (1) seeking a solution to a specific problem of direct concern, (2) enhanced personal or professional goals, and (3) attainment of material benefits.

32. The three reasons reflecting self-actualization are (1) increased knowledge of the community and how to improve it, (2) increased sense of responsibility, and (3) useful service to the community. These reasons were divided into two groups of three based on both the face meaning of the questions and the results of subjecting them to factor analysis (Varimax rotation). The factor analysis revealed that the six reasons formed two distinctly different dimensions, one conforming to self-interest and the other to community interest.

TABLE 11-7. Relationship between Community Participation and Self-Interest versus Community Interest Orientation[a]

Percent unless otherwise indicated

	Respondent's position on ICP scale[b]					
Index of community interest	0	1	2	3	4	5
Self-interest oriented	8.5	10.1	10.8	13.0	7.9	11.3
Neither self-interest nor community interest oriented	44.1	42.7	36.9	33.0	38.4	36.6
Community interest oriented	47.5	47.2	52.3	54.0	53.7	52.2
N	472	405	528	261	177	186

a. Chi-square = 15.7 with 10 degrees of freedom, significance = 0.109; Pearson's correlation coefficient = 0.024.
b. Scale ranges from least active to most active in ascending numerical order.

community orientation. Judgments about whether the former is more reflective of self-interest than the latter are necessarily difficult and value-based.

The answers to the six questions were combined into a single additive index of concern for community interest, where answers representing self-interest were considered reflective of less concern for community interest. For simplicity, categories of this index are combined to show people whose answers tend to reflect more selfishness, more community interest, or something in the middle. Overall, nearly 40 percent of the respondents fall into the middle category, indicating a balance between self-interest and community interest. Most respondents fall in the community interest category (50.4 percent), with the remainder in the self-interest category (10.2 percent).

The real issue is whether people who take part in more community participation activities are more likely to be selfish or community-oriented than people who participate less. This relationship is not strong or straightforward (see table 11-7). More (and more frequent) community participation seems to produce slightly more community interest orientation. Self-interest motivation is relatively low at all levels of community participation. This pattern does not differ according to the SES of the respondent but is essentially the same for people of lower, middle, and upper SES. Altruistic incentives are a far stronger inducement to become involved in community politics than is a concern for one's personal goals, issues, or material benefits. This is a particularly striking finding for neighborhood association participation since these associations deal primarily with issues affecting the quality of life in their own geographic areas and deal only peripherally with citywide issues.

Conclusion

One of the many arguments put forth to support advocacy of direct democracy is that the act of participating in face-to-face political activities makes people different kinds of citizens. This chapter investigated this claim by trying to determine whether community participation produces people with greater capacity to govern. The empirical results seem clear. Community participation makes people feel better about their own political effectiveness and about the ability of the local government to respond to them. It contributes to the amount of political knowledge people possess. It does not necessarily make people more community oriented and less self-interest oriented, but strong democratic activity appeals overwhelmingly to those with community-oriented motivations.

But this chapter has established more than this. It is equally clear that the face-to-face political acts of individuals tell only part of the story. When people engage in such political acts within a citywide context that reinforces these acts, the capacity consequences are generally more pronounced. This is especially true for relatively poor people. Low-SES people who engage in face-to-face political acts do not see their capacities enhanced very much; but when such people participate in the context of a citywide participation structure, efficacy and knowledge improve substantially. Middle-class and upper-class people do not seem to need any sort of citywide system in order to reap the capacity benefits of participation. For these people, to the extent that capacity improves at all, capacity benefits will accrue regardless of the local context.

On a broader scale, increased capacity contributes to empowerment. Empowerment is also enhanced by the strong "sense of community" that is felt by people who are active in neighborhood associations. The sense of belonging, of identifying with one's community, reinforces the belief that local government is responsive to individuals and their neighbors. Neighborhood associations directly contribute to the sense of community by offering a source for unified political advocacy on behalf of the neighborhood. People perceive them as organizations that defuse conflict and are open to their concerns. This is crucial in giving the neighborhood associations the image of being true community centers. They are credible, nonpartisan sources of information about neighborhood issues. By increasing people's understanding of how local politics works and of where to go with their problems, the neighborhood associations contribute to people's problem-solving skills.

What do these conclusions provide in the way of prescriptions? If it is desirable to help create a political system in which people experience improved feelings of political efficacy, expanded sense of community, strengthened belief that the government can be responsive to them, and higher levels of knowledge about the political system, then encouraging face-to-face participation solely as an individual act will not suffice. Such encouragement must be accompanied by a system carrying official recognition of community participation as a desirable and legitimate form of political activity.

Part Four
Conclusion

CHAPTER 12

The Case for Strong Democracy

WHAT CAN BE DONE to revitalize the political process? Many argue that if politics could somehow be made more meaningful, more people would begin to participate. Classical theorists, radicals from the 1960s, and contemporary communitarians claim that giving people control over their own lives will make them more involved and responsible citizens. The broader public seems to feel that people in government do not listen to them; they want government to be more responsive to their needs and they are not particular about how that gets done.

Proponents of participatory democracy see it as the vehicle for fixing what ails America. Structures of strong democracy should provide for meaningful involvement in politics where ordinary citizens make decisions about the allocation of goods and services in their neighborhoods. People involved in such activities should become more knowledgeable, more tolerant, more efficacious, and more confident in government. Government itself ought to be more responsive, setting priorities and formulating policies that more closely approximate the true preferences of the people.

This study has looked at four cities that are decentralized and that rely on structures of strong democracy to provide a high level of neighborhood government. A fifth city, San Antonio, is only partially organized and its Hispanic advocacy group, COPS, is not a part of city government. These cities offer a fair and realistic opportunity to test many of the propositions about participatory democracy. They are not, of course, perfect representations of what an ideal participatory democracy might look like. Yet when one forgoes utopian visions of such political systems, the five cities are remarkably vibrant examples of structures of strong democracy. In the four citywide systems, the neighborhood associations have substantial authority over decisions that affect the quality of life in their communities, and they facilitate participation of rank-and-file citizens in face-to-face settings.

If, as we argue, these cities are valid cases to test the various hypotheses about participatory democracy, what can be concluded about the effectiveness of these systems? Do the citywide systems of neighborhood associations prove that participatory democracy can work in large American cities? Not surprisingly, the answer is not a simple yes or no. The neighborhood associations fail in some respects but are very effective in others. Overall, though, they are positive forces that enrich and improve city politics.

The examination of the impact of the structures of strong democracy on the people and policies of the core cities has been organized around three central questions: is participation possible, does government respond, and does participation empower? Each of these will be addressed in turn.

Participation

Most discussion of political participation in America is focused on voting. The decline in voting on the national level between 1960 and 1988 stimulated a great deal of public soul-searching as to what is wrong with American politics. In comparison with most other forms of political participation, voting requires relatively little effort or reflection. Responsible citizenship requires involvement far beyond casting an occasional ballot.[1] The neighborhood associations offer an opportunity to all within their boundaries to become involved in governing their community. Citizens should not—and do not—regard them as insignificant actors in city politics. The survey results demonstrate that residents of these cities have a great deal of respect for the neighborhood associations.

The level of participation required for a form of government to be considered a true participatory democracy is unclear. Nevertheless, one of the hopes in establishing structures of strong democracy is that they will increase the number of political participants. The participation systems in the five cities do not accomplish this. The data are unequivocal: overall participation in the five cities is similar to that in the comparison groups. The structures of strong democracy do not bring people out of the woodwork.

This finding deserves some elaboration, for the data demonstrate that the relationship between participatory structure and actual participation

1. Benjamin R. Barber, *Strong Democracy: Participatory Politics for a New Age* (University of California Press, 1984).

is a complicated one. Although the focus has been on the five core cities, the entire data set was built on interviews done in fifteen cities. The overall levels of participation in these fifteen cities do not conform to the standard model in which socioeconomic status is a reliable predictor of participation. The range of participation in these fifteen cities is substantial, and citywide measures of SES do not explain the rankings. Independent of their socioeconomic standing and their structures for participation, cities differ by a great deal in the amount of political participation that takes place. Each city seems to have its own political culture that nurtures participation. Just how tradition, norms, and expectations mix with structural opportunities to facilitate or inhibit participation is not well understood by political scientists.

Even though the overall level of participation among cities cannot be predicted by their SES composition, low-income people are still far less likely to participate than middle- and high-income residents. For advocates of participatory democracy who believe that neighborhood associations controlled by the residents themselves would prove to be an inviting forum for low-income participation, the data collected for the five cities provide little comfort. Despite their openness and autonomy, it may be unrealistic to assume that neighborhood associations will overcome the class bias in American society. Other forms of political organization have also failed to mobilize the poor. The daily burdens of low-income people are powerful forces that may work to make them feel inadequate, apathetic, or alienated; such attitudes are not easily ameliorated by easier opportunities to become involved in politics. However, low-income people should not be stereotyped as having negative attitudes that push them away from politics. Life circumstances, such as problems with child care and transportation, can make participation difficult.

The idealistic image of participatory democracy propagated by its advocates suggests that evenings devoted to neighborhood politics at community meetings are broadly appealing events. For many people political meetings are anything but appealing. Only in its most utopian, futuristic form does community involvement in political meetings become uniformly attractive. In the real world, even the most open and democratic political meetings can be perceived as intimidating.[2] Also, people can be decidedly uninterested in local politics, not because they are alienated or apathetic, but because they find other pursuits more compelling.

2. Jane J. Mansbridge, *Beyond Adversary Democracy* (Basic Books, 1980).

The structures of strong democracy in the core cities seem to affect participation in one very important respect. In both the high participation and moderate participation core cities, somewhat more political activity falls into the strong participation category, which includes being involved in neighborhood or issue groups, contacting such groups, and working with others to solve problems in the community. Conversely, in the comparison cities, there is more of the weak participation activity, such as working in social or service groups or contacting government officials. Although these differences are modest, it is of real consequence that the activism in the core study cities is channeled toward the neighborhood associations. This, in turn, empowers the neighborhoods in city politics. By taking whatever absolute level of participation exists in a city and directing it toward work in the neighborhoods, the neighborhood associations ensure that there will be more demands on city hall and more incentive for city hall to respond to their needs.

In the final analysis, citywide systems of neighborhood associations do affect participation in the city. Even though they fall short in getting more people to become active in the political world and getting more low-income people involved, neighborhood associations do nurture face-to-face participation. This participation, channeled into neighborhood-based activity, changes the balance of power in the city.

Responsiveness

The fact that activism and political participation are channeled into neighborhood associations does not in and of itself prove that neighborhoods have become more powerful in city politics. What is the mechanism by which neighborhood influence is exerted?

To try to explain how neighborhood government fares in the broader context of city politics, this study has focused on the degree to which city hall is responsive to the neighborhood associations. Likewise, the research has examined the responsiveness of the neighborhood associations to their constituents. Several approaches were used to measure responsiveness, but the primary effort was directed at gauging how city officials reacted to the policy preferences of people in the neighborhoods and how the neighborhood associations were perceived by rank-and-file citizens.

No clear pattern emerged as to why the four cities created citywide systems of neighborhood associations and then proceeded to take them seriously. Neighborhood associations are common in American cities, but rarely are they found in each and every neighborhood, taken seriously, and institutionalized into a city's policymaking process. Once a citywide system is established and the neighborhood associations are given resources, authority, and significant autonomy, the stage has been set for a fundamental change in city politics. The support from city hall, even if it is only a small amount of cash and a community worker, is sufficient to keep the neighborhoods organized. The greatest difficulty neighborhoods in local politics face in influencing city hall is simply getting organized in the first place. By creating and supporting the organizational infrastructure of a neighborhood association system, a city government makes sure that each neighborhood has an institutionalized channel of access to city agencies and to the city council.

When cities resolve the collective action problem for neighborhoods and give neighborhood associations significant control over their communities, the balance of power between business and the neighborhoods is altered. Businessmen have little choice but to negotiate in good faith with the neighborhoods. In any city a neighborhood can rise up to oppose some proposed development, but what is crucial in the four citywide systems is the certainty of response by the neighborhood associations. Except for the largest development projects, a developer cannot overcome neighborhood association opposition to win approval of a proposal. Business has the incentive to cooperate with neighborhood associations and to make the compromises necessary to win their support. There is really little choice. An analysis of policy outcomes confirms the power of the neighborhoods. Private economic interests are the least frequent winners and most frequent losers in policy disputes; they are most often the party to compromise. The neighborhood associations are the most frequent opponent of business.

The neighborhood associations have decidedly less influence on citywide politics than over issues of direct concern to their individual communities. The neighborhood associations are relatively weak policy initiators of citywide issues. In the four citywide systems of neighborhood associations, these organizations are not federated in any effective manner. The analysis of the concurrence scores provides further evidence on this point. When concurrence between elites and rank-and-file citizens on citywide issues is examined, there is no relationship between levels of high participation and high concurrence. When neighborhood issues are examined, however, the high participation cities emerge with higher levels of concurrence than the moderate participation cities. Concurrence scores tap respondents' sense of priorities, so public opinion has also been analyzed to measure actual agreement between policy outcomes and citizen preference. Here again, the high participation cities show greater responsiveness.

Neighborhood opinion about neighborhood issues is heard loud and clear at city hall, not by osmosis, but by institutional arrangements that facilitate input from the neighborhood associations. Each of the four cities with comprehensive systems of neighborhood associations also utilizes some mechanism for assessing neighborhood preferences and priorities for city agency expenditures. Administrative officials at city hall rely on these feedback systems as monitoring devices to evaluate satisfaction with agency services. To varying degrees, activists from the neighborhood associations are part of citywide planning and advisory boards, and this puts them in direct contact with city officials. This is most prevalent in Portland and St. Paul, the two high participation cities. Furthermore, city officials are on call to the neighborhood associations, making appearances at the monthly meetings at the request of these groups. In short, there are rich, dense communication networks between the neighborhood associations and city officials.

City officials respond to the neighborhood associations not simply because they get lots of messages as to what each community wants, but because they know that the neighborhood associations are trusted by neighborhood residents. The surveys done for this study bear out what the administrators have learned on their jobs. Rank-and-file citizens have a very high opinion of the neighborhood associations, whether they have participated in them or not. Citizens generally believe that the neighborhood associations would offer them the opportunity to become involved on a major issue if they wanted to participate. An overwhelming proportion (88.5 percent) of citizens in the core study cities believes that no other group represents their community's interests better than the neighborhood association. Most citizens also believe that neighborhoods are treated equally by city hall.

Neighborhood associations are thus seen as the true voice of neighborhood sentiment, and administrators regard them as legitimate and effective participants in city politics. It is not that administrators do not value autonomy; in their interviews administrators indicated that they often felt restricted in their actions by the neighborhood associations. Cooperation in the four cities is achieved because administrators have substantial incentives to get along with the neighborhood associations. Being in open conflict with a neighborhood association can be damaging to one's career. The expectation is that administrators should work things out with any neighborhood associations with which they have a policy dispute. Indeed, things should be worked out before they become disputes.

These positive findings about the role of neighborhood associations in the core study cities stand in stark contrast to the way neighborhood groups and other citizen groups are generally evaluated in the literature on urban politics. Some find little effective community or interest group presence in city politics.[3] Urban politics is thus a struggle among elites, both inside and outside of government. Other studies have found that neighborhood groups generate conflict and make cities less governable.[4] And still other work documents the positive role that neighborhood organizations can play but finds that they are fragile organizations, usually without a consistent, ongoing presence in community life.[5]

Although they differ somewhat in their assessment of the exact role of neighborhood groups, it is fair to conclude that students of urban politics have not found that cities are characterized by strong neighborhood groups that are institutionalized on a citywide basis and successfully integrated into the political process. Yet these are the findings of this study for the four cities with citywide systems for citizen participation. The normal pattern found in other cities—with only some neighborhoods well organized some of the time—has enormous consequences for the way those urban governments are run. Clarence Stone found in a recent study of Atlanta, for example, that a neighborhood movement started up but faltered badly and this, in turn, enhanced the power of the downtown business establishment. In Atlanta, "all civic roads lead to CAP [Central Atlanta Progress]," the coordinating structure for the city's power elite.[6] In none of the five cities is there a downtown business establishment that dominates local politics; business still exerts substantial influence but has accommodated itself to the neighborhood associations and their control over zoning. The result of neighborhoods' empowerment is not increased conflict but a smoothly functioning policymaking system in which there is *decreased* conflict.

Citywide systems of neighborhood associations do contribute to the responsiveness of city governments. In a variety of ways, city hall has

3. Paul E. Peterson, *City Limits* (University of Chicago Press, 1981).

4. Douglas Yates, *The Ungovernable City: The Politics of Urban Problems and Policy Making* (MIT Press, 1977).

5. Matthew A. Crenson, *Neighborhood Politics* (Harvard University Press, 1983).

6. Clarence N. Stone, *Regime Politics: Governing Atlanta, 1946–1988* (University Press of Kansas, 1989), p. 133.

been shown to be responsive to the needs of individual neighborhoods because of the advocacy of the neighborhood associations.

Empowerment

What is participatory democracy's impact on individuals? Classical theorists saw participation in government as an ennobling experience, nourishing citizenship by training and educating people in the art of government. Communitarians see participation in community life as a potentially transformative experience. Working together with one's neighbors does not merely solve problems, it creates shared values and bonds to the community.

The survey research for this study provides some support for this view: participation does nurture attitudes that can be said to empower people. Participation per se is a stronger force than participation in the neighborhood associations, but the neighborhood associations contribute to the development of some empowering attitudes as well. The most striking finding of this examination of the impact of citizen participation on individuals is its effect on the sense of community. There is a strong and positive relationship between level of participation and sense of community. SES does not affect this relationship; at each level of participation low-income residents tended to have as high a sense of community as those in the middle- and high-SES groups. Participation in a neighborhood association was also strongly related to a high level of sense of community. Other forms of participation were not as strongly linked to a positive attitude on sense of community.

These findings are particularly important because of the widespread belief that there has been a decline of community in America. Studies such as *Habits of the Heart* by Robert Bellah and his colleagues find a yearning for community among Americans.[7] People want to be involved in their community, to feel a bond with their neighbors, and to be part of a collective entity with a shared purpose. Political participation is clearly one of the most effective ways of building community among neighbors. And involvement in the neighborhood associations is a particularly effective way of building community among those who are willing to participate in the political process.

7. Robert N. Bellah and others, *Habits of the Heart: Individualism and Commitment in American Life* (University of California Press, 1985).

The relationship between participation and sense of efficacy is complex because it is difficult to determine whether participation causes people to feel more efficacious or whether people who have a higher sense of personal political efficacy are simply more likely to participate. The expectation of participation theorists is that the experience of participation teaches people about the political process; as people learn more and gain experience through participation, they will come to believe they can influence the political system. The panel data indicate that participation does lead to external efficacy, the sense that the political system is generally responsive to citizens. For internal efficacy, the individual's sense that he or she can understand and influence the political system, there is no such relationship.

The surveys also show that the high participation cities do especially well in achieving high levels of trust in local government. Another important finding is that increases in knowledge about local government and neighborhood associations are positively related to increasing levels of face-to-face activity. Learning is at the core of attitudinal change, and participation theorists are correct in their suggestion that intensive political experiences add to one's knowledge of the system. The range in knowledge between those at the high and low levels of the index of community participation is considerable. Community participants learn how to get things accomplished.

The argument that increased participation enhances citizenship has been shadowed by another argument: that efforts at increasing citizen participation are dangerous because they bring out the wrong type of people. Those who are induced to participate where they had previously abstained or are encouraged to participate more intensively may be people who were best left undisturbed. In short, increased citizen participation can be a *threat* to democracy. It can destabilize society, lead to alienation by those disenchanted by their foray into the political process, and even make the political system less tolerant by stimulating participation by racist or authoritarian citizens. We find no support whatsoever for these charges. The survey results disproved each of the antiparticipation hypotheses examined.

Empowerment does come with participation. Face-to-face activity may not transform people to the degree that participation theorists have anticipated, but it does make a difference in the attitudes of people who become involved in such political activities. Other factors, of course—such as personality, childhood socialization, and attitude toward the national political system—affect attitudes toward the community and local government. Taken with this larger array of influences on an individual, face-to-face participation is a significant and impressive factor in the development of political attitudes about the individual's role in the political system.

Participatory Democracy, Representative Democracy

The citizen participation systems of Birmingham, Dayton, Portland, St. Paul, and San Antonio play a major role in the political life of those cities. Can it be said, however, that these cities are participatory democracies?

If a participatory democracy is one in which most of the adult citizens are highly active in community life and politics, then the answer is no. This, of course, is an unrealistic standard. Most of the citizens of a community are not going to be highly involved in politics no matter how open, nurturing, convenient, and democratic their local government is. Yet participatory democracy is portrayed in these idealistic terms: broad-scale, intensive participation by all types of citizens who do not mind spending their evenings debating politics. The absence of operational definitions and popular theories of what is realistically possible is a measure of just how utopian the idea of participatory democracy is. Participatory theorists can set such demanding criteria for participatory democracy because no one takes them seriously.

If the five cities are a long way from the ideal, they are also far from the ordinary. In San Antonio, COPS is an unusually successful advocacy organization. Over a long period of time it has mobilized grassroots participation to benefit residents in the solidly Hispanic section of town. The citywide systems in the other four cities facilitate direct involvement in government for large numbers of people. The 16.6 percent of the population who participate in the neighborhood associations is a significant proportion of those who participate in politics in any respect.

Still, since the neighborhood associations do not enlarge the politically active segment of the population, they are open to the criticism that they merely offer better opportunities to the politically active. Furthermore, since the politically active population in any American city will reflect the chronic class bias in political participation, aren't neighborhood associations merely convenient vehicles for those already advantaged in the political system?

The findings here demonstrate that neighborhood associations in the citywide systems are much more than a convenient mechanism for those who are already politically active, and the data do not show that they further the class bias in American politics. The public involvement programs must be seen as vehicles of not only participation but also representation. Participatory democracy is offered by theorists as an alternative to representative democracy; in the real world, institutions for strong democracy must be integrated into a system that also includes institutions of representative democracy.

Neighborhood associations are more than extensions to a city's representative electoral structure built around contests for mayor and city council. In none of the cities is the legitimacy of the neighborhood associations based on elections. Even in Birmingham and Dayton, the two cities that use elections in their neighborhood systems, neighborhood association leaders cannot be considered to have run in competitive races where they were chosen on the basis of their policy views. Rather, the moral legitimacy of the neighborhood associations comes from the sense that their leaders accurately represent the views of residents. It is widely believed that the people who are active in these organizations know their neighbors well and know the true sentiments of the community.

To diminish the accomplishment of the neighborhood associations because only 16.6 percent of the population participates would be a grave mistake. In most cities, when local elections are held independent of other elections, the number of people voting may not be too much higher than that level. Unlike voting, involvement in neighborhood associations is a very demanding form of participation. The concentration of political activism on the neighborhood level works to empower the whole neighborhood and not just the activists who go to the meetings. All the measures of responsiveness point toward the same conclusion: neighborhood associations are successful advocates for their communities.

Of critical importance was our finding, based on concurrence scores, that city officials tend not to be appreciably more responsive to participants in the neighborhood associations than to residents of the neighborhoods in general. In a variety of ways the surveys demonstrate that participants and nonparticipants alike view the neighborhood associations as open, fair-minded organizations that accurately represent the views of citizens before government. Also significant is that low-income neighborhoods have fared well under the citizen participation systems in the core study cities. The citywide systems go a long way toward getting equal access to government for all neighborhoods.

Neighborhood associations give people of all income levels more control over decisions that affect the quality of life in their communities. They perform in a way that engenders the confidence of their constituents and provide vehicles for meaningful political participation in the local community. They empower neighborhoods within the existing representative structure of city government. These are impressive accomplishments.

The City of the Future

The success of the citizen participation systems in the five core study cities is unusual. Our preliminary screening turned up few other cities that even came close to the five cities in the scope of neighborhood-based citizen participation. It is not that other cities have not tried: many have created a citizen participation system on paper only to see it fail miserably in operation.

Given the frequency of failure, does it make sense for cities to invest scarce resources to emulate the four citywide systems depicted here? The potential payoff is high, but the risk is substantial too. Involving people in systems that are ineffectual is sure to alienate them and damage the reputation of the incumbent administration.[8] Given the negative legacy of failure for citizen participation in urban politics, the paucity of inspired efforts in recent years to create new systems is not surprising. Parental control of neighborhood schools in Chicago is one visible exception to this.[9] More often than not, citizen participation has earned little more than empty rhetoric or lame efforts, such as the open office hours New York Mayor David Dinkins held for one day. Twenty-two hundred people showed up to tell him how to improve city government, and fifty-four were permitted brief audiences with the mayor.[10]

8. James Morone argues that a further risk is that reforms aimed at returning power to the people are likely to result in stronger bureaucratic institutions designed to support such endeavors. The bureaucracies endure after the efforts at direct democracy have ended. *The Democratic Wish: Popular Participation and the Limits of American Government* (Basic Books, 1990).

9. Isabel Wilkerson, "Chicago on Brink of New School System," *New York Times*, October 11, 1989, p. A18.

10. James C. McKinley, Jr., "New York Tells Dinkins How to Save It," *New York Times*, August 6, 1991, p. A1.

Building Effective Programs

Cities should not attempt to create citizen participation programs unless they are willing to meet three important conditions. First, exclusive powers must be turned over to the citizen participation structures. The primary participation structures must not be merely planning boards or advisory committees; they must have authority to allocate some significant goods and services in their communities. This means that powers must be taken away from the agencies at city hall that currently exercise such authority and transferred unequivocally to neighborhood organizations. As the four citywide systems have shown, control over zoning, a key to establishing authority over the neighborhood, should be among the powers transferred to the community.[11] More broadly, what neighborhood associations do must be integrated into the existing administrative structure of the city. Interaction between the neighborhood associations and city administrators must be routinized, so that in areas where powers are shared between neighborhood and city hall, the neighborhoods are not dependent on administrators' willingness to meet with them.

Second, accompanying such structural changes must be an administrative plan that creates sanctions and rewards for city hall administrators who must interact with the neighborhood groups.[12] If people running agencies are able to fight a rearguard action to try to prevent the neighborhood associations from encroaching on their authority, they may very well sink the citizen participation program. In the absence of proper incentives and sanctions, agency managers are the "losers" when citizen participation systems succeed; they are the ones who must give up power. Consequently, their incentives for cooperation must be realistically assessed. It has to be worth their while to buy into the system so that they have a stake in its success. Thus their personal future in city government must be tied to the success of the citizen participation system.

11. In the four citywide systems studied here, the devolution of power has been based largely on evolutionary practices rather than on statutes. Thus in these systems city hall legally retains authority over activities now carried out in the neighborhoods. Given the high rate of failure for citizen participation programs, it seems best that the neighborhood associations' powers in new programs be spelled out in law. Relying on good faith may work, but city administrators face a substantial temptation not to let go.

12. Jeffrey M. Berry, Kent E. Portney, Mary Beth Bablitch, and Richard Mahoney, "Public Involvement in Administration: The Structural Determinants of Effective Citizen Participation," *Journal of Voluntary Action Research*, vol. 13 (April 1984), pp. 7–23.

Third, citizen participation systems must be citywide in nature. Each community should have a single, officially recognized neighborhood association that represents an area with well-defined boundaries.[13] They should not be explicitly designed as programs to help low-income or minority neighborhoods. As William Julius Wilson has pointed out, the best way to help poor minority groups in cities is to create "programs to which the more advantaged groups of all races and class backgrounds can positively relate."[14] Programs that are aimed at disadvantaged neighborhoods will not have the same credibility or legitimacy as citywide programs. Although COPS demonstrates that a large area of the city can be empowered by a private organization, this model has significant shortcomings. There is substantial backlash in San Antonio against COPS among Anglos. The unfortunate racial dimension to this is exacerbated by the fact that the Anglo neighborhoods are not as well organized as minority neighborhoods.

COPS was organized for compelling reasons: low-income Hispanics had been treated very badly in delivery of city services. In the long run, however, a participation system should work to empower *every* neighborhood in city politics so as to minimize an "us versus them" mentality between neighborhoods and between racial groups. Furthermore, in most of the measurements made in the surveys, San Antonio fared worse than the citywide systems. Although part of this is surely explained by the many recent immigrants in COPS's constituency, COPS simply does not do as good a job of involving people at the neighborhood level as do the citywide systems.

If these three conditions can be met, then new citizen participation systems have a good chance of becoming an integral part of city government. Among the many other structural features that will also contribute to the success of citizen participation programs are the following:

—Ideal neighborhood-based public involvement programs should have control over some significant discretionary financial resources. Nothing will make neighborhood organizations more credible to residents than the right to appropriate funds as the organizations see fit.

13. During the start-up phase of a neighborhood-based citizen participation program, competing groups that already exist within an individual neighborhood can all claim to be the sole legitimate representative of that community. Administrators charged with building such programs must have mechanisms in place to negotiate a blending together of such groups into one officially recognized neighborhood association.

14. William Julius Wilson, *The Truly Disadvantaged: The Inner City, the Underclass, and Public Policy* (University of Chicago Press, 1987), p. 155.

—The city should provide financial support to enable the neighborhood associations to communicate with every household within their boundaries at least a couple of times a year.

—Neighborhood associations should be feeders to other citizen participation structures in the city. If there are citywide bodies that include public representatives, the neighborhood associations should be a primary source for recruitment.

—An early warning system should be built into the administrative structure of city government to provide notice to neighborhoods of pending city activities that will affect them.

—Terms of office for volunteers leading the neighborhood associations should be relatively short to work against the development of oligarchies.

—Neighborhood associations should be prohibited from involvement in electoral activity. They should be nonpartisan organizations in all respects.

Cities at Risk?

Does effective neighborhood government have a downside? We have found the warnings against expanded participation by theorists such as Schumpeter and Huntington to be unpersuasive.[15] As noted earlier in this chapter, disorder and irrational behavior are not the consequence of empowering neighborhoods. Yet another important concern comes to mind. Does neighborhood government weaken the central government to the degree that it can no longer protect and enhance broad, citywide interests? The neighborhood associations are devoted to furthering the interests of their own communities rather than watching over the city's general interest.

No evidence was uncovered to suggest that the neighborhood associations' parochial interests have damaged the broader well-being of these cities. Nor do the central governments seem seriously weakened by the devolution of some significant powers to the neighborhood associations. The administrations of the core study cities seemed to be vigorous and creative, and city officials expressed little hostility toward the neighborhood associations. Even though administrators felt constrained by the neighborhood associations, they did not regard them as the opposition.

15. Joseph A. Schumpeter, *Capitalism, Socialism, and Democracy*, 3d ed. (Harper and Brothers, 1950); and Samuel P. Huntington, *American Politics: The Promise of Disharmony* (Harvard University Press, 1981).

Another troubling issue is whether the neighborhood associations work against the long-term economic viability of central cities. Cities have no more vital problem than the pursuit of economic prosperity. The future of any city is tied to its ability to attract business enterprises that, in turn, will produce the jobs and tax revenues the city needs to maintain itself.[16] As the world moves closer to one international market economy, can American cities enjoy the luxury of neighborhoods that protect their own quality of life by using their zoning powers to keep out enterprises they find undesirable?

At first glance, the neighborhood associations may seem to be detrimental to the long-term economic health of their cities. As noted earlier, business is the most frequent loser on policy issues, and the neighborhood associations are its most frequent opponents. Our findings, however, point to a balance of power on economic issues. Neighborhoods have used their zoning powers to keep out small businesses they did not want, but in conflicts over large development projects, with much at stake for the city's economic interest, the neighborhoods almost always lose. In the cases of this type that we observed, it became clear that individual neighborhood associations are generally unable to impede projects that are important to the city's economic future. Yet more common than conflict over a large development project was cooperation and compromise between a neighborhood association and a developer. Neighborhood associations do not automatically resort to NIMBY syndrome politics every time someone wants to build a large project in their area, as in the fight against the Fred Meyer facility in Portland. Far more frequent were instances of the neighborhood associations' sitting down with businesspeople to come up with something the community could live with.

The neighborhood associations in the five cities have proven themselves to be responsible, thoughtful organizations. Rather than damaging their cities' prospects, they have enhanced the livability of their communities. Neighborhood government can go farther than it has in the four citywide systems. The powers of the neighborhood associations should be gradually broadened to give people even more control over their communities. The primary constraint on further devolution of power is the administrative capacity of these voluntary organizations; participation will have to be broadened further if new tasks are to be taken on.

16. Peterson, *City Limits*; and Stephen L. Elkin, *City and Regime in the American Republic* (University of Chicago Press, 1987).

The data here show that expanding participation is not an easy thing to achieve. Only a small percentage of people are attracted to politics per se; most will come into the neighborhood associations because they want a specific problem addressed. As tasks are added—coproduction of particular city services, for example—people who may be generally uninterested in city politics may be eager to work on a particular problem of policing, recreation, or environmental protection.

The real risk to central cities is not from giving up power to the neighborhoods but from failing to do enough to nurture the sense of community in their neighborhoods. Cities ought not to take a laissez-faire attitude toward the development of communities within their borders. To many, the image of the large American city is that of a place with many bad neighborhoods and deteriorating services. Cities can be seen as forbidding, impersonal places, but they can also be places with thriving communities at many different income levels. People want to be involved in their communities, but often do not know where to turn or what to do. As the Kettering Foundation recently reported from its conversations with rank-and-file Americans, "Apathy is *not* rampant among citizens. A sense of civic duty is *not* dead. . . . [Americans] only seek the possibility to help bring about change."[17]

Neighborhood associations are creative mechanisms for tying people into their communities. Some people, of course, will be more attracted to other kinds of neighborhood or community groups—voluntary activity that is no less valuable to the well-being of the city. Nevertheless, America needs more people involved in politics and government. In a democracy, participating in the governmental process is, paradoxically, an option and a duty. Citywide systems of neighborhood associations are an attractive alternative for those choosing the option to participate in local government. These modest, voluntary neighborhood organizations are places where the grass roots of democracy may be nourished.

17. Kettering Foundation, *Citizens and Politics* (Dayton, 1991), p. 63 (emphasis in original).

Methodological Appendix

WHEN THE PLANNING for the National Citizen Participation Development Project began, the effort was oriented toward selecting the most impressive "citizen participation efforts" across the country. No boundaries were defined for what constituted "impressive" because it was assumed that any federal, state, or local program with an outstanding reputation should be eligible for the study. Over time, however, we decided to focus only on citywide participation efforts. The two primary reasons for this were, first, the programs nominated by those who were queried were largely city-based participation efforts; and second, as the research design evolved, systematic analysis necessitated that the places studied must possess many comparable characteristics. Clearly, comparing public outreach efforts in a statewide program with those in a citywide effort creates a significant apples-and-oranges problem. Both might be very impressive in their own right, but comparing their effectiveness in reaching their target audiences raises a host of methodological difficulties.

Selection of the Five Core Cities and Ten Comparison Cities

Before beginning the search for citizen participation efforts, we established four criteria as prerequisites for inclusion in the study. First, any selected participation effort had to have direct evidence that it made an effort to contact each and every household or resident in a specific geographic area. Second, there had to be evidence that the participation effort offered an equal footing for all those who chose to participate. Third, the participation effort's agenda had to match the authority and responsibility of its targeted jurisdiction. (For example, a local nuclear freeze effort would not be included because the local jurisdiction lacks the authority to affect public policy on nuclear arms.) And fourth, there had to be some reason to believe that the effort attempted to, and actually did, influence public policy decisions.

The search for the best citizen participation efforts was formally launched by sending an inquiry to 7,500 known leaders of citizen participation efforts around the country. This group included interest group leaders, citizen activists, and government officials at all levels. People were surveyed in all fifty states. These people were asked to nominate an outstanding program for the proposed study and to provide some specific detail about the nominated program. Supplementing this questionnaire was a data bank of citizen participation programs that have been catalogued over the years at the Lincoln Filene Center. National organizations that have built reputations as networks for activists around the country were called, and recommendations were solicited from them.

This activity yielded more than 900 individual recommendations. Subjecting this pool to the four selection criteria described above winnowed the nominations down to 415. Each of the organizations that administered these efforts was then mailed a one-page screening survey. About 25 percent of these organizations had ceased to exist or otherwise did not respond, and another 30 percent were eliminated because the information they revealed showed that they failed to meet the established criteria or had ceased to exist. A combination of the available data on each group and follow-up telephone interviews with approximately 150 of them narrowed this pool down to 70 models that became part of the project's participation casebook.

Finally, applying more stringent criteria involving the citywide scale of the participation program, the frequency of contact with all city residents or households, and direct public policy impact narrowed the pool to fifteen participation programs that stood out among the rest. Striving for some geographic diversity, eliminating the most homogeneous of the cities (to ensure that the selected cities' participation efforts had to confront some of the more difficult social and political issues in contemporary urban life), and disqualifying a few that fell below the minimum requirement of 100,000 in population (imposed to guarantee that the selected participation programs would potentially affect a significant number of citizens) led to the initial selection of five cities: St. Paul; Birmingham; Portland, Oregon; Kansas City, Kansas; and San Antonio. However, when the project's advance person returned from her trip to Kansas City, she related that the program there was in the midst of a major reorganization. Because its future structure was uncertain, Kansas

City was dropped from the short list of eligible cities. Dayton, the next midwestern city on the list, was substituted. These five cities then became the focus of intensive study.

To develop the necessary baselines against which the five core cities could be compared, we selected ten additional cities. After examining the advantages and disadvantages of various sampling methodologies, we decided to pursue a city-matching methodology. Each of the five core cities was compared with other cities around the country on the basis of population size, percentage of population that was black and Hispanic, median education, level of income, and age distribution. As a result of this comparison, each of the core cities was matched with two other cities that did not differ by more than about 10 percent on any one selection criterion. The comparisons produced the following matches:

Core city	Matched cities
San Antonio, Texas	El Paso, Texas
	Tucson, Arizona
Birmingham, Alabama	Savannah, Georgia
	Louisville, Kentucky
Dayton, Ohio	Buffalo, New York
	Norfolk, Virginia
Portland, Oregon	Minneapolis, Minnesota
	Colorado Springs, Colorado
St. Paul, Minnesota	Omaha, Nebraska
	Wichita, Kansas

Thus the matched cities resembled the core cities in population characteristics and were expected to differ only in the existence of citywide citizen participation efforts.

Public Opinion Surveys

Public opinion surveys were conducted in all fifteen cities. In the five core cities full samples were taken and respondents reinterviewed after a period of time; in the ten matched cities smaller samples were taken and no reinterviews conducted. The sampling procedures were somewhat different for each group.

Sampling Framework in the Five Core Cities (First Wave)

The goal in each of the five main cities was to achieve an initial representative sample that was stratified at the neighborhood level. Because of differences in the way the local telephone companies assigned telephone prefixes and numbers, a slightly different sampling framework had to be used in each city.

St. Paul. Sampling in St. Paul was accomplished by obtaining a list of the working residential telephone prefixes from the local phone company, along with a map showing the geographic areas covered by each prefix. This map was superimposed on a St. Paul city map showing the outlines of each neighborhood or District Council area. Although telephone prefix areas did not correspond perfectly to the neighborhood boundaries, any given prefix generally covered not more than two neighborhoods. Thus the prefixes were used to maximize the probability that a given number would yield a resident from a specific neighborhood.

Each neighborhood was assigned a quota of respondents to be interviewed based on the relative size of the population aged eighteen and over. Random telephone numbers were then drawn through the following method: the 1987 St. Paul telephone directory was used to extract an actual residential telephone number with a given prefix. To accomplish this, a page of the directory was selected at random, then a column of the page was selected at random, and a position within the column of telephone numbers was selected at random. Then the residential telephone number with a given prefix closest to this random position was selected. This number was not called. Instead, three telephone numbers were generated by substituting random numbers for the last two digits. Thus, a number of 627-5544 extracted from the directory would have the last two digits replaced by a pair of numbers generated randomly. This number might have yielded the randomly generated numbers 627-5514, 627-5597, and 627-5541. These telephone numbers were then called.

Because of the lack of a perfect correspondence between the telephone prefix areas and the neighborhood boundaries, the questionnaire included two screening questions asking each respondent whether he or she lived in the city of St. Paul proper, and if so, what street intersection was nearest to his or her house. The street intersection information was used to determine, using a detailed street map of the city, in which neighborhood the respondent resided. Completed interviews were tallied by neighborhood. Interviews proceeded in a given neighborhood until that neighborhood's quota had been achieved.

Dayton. In Dayton, as in St. Paul, information from the telephone company was used to match telephone prefix areas to Priority Board areas. A map of the city's telephone prefix areas was superimposed on a map of the seven Priority Board areas. Then randomly generated numbers by residential prefix area were sorted according to the expected Priority Board area. An initial screening question was used to identify the reported neighborhood and nearest street intersection so that a precise location of residence could be determined. Then quotas for each Priority Board area were fulfilled according to the general selection criterion described above.

Portland. Portland's eight telephone prefix areas were matched to a map of the city's neighborhoods. Based on information about the percentage of working residential telephone numbers in each area, telephone numbers were randomly generated. As in other cities, completion quotas were established by neighborhood based on the relative number of residents aged eighteen years or older. Quotas were filled by reliance on respondents' identification of street intersections closest to their residences. About two-thirds of the way through the survey (after 709 completed interviews), the distribution of completed interviews was tabulated by neighborhood, and based on the difference between the original quota and number of completions, new quotas were established for each neighborhood. The final 76 interviews were conducted after selection of respondents using the 1987 *Cole Directory for the Greater Portland Area* (reverse street directory) to fill quotas in specific neighborhoods that proved to be particularly resistant to yielding the quota with random-digit dialing techniques.

Birmingham. Working with the Center for Urban Affairs at the University of Alabama at Birmingham, we developed a more efficient method of targeting respondents for Birmingham. With the benefit of the center's *Polk Street Directory* and the city's neighborhood statistics data derived from the U.S. Bureau of the Census's Neighborhood Statistics Program, a full sample of residents was selected in each of the 94 neighborhoods by name and address. As a result, interviewers were able to ask for participation of specific individuals in the survey. Consequently, no Trodahl-Carter chart was required.

San Antonio. In San Antonio, a somewhat different sampling methodology was developed. The citizen participation of interest to this study in San Antonio takes place within an area structure organized by Communities Organized for Public Service (COPS), the main citizens' group. By and large, the areas covered by COPS are the predominantly Hispanic areas of the city, which conform to parish areas of the Catholic church. Consequently, the sampling effort started with a map of the geographic areas covered by COPS in an attempt to isolate these specific neighborhoods of the city. A zip code map of the city was superimposed to match mailing addresses to the COPS areas of the city. Then lists of telephone numbers were generated for residences known to be in specific zip code areas. As a result, each generated number was classified according to whether it would reach a household within or outside of the COPS area. Again, quotas were fulfilled according to the general sampling criterion. The randomly generated interviews were supplemented by 150 interviews resulting from selection using the *Polk Street Directory*. For each of ten neighborhoods where specific non-COPS citizen groups were active, 15 respondents were selected and counted toward fulfillment of the overall neighborhood quotas.

Except for the method of selecting individual respondents, the interviewing protocol was identical in each city. In all cities except Birmingham, after reaching a party at a given telephone number, we used four versions of a Trodahl-Carter chart to systematically target a single respondent in a way that was not biased with respect to age or gender. In Birmingham, interviewers asked for the specifically sampled respondent. Every effort was made to interview the targeted respondent, including calling back a maximum of three times. The interviews were conducted between 6:30 and 9:30 P.M. local time Sundays through Thursdays unless it was determined that the targeted respondent could only be reached at a different time—that is, during the day or on a Saturday. If the targeted respondent could never be interviewed during the time frame of this study, a new telephone number and respondent were chosen as a replacement using the same selection process that yielded the initial number and respondent.

Sampling Framework in the Ten Matched Cities

The research sought to produce a single sample of about 1,500 respondents from among the ten matched cities. The sample was designed to consist of respondents from a given city in proportion to its contribution to the combined population of people aged eighteen years or older in all ten cities. In other words, if the city of Buffalo, New York, had 10 percent of the people aged eighteen years or older found in all ten cities, then the final sample would be composed of 150 respondents aged eighteen years or older from Buffalo.

Respondents were selected by obtaining from Survey Sampling, Inc., lists of randomly generated telephone numbers for residences known to have a zip code in the particular city. An initial screening question was used to verify the city of residence. Four versions of a modified Trodahl-Carter chart were again used to select the respondent within households to ensure representativeness by gender and age. The final aggregate sample of 1,530 respondents yields results with a level of precision better than ± 3 percent. In each matched city, a sample of about 150 respondents was produced; actual sample sizes ranged from 148 (in Louisville) to 157 (in Buffalo), yielding individual city results with a ± 8 percent level of precision.

Selecting Respondents and Interviewing for the Second-Wave Surveys

The citizen surveys conducted in the five core cities were designed as panel studies. Some sixteen to nineteen months after the initial interviews, the respondents were reinterviewed. At the end of the first-wave interview, respondents were asked to provide their first names for future reference. This information was used to conduct spot checks to ensure that these people had actually been interviewed and was stored for identification of the appropriate respondent in the second wave of interviews.

Using the telephone number and the first names from the original interviews, respondents were contacted again sixteen to nineteen months after the initial interviews. Personal demographic information was used to double-check to make sure that the same person was reinterviewed. No substitutions or replacements were made, and interviews were conducted only with respondents who continued to live in the respective cities. In other words, when it was determined that a respondent could not be reinterviewed, another individual was not selected to replace the first. Additionally, when we found that the first-wave respondent had moved out of the city, we made no effort to track this individual. While it may have been interesting to investigate how people viewed their cities and associated participation systems after having departed the city, this was beyond the central focus of this research, which was to examine the attitudes, experiences, and opinions of people who live in the respective cities. Very few people interviewed in the first wave refused interviews the second time.

The final first-wave sample consisted of 5,419 respondents, and the second-wave sample consisted of 3,577 respondents. The city breakdown of the first- and second-wave sample sizes is as follows:

	First wave	Second wave
Birmingham	1,100	803
Dayton	996	639
Portland	1,155	731
San Antonio	1,105	688
St. Paul	1,063	716
Total sample	5,419	3,577

Questionnaire Development

After reviewing the empirical social science literature and public opinion surveys underlying each of the conceptual variables in this study, we constructed a questionnaire using many of the same questions used in other surveys. In other words, when the focus of the project was on political efficacy and trust in government, for example, the questions used here were among the same questions used to inform the broader literature on efficacy and trust. This provided direct measures in the five cities, maximized the ability to compare these results with those from other studies, and saved time and resources in questionnaire pretest and analysis.

Questions in this study included some from the American National Election Study conducted by the Center for Political Studies of the Institute for Social Research at the University of Michigan; the General Social Survey conducted by the National Opinion Research Center; the National Survey of Black Americans, 1979–1980, conducted by James S. Jackson and Gerald Gurin of the University of Michigan; surveys on community psychology conducted by Abraham Wandersman of the University of South Carolina; citizen participation surveys conducted by Richard Rich of Virginia Polytechnic Institute and State University; and questions modified or formulated expressly for this project. (The specific questions and their sources are listed in table A-2.)

While most of the questions applied identically to all of the cities, some areas of inquiry had to be tailored to the city under study. Perhaps the most important of these areas had to do with the specific form of citizen participation in the city. The name, organization, and structure of the participation programs differed from city to city, so the questions eliciting information about the participation program were tailored to the specific city.

In St. Paul, questions asked about the city's District Council participation system in each of its seventeen districts. In Birmingham and Portland, respondents were queried about the cities' respective systems of neighborhood associations; Dayton respondents were asked about the Priority Board areas; and in San Antonio questions were asked about the COPS organization, the East Side Alliance, and the Metropolitan Congregational Alliance.

As the surveys moved sequentially from one city to the next, minor improvements were made in the questionnaire to elicit more detailed and specific information about a city's participation programs. In St. Paul, respondents were asked whether they had heard about the system of District Councils there; if the respondent had heard about the system, we asked which district area his or her home was in. Each respondent was then asked for a simple evaluation of the function of the District Council system. Finally people were asked whether they had been contacted to take part in the District Council's activities, whether they had actually taken part in activities, and if so, which activities and how frequently. In Birmingham and all subsequent city surveys, questions were added eliciting information about how people are selected to serve as officers for the neighborhood associations (or counterpart organizations) and the names of any current officers.

In San Antonio, a large portion of the population is Spanish-speaking. Although it was not possible to estimate the number of households where Spanish would constitute the sole or preferred language, preparations were made to conduct at least half of the San Antonio interviews in Spanish. This was accomplished by preparing a comprehensive translation of the questionnaire and supporting documents and relying on bilingual interviewers. Whenever a household in the COPS area was called, the interviewer was instructed to initiate contact in Spanish and conduct the interview in either English or Spanish, whichever the respondent preferred. This technique was also employed in interviews conducted with people from the two cities matched to San Antonio, El Paso and Tucson.

The second-wave questionnaires were virtually identical to those used in the first wave, with the exception that a single, lengthy battery of questions concerning reasons for participating or not participating in neighborhood associations was dropped. Questionnaires used in the ten matched cities were identical to those used in the five core cities with the exception of questions eliciting city-specific information. Since the matched cities did not have citywide systems of citizen participation, these questions were modified to elicit experiences with other types of local and neighborhood-based participation.

Elite Respondents: Selection and Interviews

The interviews with elites in the five cities were built on demands that differed greatly from those made on the citizen surveys. These interviews were seen not only as a vehicle for gathering data that could later be analyzed and quantified, but also as a means of gaining a greater understanding of day-to-day city politics. They were crucial in providing broader and deeper knowledge of how the neighborhood associations operate, as almost nothing had been written on these public involvement programs.

The elite interviewees fell into four categories: city councillors, leaders of independent citizens' groups, agency administrators, and leaders of neighborhood associations. Different procedures were used for identifying subjects in each of these groups. The city councillors were easiest to identify, and each member of the five city councils was asked for an interview. Thus, the universe of councillors was sampled, though scheduling difficulties precluded interviews with several councilpeople.

There was no way to truly sample the citizens' groups in these cities since there were no directories or listings that could be used to define the universe. A list was created for this purpose by first asking the informants during the background work for the names of citizens' groups active in city politics and policymaking. These informants were generally people who worked in the city hall office that coordinated the citizen participation systems. By the time they arrived in the cities for the fieldwork, the researchers had well over half the names of the organizations that would eventually be approached. The other organizational names came from interviewees by asking them to name any additional citizen groups that should have been contacted. Other names were gleaned from the substantive content of the interviews themselves, as respondents recounted case histories of some event or issue evolution.

An effort was made to interview a representative from all citizens' groups that could be identified in the five cities, although a handful were discovered too late in the fieldwork period for an interview to be scheduled. A more difficult problem is that in the political life of cities, many citizen groups are ad hoc organizations that spring up to work on a single issue. Some organizations, such as the local chapters of the League of Women Voters and the Urban League, have an ongoing presence in a city, but there are only a modest number of such organizations. The kind of ad hoc organizations that are run out of someone's home during an issue fight are likely to be underrepresented when interviewing is conducted over a short period of time. A number of these kinds of groups were identified, and when possible, their leaders were interviewed. Others, especially those that had not been active in the year before the fieldwork, were surely missed.

The interviews with agency administrators formed the largest pool of elite interviews. All the major agency and department heads that might conceivably have had some relationship with the citizen participation system in each city were identified. Only a few major departments and agencies fell outside this requirement, notably fire departments, sanitation departments, and city school systems. The exclusion of the school systems may seem surprising since there are many good reasons for increasing citizen participation in urban education. In each of the four cities that have officially sponsored participation programs, the school systems constituted separate political entities and in a sense had walled themselves off from involvement with the neighborhood associations. (Interviews were conducted with administrators of community school divisions in those cities that had community schools programs, since they were ostensibly open to interaction with the neighborhood associations.)

People in comparable departments and agencies were interviewed in each of the cities, although administrative jurisdictions differed considerably. The director of each of these agencies was approached, but when it was not possible to interview this person, a subordinate was interviewed instead. In some agencies, one or more additional people were also interviewed because the agency was deeply involved with the participation program and a particular division or individual played a critical role in relating to the neighborhood associations. Thus the interview pool is weighted toward those who have considerable contact with the neighborhood associations, although not toward those who might be predisposed to favorably assess these groups. The administrators in the most frequent contact with the associations are those whose actions are most constrained by neighborhood advocacy.

No precise formula was used to allocate the number of interviews between agency heads and additional administrators. Such a formula was not possible because of the reliance on the snowball method of identifying these additional administrators during relatively brief stays in each of the cities. The overall mix of administrator interviewees was about 80 percent agency administrators or their deputies and 20 percent other administrators who were extensively involved with the neighborhood associations.

The response rate to requests for interviews was excellent. Virtually all of those asked for interviews accepted, although—as noted above—in a small number of instances a deputy administrator rather than agency head was made available for the interview. Some natural attrition occurred once the fieldwork began; some scheduled interviews had to be postponed because the respondent suddenly had to do something at work. A handful of the interviews postponed due to these scheduling conflicts could not be rearranged because of the limited stay—two weeks—in each city. Overall, however, there appears to be no bias in who was interviewed as a subpopulation of who needed to be interviewed. In other words, all of the people interviewed were appropriate to the project's tasks, and there is no evidence that any specific perspective was omitted. The final samples of elite respondents are shown in table A-1.

In addition to those identified above, some individuals highly knowledgeable about city politics, such as foundation executives, business association leaders, journalists, and in one case, the mayor of a neighboring town (Minneapolis) were interviewed. These background interviews are not included as cases for the purpose of statistical analysis.

Four separate instruments were developed for the elite interviews, one each for city administrators, city council members, interest group leaders, and neighborhood association leaders. The instrument for neighborhood association leaders was used in conjunction with focus group sessions held in all the cities except San Antonio. Those neighborhood association leaders who attended filled out the questionnaires at the end of the focus group session. The other three instruments were used in more standard interview formats.

TABLE A-1. Numbers of Elite Respondents in Five Cities[a]

Type of elite	Birmingham	Dayton	Portland	San Antonio	St. Paul
City administrators	18	24	22	27	19
	(18)	(23)	(20)	(22)	(19)
City councillors	8	4	7	6	6
	(8)	(4)	(7)[b]	(6)	(6)
Neighborhood leaders and	26	30	49	46	35
support staff	(3)	(30)	(7)	(19)	(3)
Independent citizens'	19	8	19	16	27
groups	(18)	(8)	(19)	(15)	(26)
Other political observers[c]	10	11	9	4	19
	(6)	(9)	(4)	(3)	(10)
Total	81	77	106	99	106
	(53)	(74)	(57)	(65)	(64)

a. The numbers in parentheses represent the interviews conducted using the standard individual evaluation protocol and used in the quantitative analysis. Total number of completed interviews is 469. In Portland, Birmingham, and St. Paul, most of the neighborhood leader and staff interviews were conducted in focus groups, using a separate verbal and written protocol. In San Antonio, a series of phone interviews was conducted with a leader of each COPS parish organization, in addition to in-person interviews with COPS staff and leaders, and with neighborhood leaders using the standard individual evaluation protocol.

b. Portland has only 5 commission (city council) seats, but interviews were conducted just after council elections with 2 incoming and 2 outgoing commissioners for the same council seats.

c. Includes representatives of federal, state, and regional agencies; businesses; and citizens' groups with a primary focus outside the city.

The elite interview questionnaires shared many identical or comparable inquiries. A smaller number of these questions were similar to questions used in the citizen surveys. The use of many open-ended questions generated lengthy explanations of issues and processes and allowed interviewees greater latitude to provide information *they* thought was important for us to have. Interviewers were free to probe at any time during the sessions to follow up on answers or to explore additional lines of inquiry prompted by the subject's responses. Answers from one interviewee were often used to frame questions for subsequent respondents.

Since most of the questioning was open-ended, the interviews were restricted to a more limited range of topics than the citizen surveys. The questioning focused on the interviewees' evaluations of the city's citizen participation program, their assessment of citywide and neighborhood-specific problems, and their personal experience in dealing with a recent issue. As noted in chapter 5, interviewees were asked to give a detailed chronology of an issue to help build a better understanding of how the public policymaking process worked in that city. First, respondents were asked what three or four issues they spent the most time on during the previous year. After this list was recorded, one issue was selected for more in-depth questioning. Interviewees were asked for an account of the issue from the time it got on the political agenda. (Probes asked for the actual origins of the issue to help in the analysis of agenda building in city politics.) Respondents talked at length about their issue, and the probing was very aggressive to ensure as complete a picture as possible.

A few criteria were used to select the one issue from those listed by each respondent. As discussed in chapter 5, "issues" that were really internal matters (such as a departmental reorganization) rather than a public policy problem were excluded. If one issue clearly commanded the lion's share of the respondent's time during the previous year, this was the issue selected for follow-up. If a chronology of one of the issues listed had already been heard, and if there was another issue the person seemed at least equally involved with, the issue not previously discussed was selected. If, however, the interviewee had been most involved with an issue already heard about, we chose to hear it again. In the end only a small number of chronologies covered the same issue. As mentioned in chapter 5, when different histories of the same issue were examined, the discrepancies were relatively minor. This tended to confirm the decision not to hear the same case history from multiple interviewees. In those instances where there was a divergence on some point or fact, the most detailed answer was coded. If neither answer was clearly more detailed, the response was coded as "don't know." As it turned out, for the specific variables used in the analysis here, there were few discrepancies.

Since those agencies that were known to have had little to do with the neighborhood associations were excluded, there is a bias in the administrators' set of chronologies toward issues that could involve the citizen participation system. However, in selecting the issue for the detailed chronology for all groups of respondents, those issues that seemed most likely to involve the neighborhood associations were not in any way favored. It was just as valuable to find out when the neighborhood associations were not involved as it was to find out that they were participants. Although every major issue that had emerged in the five cities during the twelve months before our field research may not have been fully captured, there is no evidence that any significant issue was omitted.

Although notes were taken during the interview sessions, the interviews were taped with the permission of the respondents, and transcriptions were later prepared for analyzing and coding of all the open-ended questions. A tape recorder can conceivably make some subjects cautious since a tape is a permanent record of any inadvertent or inappropriate responses. But for several reasons, we do not believe that tape recording significantly affected respondents. First of all, the interviews were done on background. That is, interviewees were told that the information they gave would be used, but there would be no attribution—that is, they would not be quoted by name. Second, the questioning did not deal with particularly sensitive subjects. Third, the questions did not require respondents to give opinions of any other individuals. In only a few instances did respondents ask us to turn the tape recorder off while they answered a particular question. No subjects refused to allow their interviews to be recorded.

As noted above, many interviews were conducted in focus group sessions. Because of their relatively large numbers, representatives (usually officers) from neighborhood associations in most of the cities were interviewed at the same time using a focus group technique. This technique was also used to interview the community resource officers in Birmingham. All participants in a given focus group were seated around a table, and one of the principal researchers served as the moderator. Questions were put forth for discussion based on a predesigned interview schedule, although the moderator was free to change the order of the questions. These sessions were tape recorded. After the focus group discussion concluded, participants were asked to fill out a questionnaire. The focus group interviews and questionnaires were not included in the quantitative analysis.

The Reciprocal Causation Model

In chapter 11 we presented results based on a model of reciprocal causation. In the chapter itself, the results presented simply capture the reciprocal portion of a larger causal model and do not show how the model was specified. The nature of this larger model, showing how the causation was specified in the LISREL analysis, is shown in figure A-1. This model specifies the reciprocal causal relations between political efficacy at time 1 and community participation at time 2, and between community participation at time 1 and political efficacy at time 2. It also posits a causal connection between political efficacy at time 1 and efficacy at time 2, and a link between community participation at time 1 and participation at time 2. Additionally, the model specifies a connection between socioeconomic status (income and education combined) measured at time 1 and efficacy at time 1 and 2, and between SES and

FIGURE A-1. Efficacy and Community Participation: The Reciprocal Causation Model

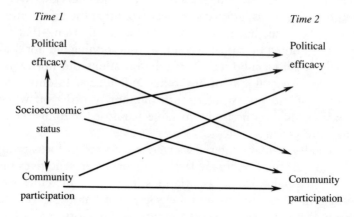

participation at time 1 and 2. Thus the model investigates whether political efficacy causes community participation controlling for socioeconomic status, and whether community participation causes political efficacy controlling for socioeconomic status.

Sources of Some Questions in the Public Opinion Surveys

As noted earlier, many of the questions included in the surveys of the general populations of the cities were culled from preexisting sources. Table A-2 lists this study's questions and their sources. Others used were either questions developed for this study or substantial modifications of questions used in other studies. The full questionnaires are available from the authors.

TABLE A-2. Questions Used in Public Opinion Surveys and Their Sources

Question	Chapter first discussed	Source
Political trust, efficacy, and sense of community		
People like me don't have any say about what government does.	11	b, d
Sometimes politics and government seem so complicated that a person like me can't really understand what's going on.	11	d
How much of the time do you think you can trust the government in [respondent's town] to do what is right—just about always, most of the time, or only some of the time?	10	a, e
Some people say they feel like they have a sense of community with the people in their neighborhood. Others don't feel that way. How about you? Would you say that you feel a strong sense of community with others in your neighborhood, very little sense of community, or something in between?	10	f
Political participation		
Have you ever worked with others in this community to try to solve some community problem?	4	a
Have you ever taken part in forming a new group or a new organization to try to solve some community problem?	4	a
People take part in organizational activities for different reasons. Please tell me *yes* or *no* for the following whether each reward might be enough reason to (*increase, start*) work with the Neighborhood Association two hours per month. Solve a problem of direct concern, increase knowledge of community, personal sense of contribution, increase personal status or prestige, increase political influence, increase sense of responsibility, friendship with other participants, enhanced personal goals, provide useful service to the community, provide material benefits.	11	f
I'm going to read a list of things that might keep people from participating in Neighborhood Associations. Each time I read one, please tell me if it is one of the things that might discourage you from (participating, continuing to participate) in the Neighborhood Association activities. Amount of time, feeling frustration, need to give up personal and family matters, interpersonal conflict with others, need to participate in meetings, the energy and effort involved.	11	f

TABLE A-2   *(continued)*

Question	Chapter first discussed	Source
Political and social tolerance		
There are always some people whose ideas are considered bad or dangerous by other people. For instance, somebody who is against all churches and religion. If such a person wanted to make a speech in your city against churches and religion, should he be allowed to speak, or not?	9	a
Should such a person be allowed to teach in a college or university, or not?	9	a
If someone in your community suggested that a book he wrote against churches and religion should be taken out of your public library, would you favor removing this book, or not?	9	a
Or consider a person who believes that blacks are genetically inferior. If such a person wanted to make a speech in your community claiming that blacks are inferior, should he be allowed to speak, or not?	9	a
If someone in your community suggested that a book he wrote which said blacks are inferior should be taken out of your public library, would you favor removing this book, or not?	9	a
Public policy and service delivery		
I am going to read a list of things which people tell us are problems in their neighborhoods. For each one, please tell me whether or not you think it is a problem in *your* neighborhood. Dangerous traffic patterns, litter and poor trash collection, poor schools, inadequate recreational facilities, theft and burglary, rape and assault, bad street maintenance, unsupervised young people, inadequate elder facilities, local businesses closing, poor police protection, inadequate public transportation, run-down housing, inadequate social services, high rents and housing costs.	5	g
Socioeconomic status		
All income, education, occupation, housing status, and personal demographics questions, used throughout the book, were taken from the 1986 American National Election Study. Some questions needed to be modified slightly by changing reference dates.		

a. General Social Survey, 1987.
b. General Social Survey, 1985.
c. American National Election Study, 1986.
d. American National Election Study, 1984.
e. American National Election Study, 1976.
f. Abraham Wandersman and others, "Who Participates, Who Does Not Participate, and Why? An Analysis of Voluntary Neighborhood Organizations in the United States and Israel," *Sociological Forum*, no. 3, vol. 2, (1987), pp. 534–55.
g. Richard C. Rich, "Participation and Representation in St. Paul's District Council System," paper prepared for the Center for Responsive Governance, Washington, 1980.

Index

Abramson, Paul R., 248n, 262n
Administration: involvement with neighborhood associations, 67–68, 295; neighborhood concerns transmitted to, 111–13; staff for neighborhood associations, 68–69
Administrative Procedure Act of 1946, 41
African Americans: citizen participation by, 85–87; citizen-government concurrence, 129–32, 133–34; and community action programs, 34; policy responsiveness to, 156–57; political opportunities in Birmingham, 94; tolerance versus participation, 221. *See also* Minority groups
Agenda setting, 102–04, 110–11, 121; business influence on, 140–42, 144–46; federal versus local, 114, 116–17; garbage can model, 114–18; haphazardness of, 103–04; neighborhood associations and, 107, 287; policy initiation sources, 106–07
Ahlbrandt, Roger S., Jr., 167, 168n
Airport and Airways Development Act of 1970, 35
Aldrich, John H., 262n
Alienation, as result of citizen participation, 198, 203–06, 213
Alinsky, Saul D., 148n, 166, 169
Almond, Gabriel A., 262n
Altman, Irwin, 167
Altshuler, Alan A., 29n, 146n, 167n
Aristotle, 9
Army Corps of Engineers, 37
Arrington, Richard, 127
Asher, Herbert, 204n
Atlanta, 289

Authoritarianism, 216–17
Axelrod, Robert, 10–11

Babchuk, Nicholas, 85n
Bablitch, Mary Beth, 44n, 212n, 295n
Bachrach, Peter, 7n, 103n
Balch, George I., 261n
Banfield, Edward C., 25n
Baratz, Morton S., 103n
Barber, Benjamin R., 2, 6, 56, 72, 73, 237, 284n
Baumgartner, Frank R., 103n, 105n
Bellah, Robert N., 3, 9n, 290
Bennett, W. Lance, 263n
Berelson, Bernard R., 196, 199, 215n
Berry, Jeffrey M., 28n, 41n, 42n, 44n, 88n, 103n, 145n, 212n, 295n
Berry, Theodore M., 26
Birmingham, 46; African-American political opportunities in, 94; budget allocations, 65; Citizens Advisory Board, 12, 57; community development block grants, 12; economic conditions in, 47; Five Points South neighborhood association, 109, 162; governmental structure, 47; Greater Birmingham Ministries, 67; information dissemination in, 60; issue concurrence in, 123, 127; issue concurrence with blacks in, 131, 132; neighborhood associations in, 12, 57; patterns of government contact in, 94; policy issues and outcomes, 162–63; population and income, 47; Turf Club racetrack, 118, 142, 143, 162; water theme park, 142
Birmingham Steel, 144
Blacks. *See* African Americans
Blumberg, Paul, 259n